When Democracies Deliver

Why do governance reforms in developing democracies so often fail, and when might they succeed? *When Democracies Deliver* offers a dynamic framework for assessing the effectiveness and durability of policy change. Drawing on detailed analyses of public sector reforms in Brazil and Argentina, this book challenges conventional wisdom to reveal that incremental changes sequenced over time prove more effective in promoting accountability, increasing transparency, and strengthening institutions than comprehensive overhauls pushed through by political will. Developing an innovative theory that integrates cognitive-psychological insights about decision making with research on institutional change, Katherine Bersch shows how political and organizational factors can shape reform strategies and information processing. Through extensive interviews and field research, Bersch traces how two competing strategies have determined the different trajectories of institutions responsible for government contracting in health care and transportation. *When Democracies Deliver* offers a fresh insight on the perils of powering and the benefits of gradual reform.

Katherine Bersch is Assistant Professor of political science at Davidson College. Her research focuses on democratic quality in developing countries, especially governance reform and state capacity in Latin America. Among her publications are articles in *Comparative Politics, Governance, Information Polity,* and the *European Journal of Development Research.*

When Democracies Deliver

Governance Reform in Latin America

KATHERINE BERSCH

Davidson College

CAMBRIDGE
UNIVERSITY PRESS

CAMBRIDGE
UNIVERSITY PRESS

University Printing House, Cambridge CB2 8BS, United Kingdom

One Liberty Plaza, 20th Floor, New York, NY 10006, USA

477 Williamstown Road, Port Melbourne, VIC 3207, Australia

314-321, 3rd Floor, Plot 3, Splendor Forum, Jasola District Centre, New Delhi - 110025, India

103 Penang Road, #05-06/07, Visioncrest Commercial, Singapore 238467

Cambridge University Press is part of the University of Cambridge.

It furthers the University's mission by disseminating knowledge in the pursuit of education, learning and research at the highest international levels of excellence.

www.cambridge.org
Information on this title: www.cambridge.org/9781108459204
DOI: 10.1017/9781108559638

First published 2019
First paperback edition 2022

A catalogue record for this publication is available from the British Library

Library of Congress Cataloging in Publication data
NAMES: Bersch, Katherine, author.
TITLE: When democracies deliver : governance reform in Latin America / Katherine Bersch.
DESCRIPTION: Cambridge, United Kingdom ; New York, NY : Cambridge University Press, 2018.
IDENTIFIERS: LCCN 2018037685 | ISBN 9781108472272 (hardback)
SUBJECTS: LCSH: Public administration – Brazil. | Public administration – Argentina. | Transparency in government – Brazil. | Transparency in government – Argentina. | Government accountability – Brazil. | Government accountability – Argentina. | Health care reform – Brazil. | Health care reform – Argentina. | Transportation and state – Brazil. | Transportation and state – Argentina. | BISAC: POLITICAL SCIENCE / Government / General.
CLASSIFICATION: LCC JL2431 .B475 2018 | DDC 351.81–dc23
LC record available at https://lccn.loc.gov/2018037685

ISBN 978-1-108-47227-2 Hardback
ISBN 978-1-108-45920-4 Paperback

Contents

Figures and Tables

FIGURES

TABLES

Acknowledgments

In researching and writing this book, I have incurred numerous intellectual and personal debts. My work benefited from the guidance of many advisors, both formal and informal. I am especially grateful to Wendy Hunter and Kurt Weyland at the University of Texas at Austin. Their patient, rigorous, and enthusiastic mentorship has had an enormous impact on my intellectual development. From my first year, when I wrote a prospectus that was the genesis of this book, Kurt's support has been unwavering, and I am deeply grateful for Wendy's encouragement of my professional and personal endeavors. Dan Brink helped me make sense of the data I brought back from the field, while Bryan Jones sharpened the theoretical insights throughout the book. Matthew Taylor provided insightful recommendations and sage advice over many years.

I thank the Center on Democracy, Development, and Rule of Law at Stanford University and the Institute for the Study of International Development at McGill University, where I was fortunate to be a postdoctoral fellow, for offering highly congenial research environments as well as institutional support. In particular, I acknowledge the financial assistance of the Program in Global Governance, funded by the Erin Jellel Collins Arsenault Trust, at the Institute for the Study of International Development, McGill University. Research for this project was made possible thanks to the generous financial support of several institutions and organizations. The idea for the project first developed while I was a Fulbright Scholar in Brazil. A Lozano Long Summer Research Grant and a Tinker Summer Field Research Grant from the University of Texas at Austin supported pre-dissertation research trips to Argentina and Brazil. A Boren Fellowship from the National Security Education Program funded my research in Brazil, and a grant from the University of Texas Graduate School provided funding for research in Argentina. I am grateful for the generous support I received from the Eisenhower Institute, P.E.O. International, and the Mike Hogg Endowed Fellowship from the University of Texas for the writing of the dissertation.

At McGill, Phil Oxhorn, Megan Bradley, Manuel Balán, Erik Kuhonta, and Laura Doering provided essential feedback along with moral support during the final phases of this project. At Stanford, my research benefited tremendously from conversations with Frank Fukuyama, Dinsha Mistree, Didi Kuo, Alberto Diaz-Cayeros, Larry Diamond, and Kate Sauders-Hastings. Versions of the argument have been presented at various workshops, conferences, and talks. I thank audiences at Brown's Watson Institute, CDDRL at Stanford University, McGill University, the University of Exeter, the Institute for Economic Policy (IPEA) in Brazil, the University of Denver, William and Mary, and Davidson College. I am especially grateful to the School for Public Administration in Brazil (ENAP), where I had to chance to present my work in 2017 and reconnect with so many of the people I had interviewed. Their response to my findings reshaped portions of the book, excerpts of which draw on my article, "The Merits of Problem-Solving over Powering: Governance Reform in Brazil and Argentina," published in *Comparative Politics* 48:2 (2016), pp. 205–25. My thanks to *Comparative Politics* and their publisher, Cambridge University Press, for permission to use this material.

I am indebted to numerous individuals and institutions in Brazil and Argentina, and I am enduringly grateful to all of the technocrats, government officials, politicians, auditors, entrepreneurs, lobbyists, journalists, scholars, practitioners, and experts who shared their time and expertise. It's impossible to thank everyone, but I am so glad to recognize the following individuals: in Brazil, Ronaldo Andreoli, Ciro Campos Christo Fernandes, Gil Castello Branco, Cláudio Cruz, David Fleischer, André Luiz Furtado Pacheco, Francisco Gaetani, Vera Monteiro, Alexandre Motta, Orlando Neto, Adriana Pacheco, André Rosilho, the Scartezzini family, Pedro Tanques, Martus Tavares, José Roberto de Toledo, Jovita José Rosa, Rodolpho Tourinho Neto, Claudio Weber Abramo, and Henrique Ziller; in Argentina, Guillermo Bellingi, Paola Bergallo, Gastón Blanchetiere, Vanesa del Boca, Armando Norberto Canosa, Hernan Charosky, Maria Eugenia Coutinho, Leandro Despouy, Carlos Gervasoni, Lucas Gonzálaz, Beatriz Hebe López, Ana

Paula Herrera, Guillermo Jorge, Oscar Luna, Santiago Nardelli, Ezequiel Nino, Santiago O'Donnell, Graciela Ocaña, José Prigue, Nicolas Raigorodsky, Roxana Rubins, and Guillermo Schweinheim. Special thanks go to the many people who anonymously shared their insights with me. In Brazil, I benefited enormously from my affiliation with IPEA. I am particularly grateful to Felix Lopez and Alexandre Gomide. Affiliations at FGV, made possible by Sérgio Praça, as well as UNB, thanks to Lucio Rennó, opened doors and made an important contribution to my research. In Argentina, I deeply appreciate Natalia Volosin for her insights and friendship. Finally, I am happy to acknowledge my dear friends, Thea Soule and Augusto Simões Lopes, and express my gratitude for their hosting me in São Paulo, teaching me so much about Brazil, and helping me see beyond my work. I also thank Bebeto and Maisa for their hospitality in Brasília, and their insights into Brazil, both shared so generously.

The advice, comments, and criticisms of many colleagues and friends shaped this book in important ways. I am grateful to Mike Albertus, Caitlin Andrews, Sandra Botero, Catherine Boone, Brett Carter, Eduardo Dargent, Zackery Elkins, Peter Evans, Riitta-Ilona Koivumaeki, Cecilia Martínez-Gallardo, James McGuire, and George Ofosu, Alison Post, Timothy Power, Jennifer Pribble, Bo Rothstein, Kathryn Stoner, and Kharis Templeman. At the University of Texas at Austin, my research benefited tremendously from the feedback of Manuel Balán, Abby Blass, Danilo Contreras, Eduardo Dargent, Austin Hart, Ilana Lifshitz, Dan McCormack, Greg Michener, Rodrigo Nunes, Daniel Nogueira-Budny, Paula Muñoz, Rachel Sternfeld, and Yuval Weber. I thank Julia Bugiel and Juan Lucci for going above and beyond as my research assistants. So many friends and colleagues deserve thanks for their guidance and support, but one stands out: Didi Kuo. When we made a pact to finish our books together, I had no idea how important our weekly accountability meetings would become. Two books and two children later, I credit Didi, ever the incisive thinker and clear-headed strategist, and our accountability system for helping me to the finish and reminding me to enjoy the race along the way.

I am also grateful to Cambridge University Press and to Sara Doskow for her interest and commitment to this project. Two anonymous reviewers provided valuable feedback.

Last but not least, I am grateful to my family. My parents and siblings instilled in me a love of problem-solving and a curiosity about the world. I thank my father-in-law for his consistent support and his appreciation of higher education. Finally, I owe more than words can express to my husband, Keith Bersch, who has moved from one side of the earth to another so that I could pursue my professional goals. He has been a rock of patience and love. Our children, Eva and Ethan, have helped me see beyond the book, and their creativity, mischievousness, and curiosity have buoyed my spirits when enthusiasm for this project has lagged. Their arrival provided a reminder that the stakes for governance reform are high: when democracies fail to deliver, the welfare of children is at stake. This book is dedicated to Eva, Ethan, and Keith.

Introduction

The Varied Advances in Quality of Governance

The piecemealing, remedial incrementalist ... may not look like a heroic figure. He is nevertheless a shrewd, resourceful problem-solver who is wrestling bravely with a universe that he is wise enough to know is too big for him.

Lindblom (1968, 27)

Me and my team, we try to fight everywhere a fight exists. We don't believe that piece-by-piece is possible to change the institution ... [W]hen you go piece-by-piece people are not able to see where you go.

It is like the intensive care unit ... If the lungs and heart are failing and you take care of only the heart, you will lose the patient. I don't have time to go piece by piece.

Dr. Carlos Regazzoni, Argentina

This book is about public sector reforms in developing democracies, what makes them successful, and the political conditions that foster success.

As seen in Latin America in the 1980s, Eastern Europe in the 1990s, and in this decade's Arab Spring, popular mobilization for democracy often raises hopes that elected leaders will attack the corruption, cronyism, inefficiency, and red tape that cripple states' abilities to deliver promised goods and services to their citizens. Indeed, in the last 30 years, politicians in developing democracies have made countless attempts to transform how, and how well, the state works. The advent of elections seemed to promise that leaders accountable to the people would sweep out corruption along with the privileged autocrats and their cronies who enriched themselves at the expense of the public interest. The results of democratic leaders' efforts to reform the state, however, varied considerably. On one hand, many countries have increased transparency, ensured greater accountability, and strengthened institutions. Yet democracies often disappoint: Even when dictators and autocrats lie dead or languish in exile, even when democratically elected leaders implement reforms, corruption often persists. Security remains precarious while the quality of roads, health care, and education is left wanting. Why do governance reforms in developing democracies so often fail? Why have some countries been able to make progress in reform and state building while others have remained mired in corruption and plagued by weak institutions?

Elected leaders, policymakers, and scholars have long argued that reforming dysfunctional institutions requires radical, non-incremental, or "big bang" change during windows of opportunity (e.g., Åslund 1994; Durand and Thorp 1998; Rothstein 2011b, 117). I call this strategy the *powering* approach, drawing on Hugh Heclo's (1974) classic term. It is no surprise that politicians seek to garner popular support by calling for forceful overhauls to sweep out corruption and enhance accountability. After all, election cycles are short, and voters elect representatives to make political institutions responsive to popular demands. A piecemeal approach is often criticized for being slow to address crises, incoherent in approach, and vulnerable to entrenched opposition.

Theories of institutional change likewise privilege the powering approach. Institutions, according to dominant paradigms, resist change. Under normal conditions, beneficiaries of the status quo block reform attempts, and "self-reinforcing" equilibria or "increasing returns" keep institutions on defined trajectories. Thus proponents argue that change requires a big push. If reforms are carried out more gradually, opposition forces will coalesce and block them; if reforms are partial or incremental, they will fail to undercut vested interests. Political entrepreneurs or reform champions, capable of harnessing political will to push change past opposition during windows of opportunity, are considered crucial for replacing dysfunctional institutional arrangements with policies that engender more salutary incentive structures. As stasis returns, such reform becomes durable and self-enforcing. Thus, according to a prominent strain of the literature, the problem is not about designing policy changes but rather pushing change past resistance. For these reasons, many scholars agree that powering is the best way to tackle reforms.

Since the third wave of democratization, Latin American leaders have applied the powering approach again and again, from Jeffrey Sachs' shock therapy in hyperinflationary 1980s Bolivia to the World Bank's support for privatization and decentralization in the 1990s. During this time, exceptional twin moments of democratization and economic crisis gave rise to sweeping transformations of Latin American states as they adopted prescriptions for radical political and economic change. In the following twenty years, diverse institutions across varied domains (ranging from social and economic policy to civil service) were created, revitalized, or restructured. Even when these exceptional moments passed, many Latin American political leaders continued to pursue institutional overhauls. Such organizational processes as budgeting, information systems, coordination mechanisms, control, and oversight were overhauled and modernized; police and security agencies were reconfigured; and new ministries were conceived to fight corruption while enhancing transparency and openness.

Yet the results call into question the powering view. Beginning in the late 1980s, political leaders who pursued the powering approach by swiftly implementing comprehensive institutional overhauls were initially commended. International financial institutions praised Argentina's rapid and extensive privatization efforts. Brazil's transformation of state-owned Petrobras was lauded for changes to contracting rules that would provide greater flexibility for the oil giant to operate more like a private company. Experts extolled Chile's radical pension reform and Colombia's comprehensive health plan as models to emulate. Each of these reforms had their critics, to be sure, but the use of, and praise for, the powering approach emerged not only from advocates of neoliberal policies but also from domestic actors supporting a variety of policies along the ideological spectrum.

Such assessments have proved premature. As Niccolò Machiavelli recognized in *The Prince* (1532), "It must be remembered that there is nothing more difficult to plan, more doubtful of success, nor more dangerous to manage, than a new system. For the initiator has the enmity of all who would profit by the preservation of the old institution and merely lukewarm defenders in those who gain by the new ones." Powering reforms did not produce the desired effect in many cases. The privatization in Argentina in the 1990s gave way to renationalization in the following decades; the sweeping changes to Petrobras's contracting rules contributed to the largest corruption scandal in Brazil's history; Chile's pension reform, once an international model, is now unsustainable and will likely require further reform. Over time, such institutional transformations have been counterproductive – plagued by performance problems, subject to backlash and credibility issues, even reversed entirely.

Indeed, the most ambitious overhauls of the state in many Latin American countries have resulted in serious, long-lasting problems. Overhauls have in some cases sparked cycles of institutional deterioration, with one set of thoroughgoing changes begetting another, in pendular fashion.

Despite the failure of ambitious powering reforms, Latin American countries have made substantial advances in many policy areas. Over the last few decades, social policies have lifted millions out of poverty, and substantial gains have been made in key areas of public health service provision. Institutions of accountability in many countries are now capable of shedding light on the highest levels of political corruption. Paradoxically, many countries labeled reform laggards – those unable to muster the political will to push through difficult but necessary changes, or where large-scale changes were watered down, stalled, or halted completely – have gone on to achieve sustained growth, improved security, sounder infrastructure, and enhanced accountability.

These seemingly paradoxical outcomes lead to two open and related questions. First, why does powering fail? And second, given that powering fails, why do countries continue adopting the strategy? By addressing these two key questions, this book answers the broader question: When and how do states in Latin American democracies transform corrupt, weak institutions into durable, accountable, transparent institutions?

This study answers these questions by examining governance reform in Brazil and Argentina. Starting in the late 1980s, executives and public officials in both countries pursued similar sets of reforms to improve the public sector and the provision of public goods and services. While both countries applied the powering approach in some cases, Argentina did so far more frequently. Tracing reforms over time in two policy areas – health and transport infrastructure – captures the interplay between reform choice and the broader forces that condition such choices. In particular, I focus on efforts to enhance accountability, increase transparency, and reduce corruption in government contracting, an area crucial for government performance.

The symmetry of this research design – looking at the same sectors of both countries over time – avoids common pitfalls of focusing narrowly on a particular policy area or a particular moment in time, which can distort or miss the broader picture. I maintain a broad focus on government contracting and service provision in the two different policy areas of health and transportation. The scope of analysis presented in the following chapters zooms out to capture high-level dramatic changes but, especially in times of comparatively more stasis, zooms in to show how more modest changes were quietly sequenced over time, resulting in greater transformations. Based on extensive field research and a wealth of personal interviews with reform decision-makers, my book reconstructs the considerations, constraints, and decision-making calculus of reform leaders. In this way, it elucidates how and why decision-makers pursued one reform strategy over another; why reforms succeeded in advancing and achieving their goals; and what made changes durable or led to their reversal over time.

The application of cognitive-psychological insights of decision-making to the study of institutional change turns conventional thinking about reform on its head. The rational choice and historical institutionalist paradigms would both predict powering reforms to be more effective than incremental approaches. When cognitive limitations are added to the analysis, however, the advantage of the powering approach becomes a disadvantage. Rapid, far-reaching changes led by politically appointed technocrats increase not only decision-makers' propensity for making mistakes but also the backlash to change. The dominant literature takes for granted the ability of political leaders to achieve their goals, underplaying the difficulties of crafting complex solutions and besting the enduring resistance that radical reforms encounter. Yet in Latin America and elsewhere, intentional and targeted incremental changes have resulted in cumulatively significant transformations. As this book demonstrates, the choice of approach to reform has important implications for the extent to which mistakes are made and enemies created.

Approaching change piece by piece and enhancing the role of state insiders – even though insider-driven change is often seen as slow, unsystematic, disorganized, and self-serving – increases the success and durability of reform and can lead to gradual transformations. Continual adjustments and modifications are improved by learning, and an incremental approach makes reform more durable and helps preserve bureaucratic autonomy, especially in weak institutional environments. This argument complements recent work on development, state capacity, social policy, and institutional reform in rejecting big-bang, one-size-fits-all approaches (Tendler 1997; Huber and Stephens 2012, 257; Abers and Keck 2013; Andrews 2013; Levy 2014; Andrews, Pritchett, and Woolcook 2017) but is unique in providing an explanation with theoretical micro-foundations for the success or failure of reform. In doing so, my argument builds on classic insights – Hirschman's (1973) "revolutions by stealth," Lindblom's (1959) "muddling through," and Heclo's (1974) account of technocrats "puzzling" through problems in developing modern welfare states – and integrates them into a dynamic framework for assessing the effectiveness and durability of policy change.

Instances of powering in Brazil and Argentina were plagued by performance problems, backlashes, and credibility issues and are subject to reversals in the long term. The deepest, most ambitious overhauls of the state, such as transportation reforms in the early 1990s, eviscerated institutions and produced enduring challenges. Targeted problem solving advanced in a frustratingly slow process, yet these cautious, gradual changes ultimately resulted in thorough transformations that tended to be more sustainable.

Even so, the powering approach was adopted far more frequently in Argentina than in Brazil. This raises a second important question: Why *do* countries continue to employ powering if it does not prove effective? More generally, why do some states tend to choose root-and-branch changes while others adopt gradual approaches? In answering this second set of questions, the effects of macro factors on policymakers' decisions are explored. Scholars employing a macro lens argue that the choices about reform strategies made by politicians and public officials are constrained by institutional or structural factors. This broad literature on development, state capacity, and rule of law, which emphasizes a variety of factors such as war, colonialism, geography, or more specific institutional characteristics, has made important contributions to understanding democracy and governance (e.g., Grzymala-Busse 2007; Spiller and Tommasi 2007; Acemoglu and Robinson 2012; Melo and Pereira 2013; Mungiu-Pippidi 2015; Soifer 2015). Such work is rarely integrated with literature on policy, public administration, or development interventions. This study integrates structure and agency to show how entrenched patterns of executive power sharing influence the characteristics of reforms and reformers.

THE MORAL OF THE STORY: THE TORTOISE BEATS THE HARE

What types of reform processes result in effective and enduring improvements? My research suggests that the approach embraced by many Latin American policymakers and international organizations – namely, swift, wholesale reform pushed through during "windows of opportunity" (i.e., powering) – does not tend to produce effective and lasting improvements. By contrast, incremental changes sequenced over time (i.e., problem-solving reforms) are more effective and durable than sweeping transformations. While powering requires selecting or designing *the* right solution beforehand, a gradual problem-solving approach allows for adjustments and corrections along the way, a far less complex task than crafting radical overhauls. Specifically, problem solving provides two crucial advantages over the powering approach.

First, continual adjustments and modifications engender an incremental learning process that allows reform tactics to evolve along the way. Instead of taking on comprehensive reform, problem solving tackles smaller problems one by one. Experienced technocrats working on smaller problems are less subject to errors in decision-making than political leaders and outsiders attempting to craft perfectly calibrated overhauls in one shot. Thus decision-makers are far more likely to reach their objectives because the targeted, problem-solving approach reduces problem complexity and enhances the role of decision-makers with greater capacity. Although such changes often advance slowly and haltingly, they can accumulate over the medium to long term and result in thorough transformations.

By contrast, powering implies selecting or designing a wholesale reform that aims to get to the root of numerous problems simultaneously. Such an extraordinarily difficult task pushes cognitive capabilities to their limits, making systematic information processing and balanced, logical calculations nearly impossible. The bounds of rationality are especially tight when sweeping reforms are undertaken by technocratic outsiders with shorter time horizons who lack the type of contextual expertise important for understanding the effects of change in a new environment.

Although insider technocrats may be more likely to pursue a gradual approach owing to their experience and distance from political power, successful reform does not require their participation. Political leaders and outsider technocrats often – but not always – take a swift, comprehensive approach because time is limited and the bounds of rationality are especially tight; yet they too can adopt a problem-solving approach. Reform strategy, not reformers themselves, emerges as the crucial variable in calculations of long-term success.

Second, small changes sequenced over time make reform more sustainable and help preserve bureaucratic autonomy, especially in weak institutional environments. Powering breaks down institutions before attempting to build them up, whereas modest, gradual change addresses problems in the existing institutional framework. And while imposition of radical change breeds resistance, problem solving relies on tactics that avoid conflict or imposition. Such tactics often proceed under the radar. Thus, support for change is built or won as reforms produce benefits, and reformers move on to the next step with a new set of beneficiaries and supporters without raising the objections of a new, anti-reform constituency. In this way, changes are woven into existing rules and practices, strengthening institutions. Moreover, insider technocrats who lead modest reforms are likely to remain at their posts when political constellations shift, safeguarding their positions and creating opportunities to extend their reforms.

My argument explains variation in the quality of governance within national states, as well as cross-nationally and longitudinally. In some countries, health agencies are islands of bureaucratic excellence while infrastructure agencies are mired in corruption; in other states, the reverse is true. As the following chapters will show, such differences are largely shaped by reform strategies.[1] In both Brazil and Argentina, the process-tracing analysis shows how attempts to achieve short-term policy goals by rapidly revamping institutions resulted in long-term problems. Although the problem-solving approach initially advanced slowly, it resulted in impressive change over time. In short, the tortoise beat the hare.

Why do countries continue to adopt powering if it does not prove effective? As the following chapters illustrate, the powering approach was adopted far more frequently in Argentina than in Brazil. Again and again in Argentina, success in the first stage of powering, wiping out the status quo, ultimately jeopardized the second stage of institutional reconstruction and consolidation. Furthermore, as time revealed, corruption and inefficiency proliferated in the new institutions, leading – perversely – to new attempts at wholesale reform. By contrast, while Brazil has adopted fewer powering reforms, problem solving has gradually, often almost imperceptibly, advanced, transforming the institutional framework in many areas. What explains the recurring choice to institute wholesale change in some countries while others so frequently opt for incremental reform?

To answer this second set of questions, the book examines the influence of political-organizational context on policymakers' decisions to embark on sweeping transformations or to proceed more gradually. I argue that entrenched patterns of executive power sharing, rooted in the long history

---

[1] As Chapter 8 addresses in further detail, such unevenness also helps shed light on the paradoxical nature of corruption and accountability in Brazil. While the enduring effects of powering facilitated the proliferation of corruption in certain areas, problem-solving efforts to rein in corruption developed in other areas, contributing to the unprecedented Lava Jato investigations beginning in 2014.

of how power is organized and exercised, account for the cross-national differences in dominant reform strategies; i.e., the choice of powering versus problem solving. *Who* reformers are and how they reach their positions have direct consequences for the choice of reform strategy. Inclusionary governance patterns (presidents sharing executive power with coalitions) result in greater reliance on problem solving, whereas exclusionary governance patterns (the ruling party dominates the executive, appointing single-party cabinets) result in greater reliance on the powering strategy. This argument builds on components of Lijphart's (2012) classic distinction between consensus and majoritarian democracies by offering a precise causal mechanism linking different forms of democracy to better results (see also Mainwaring 2001, 170).

Paradoxically, political-organizational contexts that hinder grand reform attempts may facilitate greater long-term success. This argument challenges conventional wisdom. Scholars have often highlighted the importance of decisive, efficient decision-making, emphasizing the problems of gridlock for democratic stability (Mainwaring 1993; Stepan and Skach 1993). Presidentialism and fragmented government have been thought to be the worst combination for instituting reform. My argument suggesting instead that such inclusionary governing institutions may facilitate a more effective and enduring approach to certain public-sector reform efforts.

Historically, Argentina's executive power has been concentrated in single-party cabinets, which has facilitated large-scale change. In Brazil, however, established patterns of inclusionary multiparty presidentialism have frustrated big-bang reform attempts. The absence of repeated overhauls has provided opportunities for technical experts within the Brazilian government to advance individually small but often cumulatively significant changes. In summary, the experiences of Argentina and Brazil illustrate how shared executive power tends to lead to targeted problem solving, whereas concentrated executive power facilitates powering.

The organization of executive power mediates the impact of cognitive limitations on political decision-making by shaping (1) the scale and speed of the reforms pursued, and (2) the type of individuals involved. Consequently, arguments that establish micro-foundations for reform success are situated in a broader political-institutional context, providing an integrated explanation for the development and success of public sector change.

THEORETICAL CONTRIBUTIONS

With its novel application of cognitive-psychological insights about decision-making to governance reform, this study provides a dynamic framework for assessing the effectiveness and durability of policy change. In doing so, its argument contributes to research on the foundations of decision-making.

All humans make mistakes in decision-making. This has been thoroughly established by Kahneman (2011) and others in well-documented experimental studies of cognitive shortcuts. After hearing of high-profile plane crashes, for example, we tend to overestimate the likelihood of such an unusual event. Indeed, some scholars have applied such findings to particular attributes of political rationality (Weyland 2006; 2014), and many rational choice scholars now recognize the importance of uncertainty and cognitive limitations. Nevertheless, the integration of bounded rationality into the study of politics seems to have stalled. Scholars know that cognitive limitations are at play, but how to apply this knowledge to political problems? Mappings of human systematic errors are complex. Which of the many diverse heuristics that may be applied in any given situation matter? How can one know which failure of judgment could befall political actors operating in the complex political world? Applying the insights of cognitive psychology only enhances the ambiguity and complexity of the task faced by many researchers.

Seizing on the initial insight of Herbert Simon about when and how cognitive limitations matter, my argument provides a framework for making bounded rationality tractable for a range of political questions. The extent to which decision-makers err and fall short of full rationality depends vitally on two factors: the capability of the decision-makers and the complexity of the task at hand (Newell and Simon 1972; Simon 1990). My study leverages these insights by illustrating how reform approach influences both factors. Designing and implementing profound and systematic change implied by powering is a terrifically complex task, which tends to be carried out by elected officials and their political technocrats. Such individuals are often "outsiders" to the public sector, which means they have shorter time horizons and often lack experience within the institutions they seek to reform. Problem solving, on the other hand, reduces the complexity of problems by breaking each into smaller pieces; this approach tends to be adopted by individuals with extensive experience in the public sector, drawing on networks of support within the government to enhance their capabilities. Consequently, the problem-solving approach increases the probability of reform success by reducing the extent to which reformers are forced to rely on problematic cognitive shortcuts.

Such an examination of the proponents, scale, and scope of changes reveals much more than a focus on interests alone. Indeed, interests are important, but existing arguments regarding successful institutional or public-sector reform tend to focus exclusively on pushing changes past resistance, while assuming that, with enough political will, democratic leaders can meet their objectives. Yet interest-driven actions do not ensure success; preferences are not seamlessly translated into actions. Rather, as the following chapters will show, cognitive limitations often get in the way.

My application of Simon's insight to governance reform is novel and significant because it reverses conventional thinking about reform. The rational choice and historical institutionalist paradigms both predict powering reforms would be more effective than incremental approaches. Yet swift, radical reforms led by outsiders push both of Simon's crucial factors (high complexity, low capabilities) to their limits. The tremendous uncertainty of crafting radical change in fluid environments means that decision-makers cannot anticipate all of the changes and challenges in the short or long run, especially when political leaders are rushing to push through reform plans before the next election cycle or before their political capital dries up. As a result, even well-intentioned reformers fail to reach their objectives, often resulting in subsequent overhauls. By contrast, when reform objectives are more limited and led by experts who have more than one chance at making changes, they are far more likely to succeed. The bounds of rationality loosen, and interest-driven actors are more likely to achieve their goals.

In a second step, this project embeds the arguments that establish micro-foundations for reform success in broader macro-foundations. The choice between radical transformations and modest improvements does not occur in a vacuum but rather is shaped by political-institutional context. With this argument, I contribute to efforts at theory construction within historical institutionalism by drawing on the work of scholars who focus on micro-foundations of change (for instance, Simon 1990; Baumgartner, Jones, and Wilkerson 2011) while situating these insights in organizational context (Weyland 2014).

According to my theory, patterns of power sharing play a critical role. When power is concentrated in single-party cabinets, presidents and their political appointees rely heavily on informational shortcuts in designing and implementing institutional transformations. Bounds of rationality are especially tight for such decision-makers: Election cycles are short, and high-level appointees usually come and go with the executive who appointed them. Accordingly, political actors rush to institute reform before the opposition has time to mount resistance. Thus careful planning, evaluation, and scrutiny are sacrificed for short-term outcomes, leading to ill-informed decisions. Moreover, these leaders often lack time, information, and expertise necessary to resolve problems with a proportionate solution. Hand-selected teams of like-minded individuals are also prone to the problems of "groupthink." Instead of fostering debate and deliberation, cross-checking inferences, and bringing experience from prior reform attempts to bear on current problems, they suffer from more severe distortions in judgment, with rash inferences reinforcing each other (Janis 1982; McDermott 2004, 249–56; Schafer and Crichlow 2010; Weyland 2014, 56). Conformity and cohesion are good for rapid implementation but not for identifying holes in grand reform plans. In essence, the challenges of designing radical restructurings all at once predispose reforms to new problems. Yet the rapid turnover and high level of career uncertainty of politically appointed reform teams mean that there are often few experts left to address issues after the initial overhaul. Thus in the interim between dramatic reforms, decision-makers underreact. Problems accumulate until they cannot be ignored, triggering another round of powering.

By contrast, coalitional presidentialism, which induces presidents to share executive power, means that negotiation and compromise among coalitional partners slow sweeping overhauls. Such policy proposals benefit from scrutiny and discussion; diverse perspectives lead to revision and correction. These negotiations also often result in the downsizing of initial proposals, and the process of discussion may build more coherent coalitions. Consequently, dramatic overhauls imposed by unified reform teams are less common. This kind of reform approach affords experts from within the state a much greater role in the policymaking process, often to sidestep gridlock; the relative stability extends their time horizons for effecting change, and smaller-scale reforms phased in over time are often left in their hands, as opposed to those of political leaders or high-level technocrats. Moreover, technocrats and civil servants possess technical acumen as well as access to information, enabling them to process information in a more balanced fashion. The bounds of rationality loosen when sweeping change is broken into smaller pieces and experts with longer time horizons play a greater role in crafting change. In such a context, information is processed in a more proportionate manner. As a result, we would expect fewer radical changes and more gradual transformations.

This study, then, illustrates how established governing practices mediate the bounds of rationality, going beyond state capacity arguments to explain state effectiveness (Evans, Huber, and Stephens 2017). Patterns of executive power sharing and expectations regarding coalitional formation, concepts of classical historical institutionalism, play a crucial role in this theory because they have an influence on the kinds of actors involved in the reform process and the type of reform that will likely be selected. Thus this study brings together a resurgent literature on state capacity (Geddes 1994; Kurtz 2013; Fukuyama 2014; Holt and Manning 2014) and bureaucratic capacity (Evans and Rauch 1999; Grindle 2012; Gingerich 2013; Dargent 2015; Ang 2017; Bersch, Praça, and Taylor 2017a; 2017b) with the study of micro-foundations. It is well established that bureaucratic capacity – Weberian characteristics such as meritocratic recruitment to the public sector – enhances the quality of governance. My argument suggests that it does so by enhancing the capability of reformers and limiting the scope of reform: Bureaucratic actors do not have the political power to propose dramatic transformations. These factors together enhance the quality of decisions. State capacity is then a crucial mediating variable; it is simultaneously shaped by structural factors and reform choices, which can impact bureaucratic capabilities over time.

This book also contributes to the burgeoning literature on institutional change. Extant literature has recently highlighted the importance of incremental change (Streeck and Thelen 2005; Mahoney and Thelen 2010) and patterns of frequent radical change (Murillo and Levitsky 2013). Yet we know little about the causes of different types of change (cf. Murillo and Levitsky 2014) or their consequences (Andrews 2013). The framework I develop in this study provides analytical leverage for assessing the consequences of reform, and the argument regarding the importance of political-organizational context contributes to efforts at understanding causes of different forms of institutional change.

RESEARCH DESIGN

To assess the two competing approaches to governance reform, this book examines reform strategies in Argentina and Brazil over time. In particular, it focuses on health and transportation ministries and traces efforts to improve service delivery with a broad focus on government contracting reforms over the last twenty-five years. The study draws analytic leverage from comparing cases within the same country over time, across and within policy areas (i.e., health and transport) and across systems (i.e., Brazil and Argentina). Carefully selected and controlled comparisons of reform attempts reveal the mechanisms at work and isolate aspects of reform approaches that result in particular outcomes. Exploring the questions I have posed in this study also necessitates a deep understanding of the contextual environment in which reforms are introduced. Thus the study draws on extensive field research conducted over several years (2009–13) in Argentina and Brazil – including more than 200 interviews with ministers, policymakers, politicians, auditors, civil society actors, and businesspeople, as well as World Bank officials, journalists, doctors, nurses, and construction foremen.

In these ways, the study overcomes a number of methodological challenges. First, evaluating different reform approaches requires holding numerous factors constant and varying the reform strategy. If reform approach is simply a function of the severity of the problem, for instance, then it would be impossible to assess which strategy is more effective. Although implementing experiments or identifying instances of as-if random assignment (i.e., so-called natural experiments) has become the gold standard for addressing inferential challenges (Dunning 2012), such a controlled approach is simply not feasible for complex, multifaceted, real-world public sector reforms. Above all, an experimental approach fails to capture the interplay between broader macrofactors and microfactors.

The present study instead combines comparisons at various levels. First, focusing on Brazil and Argentina permits a most-similar systems design.[2] Both countries have faced a similar set of problems and sought to implement similar solutions, but their approaches have often diverged. These neighboring countries share many similar historical, cultural, economic, and political characteristics; most importantly for this study, the structure of the state and the economy around the time of re-democratization was remarkably similar. Import-substitution industrialization meant that both states were deeply involved in economic activity and were almost solely responsible for functions such as infrastructure

---

[2] By comparing across countries with many similarities but where outcomes diverged, the method of difference applied in this study facilitates evaluation of the causal impact of the remaining differences on the dependent variable (Przeworski and Teune 1970, 32–5).

development. Social services, such as health care, were tied to public sector employment in both countries, leaving large portions of the population without adequate care. After decades of borrowing from international creditors for massive industrialization and infrastructure programs, the economic downturn of the late 1970s and 1980s meant that Latin American countries such as Argentina and Brazil could no longer finance their debt.

Beginning in the late 1980s, Argentine executives implemented numerous ambitious, rapid, and far-reaching state reforms. Conversely, in Brazil, a similar set of large-scale reforms was weakened, stalled, or halted completely. Argentina tended toward the powering approach, implementing changes with alacrity, whereas Brazil often adopted a problem-solving approach. These cases, then, exemplify the two different reform strategies with particular clarity and help illustrate the importance of macro foundations such as political-organizational context.[3]

Microfactors are also at play, and sometimes executives do have a greater degree of choice in the approach they adopt. To complement the most-similar systems design, within-case comparisons trace processes of policy design and implementation within the same country over time and across policy areas (health and transportation). This analysis surmounts the classic challenge of too many variables and too few cases (Lijphart 1971). Moreover, the approach applied in this study is particularly appropriate for illustrating how broader macrofactors intersect with microfactors. While Brazil tends toward problem solving and Argentina tends toward powering, this is not always the case. I use matched comparisons of attempts to increase transparency, reduce corruption, and enhance accountability to show that powering and problem solving occur in both countries. Comparisons of reform episodes allow for within-case tests of the proposition that incremental reforms sequenced over time result in more effective and enduring outcomes by holding constant background factors. They also provide a way to trace the mechanisms that connect the type of reform approach to outcomes so as to analyze both within-country and cross-country variation.

Detailed case studies, which document changes over a quarter-century, address a variety of other obstacles common in previous studies of reform and development in Latin America. Too often, scholars, public officials,

---

[3] To probe the comparative extension of this analysis, Chapter 8 assesses the broad contours of state reform efforts in five additional Latin American countries: Chile, Colombia, El Salvador, Uruguay, and Venezuela.

and development personnel focus on the passage, implementation, or initial effects of an important policy. Victory is declared prematurely and gradual transformations overlooked. Viewing reform along a longer time horizon and relying on process tracing reveals previously obscured mechanisms that are crucial for understanding how to create lasting improvements. Process tracing – the technique of looking for the observable implications of hypothesized causal processes – is particularly appropriate for the sequential isolation of causal factors throughout the unfolding stages of reform (George 1979; Bennett 2008). The outcomes of early reform decisions condition later decisions; instead of ignoring the importance of temporal sequence, process tracing makes such path dependencies a part of the longitudinal analysis of reform politics.

I apply a qualitative approach because many of the theoretical factors highlighted in my study are difficult to quantify. Above all, identifying instances of problem solving requires in-depth field research and extensive knowledge of the institutional landscape. Classifying whether a major reform effort is problem solving can be difficult without careful case studies. Well-known reform efforts, such as the *Plano Real*, which ended hyperinflation in Brazil, might at first blush be considered powering. Upon further examination, however, the plan appears part and parcel of a long problem-solving sequence of reforms. That is, without contextual knowledge provided by case studies, many reform efforts look like big bangs but are, in fact, preceded and followed by slow, sustained efforts that made the dramatic changes effective and enduring.

Deep contextual knowledge is also important for understanding the informal rules and practices that affect change in the real world. Legislation and formal rules are often used to quantify policy change or to study reform. While legislation is important, formal rules often obfuscate the actual practices that govern the actions of public officials. Rules on the books are often not enforced and informal practices are often required to make existing rules functional. I conducted my research and interviews with an eye toward understanding formal and informal rules and practices, turning points, and changes that actually improved transparency, efficiency, accountability, or access in the provision of goods and services. This meant that, after a careful review of the existing literature and World Bank documents, I started my fieldwork with what I thought was a solid understanding of the reforms that I would study and a sense of whether or not they were successful. Once in the field, I was quickly disabused of that notion by open-ended interviews that revealed a set of reforms and realities largely overlooked in the existing literature.

To guard against biased assessments, I conducted interviews with reform proponents and opponents, auditors, experts, former public and private sector workers, whistleblowers, construction workers, and a variety of other individuals until a consistent narrative of reform emerged. In many cases, consensus did not emerge, but interviews brought into sharper relief points of disagreement and opposition. Finally, in other cases, interviewees provided subtle – and not so subtle – indications that it was too dangerous to proceed with a particular line of questioning. And many interviewees in this study wished to remain anonymous. While a researcher can only go so far in understanding the subterranean world of government contracting, this approach yielded insights that would have been impossible to draw by quantifying reform efforts.

Finally, a narrow focus on a particular policy area or a particular moment in time distorts an assessment of change; it misses the broader picture. Specific improvements, such as increasing transparency in public procurement, are often trampled by more radical institutional transformations, such as infrastructure privatization. By lengthening the scope of analysis and analyzing government contracting and service provision in two different policy areas over 25 years, this study captures the interplay between major and minor attempts at transforming public-sector institutions in Brazil and Argentina.

Key Concepts: Governance Reform and Reformers in Developing Democracies

The concept of "governance reform" used in this study focuses on intentional actions undertaken by the executive branch and public officials in developing democracies to improve the public sector and the provision of public goods and service delivery. Over the past decades, the use of the term "governance" has expanded rapidly – so much so that some scholars have questioned its usefulness (Grindle 2010). In response to the disappointing outcomes of state and neoliberal reforms of the 1990s, "governance" became a broad residual category used to explain unexpected outcomes, an ambiguous term that often substitutes for something else (Bersch and Botero 2014; Rose-Ackerman 2017). When the scope of governance reform is defined, however, it provides a way to understand the variegated effects of reforms, which often are meaningless when analyzed in isolation.

The definition of governance reform used here focuses attention on the state, the executive branch. It is important to note that this study does not test the argument in developed democracies, where institutions tend to be far stronger than in the developing world. Nor does it apply to states in moments of regime transition or in the midst of violent conflict. Instead, it emphasizes that, in stable democracies in the developing world, many of the most salient decisions for the public occur when laws are translated into practice in the executive. Governance reforms – often labeled public sector, public administration, state, or service-delivery reforms – focus on such goals as strengthening institutions, enhancing transparency, improving access, ensuring impartiality, and improving service delivery in a variety of policy areas that range from health to transportation to education.[4] Misguided theories of state reform applied to service provision in these areas have devastating consequences – from promised wells, medication, and books that never materialize to subway-car collisions and epidemics. Such catastrophes are often not failures of legislatures per se, which play a crucial role in determining the priorities of an administration (e.g., where to allocate the budget or what to build), but rather of well-intentioned reforms executed by the state – the executive branch, its ministries, and agencies that wield power over the delivery of services, security, and regulation.

Given the diversity of governance reforms, this study measures success based on the broad objectives of reformers and evaluates whether strategies result in both effective and enduring changes. In this way, one type of policy is not privileged over another. The analysis remains agnostic about whether the public or the private sector plays a larger or smaller role in the provision of public goods and service delivery. The standard of policy effectiveness adopted here, therefore, evaluates the performance of a government's reforms on issues that the reformers define as areas of priority, whether they focus on expanding coverage or enhancing efficiency. To evaluate endurance, I look not only at the ability to accomplish goals in the short-term but also at whether changes are sustained over time, enduring at least two turnovers in the administration.

Defining success in terms of reformers' objectives raises the question of who governance reformers actually are. Scholars of governance reform have focused on the president and high-level technocrats, generating

---

[4] While problem solving can lead to impressive public sector changes, it is important to note that not all areas that affect the public sector ought to be left, or can be left, to experts within the state. Problem solving reaches its fullest potential only by working with representative political institutions and civil society. See Chapter 8 for additional considerations regarding problem solving and democratic accountability.

numerous studies on the importance of technocrats in Latin America (Grindle 1977; Centeno 1994; Teichman 1997; Dargent 2015). What distinguishes a technocrat is expertise (Centeno and Silva 1998, 2; Dargent 2015, 13; Teichman 1997, 32). Yet authors who write about technocrats as those who have acquired expertise outside the bureaucracy and at foreign universities (Teichman 1997, 32) are often only referring to *outsider* technocrats. Indeed, such individuals play an important role in reform, but emphasis on outsider technocrats often masks important differences between reformers. High-level, and often foreign-educated, technocrats generally come and go with the president who appointed them. Thus they are outsiders to the public administration and tend to be politically affiliated with a particular president or party. Such individuals are labeled here as "technocratic outsiders" or "political technocrats."

The focus on outsiders overlooks insider (bureaucratic) technocrats, who often play an important role in advancing reforms. Often overshadowed by flashy political technocrats or mistaken for stodgy bureaucrats who resist change, bureaucratic technocrats (i.e., permanent technocrats or technocratic insiders) are the protagonists of many of the reforms highlighted in this study. Such an individual is a technocrat or a civil servant, who is recruited meritocratically and whose tenure in the public service does not hinge on political turnover. This distinction between insider and outsider technocrats adds a new dimension to literature on reform and technocrats.

Political technocrats tend to be proponents of powering, whereas bureaucratic technocrats tend to spearhead problem solving. Yet in my theory reform type is independent of other factors: The type of reform proponent does not determine reform approach. The conceptual separation of reform type and reformers also has important implications for the scope conditions of the argument. Outsiders – politicians and political technocrats – can acknowledge their limitations and seek to problem solve. This makes the theory relevant for countries with low levels of bureaucratic capacity and those countries that lack the type of insider technocrats that are highlighted throughout. Confronted with weak institutions, outsider reformers who understand their short time horizons and thus seek to work within the institutions they inherit will be more successful than those who attempt to bypass or transform existing institutions.

Finally, the objectives of governance reforms may vary significantly in their level of ambition. While some reformers set small, achievable goals (e.g., experimenting with a new contracting approach), others set their goals quite high (e.g., privatization of public infrastructure). Thus if reformers' goals are the yardstick of success, then sweeping reforms may fail at achieving their ambitious goals but may bring about more improvements than reformers who are successful in achieving one small change. Evaluating meaningful success also requires evaluating changes over longer stretches of time, taking into account the specific, immediate goals of reformers as well as the broader goals. Focusing on changes over time illuminates how reformers make progress toward more ambitious goals or alternatively whether radical reforms are reversed. The case comparisons in Brazil and Argentina also facilitate this approach. Because both countries faced similar challenges, reformers focused on similar broad goals, even if they relied on very different strategies.

ORGANIZATION

The first section of the book presents a theory of state building, explaining why some reform strategies result in sustainable improvements (Chapter 2) and describing the political conditions under which policymakers tend to adopt such successful strategies (Chapter 3). Alternative arguments are discussed to demonstrate the flawed logic behind conventional wisdom regarding state reform and establish the merits of an alternative approach (i.e., problem solving) that draws on cognitive-psychological insights about decision-making. Incremental changes sequenced over time, in response to failings in previous policy, provide two crucial advantages over wholesale, rapid change: (1) Continual adjustments and modifications benefit from learning; and (2) an incremental approach makes reform more durable and helps preserve bureaucratic autonomy, especially in weak institutional environments.

The choice of reform strategy and mechanisms elaborated are then explored in a political-organizational context, showing how established patterns of governing create variation in the type of reform strategy pursued. Whereas executive power in Argentina concentrated in single-party cabinets facilitates large-scale change, executive power sharing in Brazil frustrates big-bang reform attempts. In the context of Brazilian coalitional presidentialism, however, relative stability and the diversity of actors in the policy process create space for technocrats within the state to make small changes that accumulate over time. Thus I argue that established patterns of governing, rooted in the long history of how power is organized and exercised, account for the cross-national differences in the predominant reform strategies – i.e., the choice of powering versus problem solving.

The second section of the book analyzes public sector reforms. Chapter 4, on transportation in Argentina, documents the powering overhaul in the early 1990s; it shows how ideal-type models failed to account for changing conditions and unforeseen circumstances, and how the very process of imposing changes weakened institutions, prompting a fresh set of radical reforms in 2012 that reversed those of the 1990s. This chapter demonstrates how powering creates its own unhealthy dynamic: failing to produce the expected results, but also making it very difficult for subsequent reformers to come in and begin a process of successful problem solving. Thus this case study establishes a baseline by detailing the effects of draconian, almost immediate transformations.

Chapter 5, on transportation in Brazil, demonstrates how political-organizational context affects the adoption of the powering approach highlighted in Chapter 4. Coalitional presidentialism, which induces Brazilian presidents to share executive power, impeded most attempts at radical change, limiting the scale and speed of reform. For the few changes that did advance, however, a broader-based consensus was forged, and plans were subjected to the scrutiny of a diverse set of interests and experts. Moreover, smaller-scale changes opened up greater space for experts within the state to use their longer time horizons and technical acumen to gradually sequence individually small but often cumulatively significant changes. Chapter 5 demonstrates that even though powering in Brazil has been a rare occurrence, when radical change did occur it left negative and enduring repercussions.

The findings of Chapter 6, on health in Argentina, corroborate the failures of comprehensive planning required of powering. The within-country comparison of transportation and health in Argentina provides useful analytical leverage in assessing the extent to which the speed and depth of reforms affect outcomes. This chapter shows that change to the health sector did not cut as deeply nor go as far as it did in transport, but areas of comparatively greater stability were more successful at fostering gradual changes down the line. The subsector in which the *most* drastic changes were made – health care for pensioners – ultimately witnessed the most disappointing outcomes over time. Thus Chapter 6 substantiates the negative correlation between reform speed/depth and success and shows how delayed and stalled powering reforms can give rise to gradual, problem-solving efforts in some key areas.

Chapter 7 shows that health reforms in Brazil have proceeded even more gradually and with particularly high success. The multiplicity of actors involved in the policymaking process often diluted, delayed, or halted changes. This reduced the scale of the changes attempted and thus the complexity of reforms attempted at any given time. The sequencing of change also allowed for learning that ultimately increased success.

Chapter 8 summarizes the theoretical and empirical insights of the book while highlighting the relevance of this study to the unfolding, unprecedented corruption scandals in Brazil. It then places the cases examined in comparative perspective, by assessing reform processes in the Latin American cases of Chile, Uruguay, Colombia, El Salvador, and Venezuela, and by considering the implications of applying the theory to developed countries or non-democratic regimes. Finally, the broader theoretical implications of the argument are considered in discussing the application of bounded rationality to studies of policy change and highlighting the connections between historical institutionalism and bounded rationality.

2

The Merits of Problem Solving over Powering

The best is the enemy of the good.

Voltaire

The return to democracy in Latin America has been followed by countless attempts to transform the public sector. In many countries, civil service laws have been redesigned, yet cronyism persists; transparency systems implemented, yet opacity prevails; and new constitutions written, only to be rewritten. Why did such impressive efforts fail to bring about the anticipated results? What reform processes result in effective and enduring improvements?

This chapter provides the microfoundations for the theoretical framework presented in this book, arguing that problem solving provides two crucial advantages over powering: (1) continual adjustments and modifications benefit from learning; and (2) an incremental approach makes reform more durable and helps preserve bureaucratic autonomy. After examining insights and inadequacies of existing approaches to the understanding of advances in the quality of governance and reform, the I make the case for incorporating microfoundations of change into broader macro assessments of institutional development by focusing on reform strategy. The following sections of this chapter establish the differences between reform strategies and their microfoundations.

Chapter 3 follows this discussion of powering and problem solving with a chapter on institutional context and historical legacies, which explains how political-organizational macrofactors influence the choice of reform strategy. It complements the present chapter both by reviewing historical institutionalist literature and detailing how exclusionary and inclusionary institutions contribute to the reform strategy. In doing so, Chapter 3 will show how established patterns of executive power sharing create variation in the reform strategy pursued and will demonstrate how my theory of reform combines structure and agency.

INSUFFICIENCY OF EXTANT APPROACHES

The existing literature focuses on broad structural and institutional features to try to explain effective states, account for a wide range of governance outcomes, and determine the conditions for successful reform. We can gain important insights from these approaches, but they must be combined with an analysis of the underlying micro processes of reform to form a truly compelling account of contemporary Latin American state development. While structural and institutional theories contribute to the general conditions that may affect institutional quality, they focus primarily on cross-national or cross-regional variation. This fails to capture within-country variation, which is often more significant. They also tend to overlook the importance of the executive branch, which in Latin America plays a dominant role in policymaking. Thus, while these theories provide important insights into understanding the conditions for successful reforms and may be empirically accurate in specific cases, reform strategy is a crucial and overlooked factor that deserves considerable attention as it independently increases the chances for successful reform.

Structural Theories

Theories focusing on structural factors predict progress in state building, and thus reform efforts, as by-products of system-level trends. Economic growth has long been thought to foster the emergence of strong institutions and capable states (Lipset 1960; Leff 1964; Leys 1965; Demsetz 1967). Despite scant empirical evidence for modernization theory, variants of the argument emerge in a wide variety of claims about how corrupt, inefficient states become clean, capable, modern nations and how economic growth spurs greater transparency, accountability, and participation (e.g., Goldsmith 2007, 165). Surely very low levels of development and resources can make any reform effort more challenging, but modernization theories fail to explain much of what we see in Latin America. After all, Chile was considered an impoverished colonial backwater yet has gone on to lead the region both in terms of economic growth and institutional strength, surpassing wealthier and more institutionalized colonial centers. Such theories would also predict that Argentina – which during the early half of the twentieth century maintained some of the highest levels of GDP, education, and tax collection capabilities in the region – would today rank near the top of Latin American countries in terms of state capacity. Despite initial advantages, however, Argentina has underperformed in many areas (Kurtz 2013, 3–16; Fukuyama 2014, 274–84). In these and many more cases, modernization theories have not been borne out in Latin America.

Some scholars suggest that persistent cycles of economic crisis create variation in reform trajectories (Levitsky and Murillo 2013). According to this hypothesis, Argentina's recurring crises, and particularly the severe economic collapse of 2001, explain its disappointing reform track record, whereas Brazil's gains in institutional strength reflect periods of greater economic stability. Yet the Argentine crisis was largely the *result* of decisions made during periods of high economic growth.

Indeed, structuralist arguments in general raise a series of pernicious questions regarding endogeneity: Does economic growth increase institutional quality? Or does institutional quality increase economic growth and preclude economic crises? The weight of the evidence seems to suggest that institutional quality is an important cause of cross-country differences in economic growth and prosperity (Acemoglu, Johnson, and Robinson 2001; Acemoglu et al. 2005; Dollar and Kraay 2003; North 1990; Kaufmann and Kraay 2002; Knack and Keefer 1995; Rodrik, Subramanian, and Trebbi 2004). Economic growth matters for state building but is not decisive, and theories roughly based on modernization provide unconvincing explanations for reform trajectories in Latin America.

A variety of other structural factors – ranging from distance to the equator, colonialism, resource wealth, and war – have been invoked to explain the continued poverty and underdevelopment of certain nations (Diamond 1997; La Porta et al. 1999; Mahoney 2001; Ross 2001; Sachs 2006; Teorell and Rothstein 2013; Tilly 1990; Doner, Ritchie, and Slater 2005). Yet resource-curse arguments must contend with the reality that countries awash in natural resources (Chile, Canada, the United States, Norway) have used that wealth to enhance political and economic development. Colonialism may explain variation between world regions but falls short when applied to Latin America, which shares a common colonial heritage. Similarly, it is difficult to apply Tilly's theories to Latin America, with its conspicuous absence of war – save for nineteenth-century wars directed at destructive domestic ends that did not contribute to state building as in Europe (Centeno 2002).

Structural forces certainly do matter. After all, many early state-building efforts seem to have enduring consequences. Countries such as Chile and Brazil that invested in state capabilities continue to have some of the strongest states in Latin America. Two recent studies of state building in Latin America by Marcus Kurtz (2013) and Hillel Soifer (2015) provide compelling explanations for these cross-national differences in state capacity. They suggest that socio-political dynamics at key historical moments shape long-run outcomes. While Kurtz shows the importance of the post-independence consolidation of institutions and the timing of mass political incorporation, Soifer underscores how fragmented regionalism led to the rejection of state building.

The argument presented in this book in no way diminishes the importance of the broad set of factors that contribute to state capacity and governance reform. At the same time, arguments that emphasize historically determined, path-dependent consequences fail to account for change and within-country variation in capacity. As recent scholarship has shown, within-country, cross-agency diversity in capacity often trumps cross-national variation (Gingerich 2012; see also Bersch, Praça, and Taylor 2017a). While higher levels of capacity increase the chances of successful reform, state capacity and civil-service structure are not given but are themselves subject to change. In fact, reform type has a significant effect on bureaucratic quality, and improvements are possible even in areas of weak capacity.[1] Thus, while prior levels of state capacity matter, reform strategy independently increases the chances for successful reform and helps explain within-country variation.

In summary, structuralist theories are better at explaining variation between world regions, but they are insufficient when invoked to explain variation within countries or between countries that share many structural characteristics. Moreover, factors that Latin American countries do not uniformly share, such as depth or frequency of economic crises, are more likely the result of improved institutional quality than the cause.

---

[1] Whereas powering may further weaken what civil service protections do exist, problem-solving has a salutary impact by building bureaucratic capacity over time. Thus, while existing civil service systems matter, I will show how change and improvements are possible in areas of weak capacity and how one reform type, problem-solving, can strengthen capacity over time.

Institutional Theories

Interest-Driven Theories and Political Insurance

Interest-driven theories, specifically theories of political insurance, claim that high levels of electoral competition result in successful reform. Such theories are informed by the rational choice paradigm: politicians are strategic actors who aim to maximize their chances of winning elections (Geddes 1994); to do so, elected officials weigh the costs of governance reforms (e.g., loss of access to state resources and patronage) against the benefits (e.g., increased state capacity and governance outcomes). Insurance theories of reform argue that if the electoral defeat of an incumbent is imminent, the officeholder will seek reforms that increase accountability and transparency as a way to tie the hands of his or her successors (Moe 1990).[2] Thus, where electoral competition is high and political turnover is frequent, we should expect strong institutions.

Interest-driven arguments have often been applied to foundational moments like the creation of courts. For instance, Ginsburg (2003) argues that fragmentation increases political uncertainty, which encourages designers to create strong, autonomous courts that can protect them when they are out of power. Chavez (2004) also shows that electoral uncertainty and fragmentation shape the creation, design, and operation of high-level courts. Scholars have used a similar logic in a number of other areas. For instance, in their analysis of freedom of information laws at a subnational level in Mexican states, Berliner and Erlich (2013) claim that electoral competition is a major driver of transparency reforms. Studying postcommunist state reconstruction, Grzymala-Busse (2007) argues that even opportunistic political parties will limit their corrupt behavior and abuse of state resources when faced with strong political competition. In all of these instances, uncertainty – whether due to political fragmentation, political competition, or future loss of political control – motivates rulers to strategically limit their own power.

The insurance arguments suit some institutional and policy domains better than others. That is, such theories may apply to the creation of powerful courts during highly uncertain foundational moments or to institutions of horizontal accountability among government officials,

---

[2] In Moe's words, designers "do not want 'their' agencies to fall under the control of opponents. And given the way public authority is allocated and exercised in a democracy, they often can only shut out their opponents by shutting themselves out too. In many cases, then, they purposely create structures that even they cannot control" (Moe 1990, 125).

but they are less useful for explaining variation in the effectiveness and endurance of state reforms initiated by the executive.

First, the logic of political insurance unravels when considering office-holders' strong demands for campaign financing, casting doubt on the sequence of events that could induce the governing party to implement accountability or transparency reforms. According to the logic of political insurance, a governing party would only implement reforms when certain of its own impending electoral doom. Yet one would expect that, at precisely this vulnerable electoral time, a vulnerable party would be inclined to use public resources to fund electoral prospects.

Second, let us suppose that uncertainty did induce an executive to advance reforms that limited its own power and discretion (e.g., institutional mechanisms to enhance accountability or transparency). Designing such changes, especially in the midst of an impending electoral defeat, assumes comprehensive rationality to tackle a complex task. That is, insurance arguments assume a seamless translation between interest and outcomes: if an executive wishes to increase transparency and account-ability plus has the power to implement reforms, such theories largely assume he or she will be able to design or select effective mechanisms. Insurance theories, then, confer a great deal of computing power on decision-makers, who are likely cognitively constrained by a lack of time, information, attention, and resources. Thus decision-makers are more likely to create imperfect reforms leading to unintended conse-quences. Furthermore, political insurance arguments rest on the dubious assumption that if rules are adopted, they will be sustained over time. If the governing party passes a reform only when it foresees defeat, then there is little time to implement the changes. Even if lame ducks carry out reforms, little prevents an incoming governing party with enough legisla-tive support from reneging (Moe 1990).

While political insurance arguments may apply to some policy and institutional domains, they fail to adequately explain effective and durable governance reforms. Many of these theories are valuable, however, in that they provide insights into the motivations for policies that limit the executive's discretion and the role of fragmentation in shaping the reform processes (Chavez 2004), a point discussed in further detail in Chapter 3.

Formal Institutional Theories

A final set of theories focuses on strategic choice but expects reforms to be shaped by formal political institutions. Formal rules, according to the rational-choice framework, constrain behavior by defining the set of choices actors can select to maximize their self-interest (Shepsle 1989).

Such arguments have been used to claim that presidential systems produce political instability and gridlock. Linz (1994) influentially argued that presidentialism is less conducive to democratic stability, because it engenders a winner-takes-all dynamic that polarizes competitors and leads to deadlocked, zero-sum politics. He expected presidentialism to be particularly pernicious in Brazil. Similarly, scholars like Mainwaring (1999) and Ames (2001) have drawn attention to perceived deficiencies of the Brazilian party and electoral systems. Brazil's open-list proportional representation, high average district magnitude, and federal structure result in extreme multipartism and high levels of political fragmentation (Mainwaring 1999).[3] This combination of multipartism and presidentialism was to exacerbate the "perils of presidentialism" by complicating interparty coalition building and was labeled the "difficult combination" (Mainwaring 1993; Stepan and Skach 1993).

Empirical evidence in Latin America challenges these arguments. Countries with the "wrong" formal institutions, such as Chile, Uruguay, and Brazil, lead the region in rankings of government effectiveness and rule of law (Kaufmann, Kraay, and Mastruzzi 2010). Accordingly, a revisionist literature seeks to explain the success in Brazil and the comparative failure in Argentina to sustain high-quality policies. This literature provides valuable contributions but has important weaknesses. Focusing on Argentina, for example, Spiller and Tommasi (2007) hold that specific institutional arrangements result in low-quality policies, emphasizing the importance of intra-temporal cooperation for high-quality policies. They argue that having strong governors who seek fiscal favors from the executive, in addition to legislative careers at the provincial instead of national level, results in a shortsighted executive and an unprofessional legislature; this in turn reduces intertemporal cooperation and leads to lower-quality policies. Such an argument could plausibly address the low quality of policies in Argentina but does not explain why Brazil has done better in many areas. After all, governors in Brazil

---

[3] The pattern of cabinet sharing in Brazil cannot, however, be attributed solely to the existence of proportional representation or to its electoral system. As Colomer (2004) details, the choice of electoral system is best understood as a consequence of the expectation and calculations of the established political leaders. Proportional representation systems were adopted in pluralistic constituent conventions or by political agreements among multiple political parties that expected to compete in uncertain elections and to share power in multiparty cabinets (Colomer 2004, 86).

are also powerful, and the legislature is a focal point for fiscal favors (see González 2010).

Spiller and Tommasi's analysis has been extended to other countries in Latin America. Scartascini, Stein, Tommasi, and their co-authors argue that the institutions defining the policymaking process shape the incentives of political actors, which in turn conditions the quality of policies (Stein et al. 2006; Scartascini, Stein, and Tommasi 2010). These authors highlight the aspects of the formal institutional framework – ranging from brief legislative careers (Jones et al. 2002; Saiegh 2010) to low bureaucratic capacity and autonomy (Zuvanic and Iacoviello 2010) – that can decrease the quality of policies (Stein et al. 2006; Scartascini, Stein, and Tommasi 2010). Such factors, along with the role of intertemporal cooperation, are indeed crucial in determining the quality of public policies.[4]

Likewise the revisionist literature on Brazil makes some important contributions. Figueiredo and Limongi (1999; 2000), among the first to revise the pessimistic expectations regarding Brazil's institutional structure, argue that the institutions that shape presidential power and centralized leadership in the lower house ameliorate political instability and gridlock. Similar arguments about the success of multiparty presidentialism in Latin America point to the importance of a strong executive and institutions of accountability able to check the president (Melo and Pereira 2013).[5] Other scholars have highlighted the importance of multiparty cabinet composition for securing governability (Deheza 1997; Amorim Neto 1998) or the importance of the executive toolbox – distributive politics and coalition formation – for maintaining legislative support (Cheibub, Przeworski, and Saiegh 2004; Raile, Pereira, and Power 2010; Chaisty, Cheeseman, and Power 2014).

The problem with the literature on the quality of policies and multiparty presidentialism in Brazil, however, is its failure to address arguably the most important actor in policymaking: the executive. The quality of many public policies is ultimately determined by the executive, as are bureaucratic capacity and autonomy (Ames, Carreras, and Schwartz 2012). Focusing on the legislature (Cheibub, Przeworski, and Saiegh 2004; Raile, Pereira, and Power 2010; but see Bersch, Praça, and Taylor

---

[4] While their emphasis on cooperation and the importance of historical institutions for the policymaking process is well placed, their analysis fails to demonstrate why we would ever see countries move out of a dysfunctional equilibrium.

[5] Existing analyses argue that a strong web of accountability is a precondition for the success of multiparty presidentialism (Melo and Pereira 2013). However, such arguments fail to explain where such a web comes from or how strong checks and balances develop.

2017a; 2017b for exceptions) obscures the fact that important questions of the state are exclusively in the domain of the executive and his or her cabinet. Cabinets in presidential systems are accountable not to the legislature but to the executive; therefore, they are largely outside of the formal institutional framework (Martínez-Gallardo 2010, 120). Instead of opening up the black box of the state, existing analyses highlight correlations between multiparty presidentialism and democratic sustainability (even success) without explaining why multiparty presidential democracies have been more successful than critics presumed.

In sum, formal institutional arguments are still often at odds with empirical realities, as demonstrated by the revisionists who have attacked Linz's link between presidentialism and instability. This newer literature does well to shed light on the importance of cooperation for high-quality policies and the strategies presidents use to induce politicians in fractious legislatures to work together. Yet arguments fail to identify the reasons cooperation occurs within the executive and the causal mechanisms that connect institutional differences to governance outcomes (cf. Bersch, Praça, and Taylor 2017b).

Both structural and institutional arguments have contributed to our understanding of state building and the quality of institutions on a regional or cross-national basis; however, a focus on such broad trends fails to provide meaningful insights into what might be done to reduce corruption, enhance state capacity, or advance development in the meantime. In short, such high-level arguments leave little room for individual agency. Indeed, if structural forces such as economic development or historical factors determine the quality of institutions and the trajectories of state building, the hands of political leaders and practitioners are tied. Political actors' efforts to improve the quality of institutions, build capacity, or spur economic growth would be ineffectual in the face of these broader trends. We know, however, that politicians' actions and leadership substantially affect the quality of institutions and longer-term trajectories, for better or worse.

Most scholars would agree, for instance, that Venezuelan President Hugo Chávez and his successor Nicolás Maduro have had an indelible effect on the quality of institutions and the trajectory of the country. While structural or institutional factors may have given rise to Chavismo, the leadership and strategic choices of the man himself were crucial. If leadership can have such problematic consequences for the quality of governance, then it can also presumably strengthen institutions as well. Moreover, understanding the effects of such reform choices would provide analytical leverage for explaining within-country variation. Scholars have long noted that within a single nation-state some areas of the government are "instruments of unfettered patronage" (Whitehead 2006, 96) while others are "islands of excellence" (Martins 1985; Willis 1986; Schneider 1987; Geddes 1994; Evans 1995, 257; Bersch, Praça, and Taylor 2017a; 2017b). Structural and institutional arguments fail to explain such within-country variation for one key reason: They leave little room for leadership and strategy.

REFORM STRATEGY: A THEORY OF EFFECTIVE AND ENDURING REFORM

Which reform processes result in effective and enduring improvements? A prominent line of argument emphasizes political will and argues that the surest way to reform the state is swift, wholesale change (e.g., Åslund 1994; Durand and Thorp 1998; Graham and Naím 1998; Rothstein 2011a, 246; 2011b, 211; Sachs 1993; 1994). Drawing on Heclo (1974), I call this approach powering. The goals of such forceful overhauls – such as restructuring pension plans or reducing the number of civil servants – are clear and comprehensive from the outset. Proponents argue that corruption and inefficiency can be eliminated by replacing dysfunctional institutional arrangements with policy programs that engender more salutary incentive structures. Under normal conditions, however, societal interests have a stranglehold on institutions; thus, change must be imposed by driving rapid, far-reaching reforms past beneficiaries of the status quo. If reforms are carried out more gradually, opposition forces will coalesce and block them (Graham and Naím 1998, 336). If reforms are partial or incremental, they will fail to undercut vested interests focused on preserving the status quo (Rothstein 2011a). Consequently, political entrepreneurs and reform champions are crucial for harnessing political will and power to push change past opposition forces during windows of opportunity. Reforms successfully shepherded through the challenging phase of initial implementation, adherents posit, will become durable and self-enforcing.

A second set of scholars disagrees with the powering thesis. They illustrate that institutional reform is often the product of gradual change, resulting from efforts to address problems within the established policy-making process (Hirschman 1973; Heclo 1974; Abers and Keck 2013; Lindblom 1959; Taylor 2009; Andrews, Pritchett, and Woolcock 2017). I refer to such reform as problem solving, advances that seek to resolve

policy problems and puzzles.[6] Whereas powering pursues an ideal program and has clear, comprehensive goals, problem solving focuses on
existing programs. Its objectives arise from addressing problems caused
by the current policies in practice. Problem solving implies that substantial
changes are achievable by sequentially advancing small, novel, partial, or
indirect alterations, often quietly and under the radar of political and
social forces. Instead of pushing wholesale reform through at "critical
junctures," proponents of problem solving take advantage of any opportunities and use the complexity of policy areas to advance individually
minor but cumulatively significant changes. Administrative officials often
convince politicians to agree to an incremental step, planning and hoping
that the "one little step" sets in motion a sequence of steps that add up to
significant transformation. This "reform-mongering" approach, as
Hirschman labeled it, can result in a "non-spectacular, stealthy style of
change" with impressive results over the long run (Hirschman 1971, 335).

Tackling Problems versus Applying Power

The concepts of powering and problem solving offer a lens on theories of
reform strategy. Powering assumes a homeostatic equilibrium able to
maintain itself against external "disruption," whereas problem solving
assumes a more flexible equilibrium. Although proponents of powering
argue that a strong push is required to bring significant change, problem
solving starts from the premise that incremental change is achievable
within the existing sociopolitical environment. And if powering confronts
opposition head-on, problem solving tends to avoid it. Two attributes are
particularly important for distinguishing powering from problem solving:
aspirational level and time frame. Powering reforms overhaul institutions
within a short time frame, usually during the term of political leaders;
problem-solving reforms make incremental modifications over a longer
period of time, and tend to be spearheaded by actors within the state.[7]

---

[6] I thank Bryan Jones for suggesting this term. "Problem solving" is used broadly in
cognitive and political science literature and is greatly influenced by Herbert Simon's
later work with Allen Newell on complex tasks (Newell and Simon 1972; Simon 1996;
see especially Bendor 2003, 457). I elaborate a specific meaning for the term here that
draws on this earlier work. In other places I have labeled the same concept as "puzzle
solving," drawing on Hugh Heclo's (1974) distinction between "powering" and "puzzle
solving."

[7] My elaboration of these terms draws on seminal studies of reform and institutional change
(e.g., Lindblom 1959; Hirschman 1973; Heclo 1974). The problem-solving approach also
shares important similarities with Andrews, Pritchett, and Woolcock's (2013; 2017)

TABLE 1 *Types of Reform*

	Powering	Problem Solving
Objective	The goal is clear – must be imposed against opposition	The exact goal is unclear; broad principles guide flexible reform process
Aspirational Level	Wholesale and rapid; based on ideal models	Incremental and sustained; Based on experiential learning
Strategy	Sweeping use of political power to break through logjams	Finding space and using technocratic capacity to make gradual advances
Time Frame	Completed within executive's term	Sequenced over time across presidential terms
Outcome	Episodic – depending on power balance	Enduring

Table 1 expands on these distinctions. The different purposes and causal processes are formulated in ideal-typical terms, but it is important to note that any particular reform may fall on the spectrum between powering and problem solving.

In the early 1990s, advocates of powering highlighted the importance of the exceptional economic and political crises in Latin American and post-communist countries for tabula rasa state overhauls.[8] When these extraordinary situations passed, scholars began to shift attention from macroeconomic reforms to strengthening the state (Naím 1994), de-emphasizing the importance of "exceptional" crises and instead underscoring the crucial role of political entrepreneurs in imposing change – regardless of opposition – during "limited windows of opportunity" (Bunse and Fritz 2012, 6). The commitment of strong political leaders became the crucial element for successful reform (e.g., Grindle 2004, 20; Bunse and Fritz 2012,

---

"Problem-Driven Iterative Approach (PDIA)," such as the emphasis on experimentation and iterative feedback and the rejection of one-size-fits-all solutions. The argument of my book is unique, however, in addressing issues of governance or public-sector reform (rather than addressing development more broadly), explaining the political conditions that shape reform approach, and providing theoretical micro-foundations that explain the success or failure of reform. Thus, Andrews, Pritchett, and Woolcook's (2017) excellent handbook for development practitioners can be seen as a complement to this book's more theoretical argument, which is supported by detailed evidence in two countries over time.

[8] See the special issue of *Journal of Democracy* (October 1994) on reform and democracy.

34–5). Such leaders, together with technocratic reform teams or "change teams," would have the capacity to push complex overhauls of state institutions past resistance (Durand and Thorp 1998, 5; Graham and Naím 1998, 336; Grindle 2004, 187).[9] "Technopols" became the new term for the marriage of technocratic skill and high-level political power (Domínguez 1997). Such political leaders and their handpicked experts, here referred to as "outsiders" or "political technocrats," were seen as crucial for bringing about political and economic transformations (Grindle 1977; Camp 1985). As recent analyses have pointed out, the focus on political will and the importance of political technocrats for ensuring reform outcomes remains pervasive in the development community and among International Financial Institutions (IFIs) (Andrews 2013, 7–15).

By contrast, problem solving implies that existing state actors (i.e., "insiders") can drive the reform process without significant realignment of political forces (Taylor 2009), advancing marginal changes gradually and without directly confronting powerful resistance (Hirschman 1973). The underlying assumption of a flexible equilibrium allowing the possibility of implementing partial changes, observing their impact, and making necessary corrections along the way. The process is not dramatic, nor is it led by political leaders or technopols with the ear of the president; rather, technocrats or higher-level public servants fulfilling their regular professional duties are often the quiet backers of these modest changes.[10] This process does not require breaking through resistance with force; instead, it is a process of "muddling through," to use Lindblom's (1959) term – of learning from addressing previous policy concerns by making adjustments and corrections over time, thereby assessing what is effective and what is not.

A variety of factors provide momentum for problem-solving reform efforts, running the gamut from proactive strategies to more passive approaches. Nóbrega (2005) and Taylor (2009) illustrate the importance

---

[9] While these scholars emphasize the importance of strong political executives for successful reform, they cannot all be unequivocally labeled as adherents of the powering view. Grindle, for instance, recognizes the challenges that imposed reform later creates for sustainability (Grindle 2004, 189–94).

[10] Scholars such as Huber and Stephens (2012) also advocate for more incremental policy change as opposed to dramatic change; however, their account does not attribute change to technocratic actors but rather to "bottom up" pressures (257). Mahoney and Thelen's (2010) power-distributional theory of institutional change recognizes the importance of gradual change but says little about which types of processes engender effective and enduring change (1–37).

of broad principles or a common end goal, which serve as a north star for disparate reformers (Mailson da Nóbrega in Taylor 2009). Other scholars highlight the strategies reformers use to "smuggle" broader changes into the policy process, like convincing politicians to agree to an incremental step, hoping that "one little step" eventually leads to significant transformation (Hirschman 1973), or drawing up desirable policies and including them in remotely related legislation (Nóbrega and Loyola 2006; see also Taylor 2009).[11] In other works, Hirschman (1967, 78) notes that pursuing ambitious objects lead to "voyages of discovery," with creative solutions emerging from solving problems that turn out to be more difficult than expected, observing that "[people] engage successfully in problem-solving [when] they take up problems which they think they can solve, find them more difficult than expected, but then, being stuck with them, attack willy-nilly the unsuspected difficulties." Such types of change have a clear direction, even if the means to get there are flexible. Still other approaches have no grand plan but rather commit reformers to brainstorming new changes that incrementally alter the "rules of the game" (Praça and Taylor 2014).[12] In contexts with limited reform capacity, Hausmann et al. (2005) highlight the strategic importance of removing bottlenecks, or "binding constraints," starting with reforms that tackle the largest and moving piecemeal to the next. Instead of addressing the largest economic distortions, this reform style eliminates bottlenecks with the largest negative impact on social welfare and economic development.

At the most passive end of the reform spectrum are incremental approaches, such as Lindblom's classic "muddling through" or approaches that advocate iterative feedback (Andrews, Pritchett, and Woolcock 2013).[13] Many American scholars have criticized Lindblom's incrementalism for a lack of goal orientation (e.g., Behn 1988, 649), with some claiming that incrementalism "would have us cross and recross intersections without knowing where we were going" (Forester 1984, 23; see also Weiss and Woodhouse 1992 for critiques and rebuttals). Yet directionless, reactive change that does not seek improvements should not

---

[11] This became known in the Central Bank as "smuggling" (Nóbrega and Loyola 2006, 83, fn.12).

[12] For instance, Praça and Taylor (2014, 30) cite Brazil's National Strategy for Combating Corruption and Money-Laundering (ENCCLA) as a successful accountability institution for its ability to bring together its constituent organizations to share information and generate gradual institutional change.

[13] Lindblom advocated limiting analysis to "any calculated or thoughtfully chosen set of stratagems to simplify complex policy problems" (1959, 518).

be conflated with problem solving. After all, Lindblom (1959, 86) himself recognized that incremental analysis could help harried policymakers pursue relevant long-term goals. A range of other strategies exists between those that work toward one policy objective and those with more modest incrementalist approaches. Thus problem solving is not an integrated strategy; rather, as an applied theory,[14] it employs a range of strategies to make change politically and cognitively feasible.

How can this slow, arduous process possibly produce advantages over powering's promises of rapid, comprehensive, and enduring change? An evaluation of the limitations of the powering approach lends insight into problem solving's merits. The powering argument is based on two assumptions that are often unrealistic and unpromising in the real world: (1) It is possible to rationally design or select the appropriate reform; and (2) once implemented, dramatic, comprehensive reforms will persist as new vested interests begin to defend the status quo.

Limitations in Designing Wholesale Change

The powering approach, which implies comprehensive rationality, over-estimates the ability of political actors and decision-makers to find the appropriate solution. If political actors were to select a reform rationally, according to the rational choice institutional approach, they would rank order their goals and systematically evaluate the best means to achieve those ends. This approach is daunting when planning an overhaul to a program, agency, or ministry that aims to root out numerous problems at once. Such change is very different from simply adjusting the levels of existing policy (e.g., increasing the number of Medicare recipients). It implies that it is possible to identify and systematically assess different reform alternatives by performing careful cost–benefit analyses. Especially for the most complex problems, however, the constraints on policymakers' time and information, along with the considerable uncertainty they face, make the extensive planning required unlikely to be carried out in a systematic and balanced manner (Tetlock 2005). Indeed, the selection and execution of powering reform is not like playing chess, where the rules of the game are fixed and agreed upon by the players ahead of time. Instead, the rules themselves are up in the air. Powering implies creating a new game from scratch and forcing players, who were engaged in a prior game, to use an entirely new set of rules. That is, powering implies understanding *ex ante* where opposition will emerge and what

---

[14] On this point, see Bendor 2015, 198–9.

strategies that opposition will adopt in reaction to reforms. This is virtually impossible to do.

To execute these feats in such a complex task environment seems to require an omniscient and omnipotent political actor with extensive informational, computational, and financial resources. In short, it requires comprehensive rationality in an extraordinarily demanding task environment. We know, however, that humans rarely meet the standard of full rationality and are instead boundedly rational (see Jones 1999; Bendor 2003). As Lindblom (1959) argued long ago, rationally designing wholesale comprehensive reform assumes "intellectual capacities and sources of information that men [and women] simply do not possess" (80). Instead of proactively seeking out alternatives, calculating advantages and disadvantages, and maximizing their utility by selecting the solution that ranks highest in terms of costs and benefits, policymakers commonly rely on heuristics that facilitate the process of making choices, often by seeking a satisfactory solution rather than the optimal solution (Simon 1955; Bendor 2003).

The extent to which actors rely on cognitive shortcuts depends not only on the task environment's structure but also on actors' computational capability, which act together, according to Herbert Simon, like "scissors [with] two blades" (Simon 1990, 7; Bendor 2003, 435). Thus, while all decision-makers confront such limitations as a lack of time, attention, resources, information, and intellectual and computing capacity to rationally evaluate complex problems (see Jones 1999, 305–9), some face tighter bounds than others. Elected officials are particularly disadvantaged, as politicians do not have the resources to be experts in more than a few areas. Their attention span is short (Jones and Baumgartner 2005) and frequently jumps from economic crisis to health care to agricultural policy and so on. And while political technocrats may have impressive academic credentials, their fate is often linked to the political actor who appointed them, resulting in shorter time horizons and an absence of the expertise important for understanding the effects of change in a new context – experience working in the government. Consequently, relying on "outsiders" to implement radical changes in new contexts heightens ambiguity, uncertainty, and unintended consequences. Thus comprehensive reforms often fail to replace problematic institutional arrangements with functional alternatives; instead, they engender new dysfunctionalities (see also Scott 1998).

Problem solving, designed to cope with a world of bounded rationality, is more realistic and consequently more promising. The limitations of decision makers are less acute for the proponents of problem solving. Newell and Simon (1972) long ago noted that problem-solving performance varies greatly. In chess, they argue, there are both grandmasters and duffers. What separates the two is expertise, which allows the grandmasters to remember action rules and recognize repeated patterns. Duffers, however, are lost in time-consuming attempts to compute their next play (Simon 1990, 8–11). The rules of chess, of course, are more fixed and predictable than twenty-first-century policymaking, which requires knowledge of informal rules governing the larger context within which reforms occur.

Such expertise is developed by the study of an area over time. And time is what accounts for the variation in the capabilities of powering versus problem solving: Political actors have many issues on their plates and tend to have short time horizons, whereas bureaucratic technocrats and civil servants are able to gain experience and expertise in a given area over time, including knowledge of problems caused by previous policies. As a result of this contextual understanding, they are frequently in a better position to evaluate problems and to design solutions in a particular policy area than are their elected counterparts.

Moreover, problem solving divides complex problems into smaller steps, thereby simplifying the task environment. Instead of taking on comprehensive reform, problem solving tackles smaller problems one by one. Efforts to resolve these smaller problems draw on decision-makers' existing knowledge and experiences. This approach does not assume that definitive solutions to complex problems exist; solutions are instead discovered by comparing locally known alternatives with the status quo (Lindblom 1959). The improvement may not be the best possible solution, but it is better than the status quo: It is attainable, and, most importantly, it is improvable.

Taken together, these two advantages of problem solving – its fit with the capabilities of decision-makers and its simplification of the task environment – result in learning over time.[15] In the sequential process of solving smaller problems, reformers acquire a repertoire of pragmatic moves and their results, increasing their ability to recognize solutions to a given problem (Simon 1990; 1996). In this way, problem-solvers work around the opposition one step at a time. Changes often build on

[15] For a definition of learning, see Hall (1993, 278).

themselves and cumulatively create a thorough transformation of the original policy framework. Consequently, state actors improve their ability to address harder questions, building their expertise, learning about different types of reforms, and discovering what it takes to guide reforms past opposition. While the advocates of powering search for magic bullets, problem solving engenders an incremental learning process that allows reform tactics to evolve along the way.

Challenges to Powering's Durability

The second assumption of powering – that, once implemented, reforms will persist as new vested interests begin to defend the status quo – also regularly fails. Powering has two goals: the elimination of the status quo; and the establishment and consolidation of a new approach. These two goals, however, create a contradiction in which successfully eliminating established arrangements endangers the chances of consolidating reforms.

Consider a powerful president intent on sweeping out corruption in health-care provision. By bringing in outside experts and teams, the president may successfully overcome resistance, uproot the status quo, and establish a new approach. These changes, according to the powering logic, will generate a new set of vested interests that will defend the policy changes. Deep-cutting reforms that usher in transparency or clean government, however, entail concentrated costs for opponents – often creating a backlash. Thus, when a new president takes office, she is likely to respond to the backlash and empower opponents before supporters of the diffuse benefits can organize a defense. Why, then, right after an entirely new policy framework is installed, would relevant actors believe it has staying power? Most often, the defenders of the new program (diffuse benefits) are weaker than the prior defenders of the status quo (concentrated benefits). Counter-reforms will then face even less resistance. Therefore, the *paradox of powering* is that triumph in the eliminatory stage hinders the probability of enduring, consolidated reforms. Gonzalo Sánchez de Lozada in Bolivia, for example, won the battle of implementing shock therapy in the hyperinflationary 1980s only to lose the war: powering through in Bolivia led to immense pushback, including the removal of President Sánchez de Lozada and the election of Evo Morales.

Moreover, the more "normal" the conditions under which powering is imposed, the more the paradox applies. War, earthquakes, or hyperinflation may effectively wipe out resistance to change without generating concentrated costs and backlash. In the absence of crisis, however, proponents of powering emphasize political will or a political leader's ability to cast a problem as a "crisis." In non-crisis periods, political technocrats – teams of experts or new political appointees who have the expertise and "will" to execute the changes – are brought in to implement reforms (Durand and Thorp 1998, 140). Yet political capital often runs out well before a reform's diffuse beneficiaries are able to defend it against a new leader who abandons her predecessor's unconsolidated reform efforts. Over time, this process chips away at bureaucratic capacity and experience, reduces the possibility of learning from past mistakes, and leaves reforms without defenders.

When reform efforts predictably fail, powering changes are often discarded as a "partial" solution that failed to strike at the heart of the problem. The search for a comprehensive model begins anew (see Hirschman 1973, 240–1). Levitsky and Murillo label frequent and radical institutional change "serial replacement" (2013, 95; 2014). Although these authors are referring to such overarching institutional changes as constitutional replacement, the same concept can be applied to public-sector reform. In weak institutional environments, then, powering can be particularly damaging to learning and institutional development.

By contrast, problem solving engenders stability. Modest, achievable improvements do not rely on powerful politicians or their political technocrats; they rely on professionals with a deep understanding of existing problems and their political context. These professionals encounter issues and have enough experience to understand what is achievable. Instead of relying on power, problem solving emphasizes technical expertise and contextual knowledge. Instead of seeking to break the existing status quo, problem solving relies on tactics that avoid conflict. Thus, the technocratic insiders who lead modest reforms without strong political backing are likely to remain at their posts when political constellations shift, safeguarding their positions and creating opportunities to extend their reforms. Unlike powering, which often meets strong resistance after the political will that gave rise to the changes evaporates, problem solving tends to endure.

The differences in approach raise an important question: Are the strategies elaborated here merely different responses to different problems? After all, powering seems more proportionate to the pressing nature of a true crisis, whereas problem solving seems better suited to addressing minor issues. In fact, problem solving (or elements of the approach) can be applied to even the most severe, urgent problems by relying on inside experts and sequencing reforms. Even in areas of particularly weak capacity dominated by patronage, political leaders can initiate a problem-solving approach by recruiting civil servants meritocratically rather than appointing outside experts likely to be replaced by the next government. Thus the differences in approach are not simply responses to different problems but can be applied to a range of different challenges.

In sum, problem solving reduces the complexity of the large problems that powering seeks to solve and is more promising because insider technocrats are often less bounded than political actors. Additionally, the sequencing of reform contributes to learning over time and creates a dynamic in which experts within the state can advance change without inciting opposition and remain in a position to defend and extend their reforms. Finally, if the problem-solving process is successful, there is no need for wholesale reforms.

CONCLUSION

Contrary to conventional wisdom, problem solving (incremental changes sequenced over time) is more effective than powering (swift, ambitious overhauls pushed through by political leaders). Insights from bounded rationality reveal that the problem-solving approach is more promising because it allows for modifications and corrections along the way. Such changes are based on learning from previous reforms. Thus, the problem-solving approach does not require decision-makers to design or select perfectly calibrated comprehensive reforms in one shot, a complex task that places extraordinary demands on comprehensive rationality.

The argument that problem solving is more effective and enduring raises another set of important questions. Reform type, after all, is not determined randomly, nor is it always a matter of choice. What leads governments to power or to problem solve? If powering is ineffective over the long term, why do states keep powering? Of course, states do not only power or only problem solve; they may pursue both strategies (Hall 1993). At the same time, one type of reform or another is often more prevalent. What, then, causes these differences in reform approach?

3

An Explanation of Reform Type

The theory of effective and durable reform advanced in Chapter 2 drew on bounded rationality to argue that problem complexity and the limited capabilities of decision-makers affect reform outcomes. Comprehensive attacks on problems via powering prove less effective and tend to be less durable than gradual problem-solving efforts. Such a theory does not, however, explain under what conditions governments tend to power or problem-solve. To account for the choice of reform strategy, the mechanisms of bounded rationality must be embedded in a political-organizational context to illuminate how established patterns of governing create variation in the type of reforms pursued.

Established patterns of governing, rooted in the long history of how power is organized and exercised, account for the cross-national differences in the predominant reform strategies – i.e., the choice of powering versus problem solving. These entrenched patterns influence policymakers' decisions either to embark on sweeping transformations or proceed more gradually. In short, executive power concentrated in single-party cabinets facilitates efforts at large-scale change, while executive power sharing frustrates sweeping overhauls. While powering changes are difficult in contexts of coalitional presidentialism, relative stability (due to the absence of repeated, dramatic overhauls) and the diversity of actors involved in policymaking provide opportunities for insider technocrats to advance individually small but often cumulatively significant changes. Exclusionary governing patterns in Argentina tend to foster presidents' selection of powering, whereas inclusionary governing patterns in Brazil tend to result in the predominance of the problem-solving approach.

This argument resonates with a wide-ranging literature that suggests good governance is a by-product of political contention among a variety of actors, attenuating the power of any one group. For example, Acemoglu and Robinson (2012) argue that inclusive institutions, in which many people take part in the governing process, check the ability of a small group to exploit the rest of society. Johnston's (2014) study of corruption concludes that good governance efforts are a byproduct of power struggles and political contention,[1] which challenge monopolies of power. In a similar vein, scholars studying Brazil have highlighted how multiparty presidentialism has contributed to the development of strong institutions of accountability (Melo and Pereira 2013; Praça and Taylor 2014) and governability (Deheza 1997; Amorim Neto 1998), using a variety of tools to maintain legislative support (Cheibub, Przeworski, and Saiegh 2004; Raile, Pereira, and Power 2010; Chaisty, Cheeseman, and Power 2014). By contrast, Argentine scholars point out how the absence of coalitions reduces cooperation over time and thus the effectiveness of governance reforms (Stein et al. 2006; Scartascini, Stein, and Tommasi 2010). My argument builds on such insights but crucially connects broad macrofactors to micro-foundations that motivate reform decisions to show that entrenched governing patterns influence both the complexity of the change attempted and the collective capabilities of the reformers – both sides of Simon's scissors.

HISTORICAL INSTITUTIONALISM AND BOUNDED RATIONALITY

The classical version of historical institutionalism explains continuity, not change. Critical junctures – rare moments of uncertainty when the rules of the game are in flux, followed by long stretches of continuity – can reveal, for example, how the type of regime under which a party develops has indelible effects on its long-term growth and development (Collier and Collier 1991). Yet such arguments emphasize that, after short bursts of change, institutional stasis returns; new vested interests begin to defend the status quo and the rules of the game "lock in," generating "increasing returns" to existing institutional arrangements (Pierson 2000). This emphasis on long periods of continuity fails to account for ongoing, incremental change as well as frequent, radical change.

---

[1] For an in-depth examination of his argument, see chapter 2 of his 2014 book.

More recent variants of historical institutionalism have sought instead to emphasize that institutional change often occurs outside the context of critical junctures. Scholars such as Mahoney and Thelen show that gradual and incremental change, in which actors build upon, displace, subvert, or redirect institutional rules, is actually quite common (Streeck and Thelen 2005; Mahoney and Thelen 2010).[2] Levitsky and Murillo (2013; 2014) also demonstrate that change is quite common, calling attention to a very different process that focuses on overarching institutional changes, such as constitutional replacement. They argue that, in weak institutional settings, radical overhauls of institutions are indeed a frequent occurrence; they label this phenomenon "serial replacement."

Revisionist historical institutionalism succeeds in highlighting the empirical realities of change and hypothesizing the factors that might shape such change but stops short of developing a full theory to explain the reform patterns it illustrates. For instance, Mahoney and Thelen (2010) claim that veto possibilities are crucial in either accelerating or hindering the pace of reform. Weak veto possibilities, paired with low levels of discretion in interpretation or enforcement of rules, result in patterns of institutional displacement. Yet strong veto players and high levels of enforcement more commonly lead to a slow "layering" of new rules over the existing institutional framework (Mahoney and Thelen 2010, 19). Although they argue that problems of rule interpretation and enforcement create opportunities for change, they fail to adequately address what happens in such gaps, suggesting only that power-distributional conflict drives change (ibid., 4). Moreover, for many of the episodes of "problem-solving" reform, there simply is no obvious power-distributional shift that corresponds to institutional change. These authors highlight the role of such actors as "subversives" who infiltrate the state apparatus in order to layer new rules, but their approach fails to explain where these actors come from. Nor do they explain why such subversives have a leg up in advancing such

---

[2] Gradual change is also highlighted in early policy process models developed in the American context – e.g., incremental adjustment from the status quo (Wildavsky 1964) or "mutual partisan adjustment" (Lindblom 1959). The Mahoney and Thelen (2010) classification includes four types of gradual change: displacement, the "removal of existing rules and the introduction of new ones" (15–16); layering, in which new elements are added to existing institutions; drift, when changing circumstances alter the impact of existing rules (17); and conversion, in which "rules remain formally the same but are interpreted and enacted in new ways" (17–18).

reforms. Mahoney and Thelen offer more of a classification scheme than a causal theory.

Levitsky and Murillo (2014) argue that in Latin America, where institutions are often weak, processes such as layering, drift, and conversion are less common than radical and recurrent change (192). Radical and recurrent transformation characterizes the powering reforms in Argentina quite well. In Latin America, however, substantial cross-national variation exists, and this generalization cannot be easily extended to countries like Brazil and Chile. Brazil, especially in the 1990s, would be characterized as a weak institutional environment in which the policy process on a wide variety of issues took the form of gradual change.[3] Why, then, do we see radical and recurrent change in Argentina and gradual change in Brazil? Why have some countries in Latin America been able to escape serial replacement?

Levitsky and Murillo's (2013; 2014) work on overarching institutional changes helps explain why serial replacement occurs more often in certain contexts than others. Relevant factors include regime instability, electoral volatility, social inequality, institutional borrowing from abroad, rapid institutional design, crises, and the de facto weakness of formal institutional veto players. Additionally, they present valuable insights into conditions that lead to failures: "[W]hen powerful actors are excluded from the rule-writing process, they are likely to attack fledgling institutions early on. Consequently, new institutions are unlikely to endure long enough to gain broad public legitimacy, stabilize actors' expectations, or generate the kinds of vested interest and institution-specific investments that increase the costs of replacement" (Levitsky and Murillo 2014, 201). Ultimately, however, they do not develop a complete theory that would explain why we tend to see serial replacement in some countries and gradual layering in others.

In sum, revisionist historical institutionalism clarifies the empirical realities of reform and offers hypotheses on different patterns of such reform yet is unable to fully address the causes and consequences of change. This shortcoming stems in large part from the absence of strong micro-foundations that bridge the divide between structure and agency.

The work of Jones and Baumgartner (2005; 2012) makes an important contribution here. Their "general punctuation thesis" emphasizes

---

[3] Thus, gradual reforms are not only a product of the developed democracies that Mahoney and Thelen (2010) study.

the role of human limitations in processing information within a policymaking system (2005) and demonstrates how bounded rationality can serve as a micro-foundation for classical historical institutionalism. Under normal circumstances, information regarding policy problems is largely ignored and responses delayed due to the overabundance of data and limits on human attention. Thus the policymaking process typically appears to be stable, unchanging, or incremental. As the pressure to address a particular problem accumulates, however, and as attention shifts to the issue, policymakers often overreact, causing disjointed and episodic change. The response is then disproportionate to the problem (2012, 7).

Institutional change appears to follow a critical-juncture model with exceptional changes followed by long periods of stasis. As Jones and Baumgartner point out, however, disjointed policy responses are "part and parcel of the same policymaking process that generated the periods of stability" (ibid.). Problems are ignored until they become so acute that something finally *must* be done, resulting in a disproportionate response. This pattern of underreacting, then overreacting, creates a leptokurtic distribution characterized by many minor changes and some major breakthroughs. A leptokurtic distribution has a higher central peak, more outliers than a normal distribution, and an absence of medium or proportionate changes – the type of changes that actually solve problems. Essentially, such a distribution reflects a "punctuated-equilibrium" or critical-juncture pattern, with dramatic and rare shifts followed by periods of continuity (ibid., 7–8).

Thus, Jones and Baumgartner's general punctuation thesis can be used to set the traditional approach of historical institutionalism on cognitive psychology's well-corroborated findings regarding information processing and human choice. By drawing on the more empirically solid microfoundation of bounded rationality, their approach integrates periods of stasis with bursts of change. At the same time, their thesis alone cannot explain the cross-national variation observed by Levitsky and Murillo. Why is serial replacement ubiquitous in some contexts and gradual layering or conversion in others? What explains variation among countries or even time periods? What factors might tighten or loosen bounds of rationality?

To explain variation in information processing, Kurt Weyland's (2014) research on diffusion waves in European democratization demonstrates how organizational developments mediate the bounds of rationality. Before mass political organizations arose, citizens relied on informational shortcuts to decide whether to rise up and emulate foreign challenges to autocrats. Bounds of rationality were especially tight for such citizens, and they often made hasty, ill-informed decisions. With the advent of mass organizations, however, regular citizens began to take cues from representative leaders able to process information in a more proportionate fashion. Thus, the bounds of rationality loosened as citizens became tied to organizations with leaders who had access to information and possessed greater processing capacity. In this way, Weyland explains how organizational developments condition the bounds of rationality. Drawing on Simon's early work about how organizations can compensate for cognitive limitations by enhancing information processing (Simon 1976; Bendor 2010, 165–9), such research provides insights into how bounded rationality can be embedded in organizational contexts in order to explain collective variation in capabilities and even task environments.

This project's argument contributes to efforts at theory construction within the historical institutional paradigm by drawing on the work of scholars who focus on micro-foundations of change (e.g., Simon 1990; Baumgartner, Jones, and Wilkerson 2011) while embedding such insights in organizational context (Simon 1976; March and Simon 1993; Weyland 2014). Serial replacement results from consistent overreaction to information in some contexts, with comparatively more stasis in other countries that tend to process information in a more balanced, proportionate manner. In particular, powering reforms, which frequently fail to consolidate, produce crisis. Crisis produces the overreaction to information, generating a new round of powering and setting a pattern of serial replacement. By contrast, problem solving relies on organization, which loosens the bounds of rationality, yields higher-quality decision-making, and promotes effective information processing (Simon 1976). Problem solving allows decision-makers to be more evenhanded, avert crises, and contribute to a pattern of gradual change. What causes this cross-national variation in organizational capabilities?

ESTABLISHED PATTERNS OF GOVERNING: AN EXPLANATION OF REFORM STRATEGY

Established patterns of governing shape cross-national differences in the predominant reform strategies. Inclusionary governing patterns (wherein presidents share executive power with a coalition) result in greater reliance on the problem-solving strategy, whereas exclusionary governing patterns (with presidents appointing single-party cabinets) result in greater reliance on the powering strategy.[4]

Consistent patterns of inclusion in Brazil and exclusion in Argentina have emerged over time. Argentine presidents, who win with slim majorities, have routinely governed in an exclusionary manner: They concentrate executive power in single-party majority cabinets at the expense of other parties, appointing primarily members of their own party or faction to the cabinet and positions within the executive branch (Teichman 1997, 32; Lijphart 2012, 3). By contrast, scholars of Brazil increasingly recognize that coalitional presidentialism, *presidencialismo de coalizão*, has become the established governing approach (Abranches 1988; Melo and Pereira 2013).[5] Recent literature investigates how discretionary appointments, in addition to other executive "tools" such as pork and budget amendments (Raile, Pereira, and Power 2010), are provided to political allies in tacit exchange for legislative support (Meneguello 1998). In this way, presidents, like European prime ministers, fashion multiparty cabinets and legislative coalitions. Brazilian presidents, unlikely to have a majority in Congress, have consistently shared government responsibilities with broad multiparty coalitions (Lijphart 2012, 3).

While formal electoral rules provide incentives for coalition building by conditioning the size of presidents' legislative majorities, they do not ensure the development of informal practices that facilitate such coalition building.[6] As highlighted in Table 2 (see the index of coalitional necessity), presidents who have a minority in the legislature have incentives to build coalitions to secure passage of their legislative agenda. Indeed, Brazil

---

[4] This argument builds on Lijphart's distinction between "concentration of executive power in single-party majority cabinets versus executive power-sharing in broad multiparty coalitions" (2012, 3), but crucially adapts it to the Latin American context where some presidential systems have multiparty cabinets in which other parties have considerable policy-making authority (cf Lijphart 2012, 94–6; Mainwaring 2001, 172).

[5] Coalitional presidentialism is defined by Chaisty, Cheeseman, and Power (2014) as "a strategic response to the institutional dilemmas posed by the coexistence of a presidential executive with a fragmented multiparty legislature. In order to win support for the legislative agenda of the executive, presidents must behave much like prime ministers in the multiparty democracies of Western Europe: they must first assemble and then cultivate interparty coalitions on the floor of the assembly. The objective of the president is to foster the emergence of a legislative cartel which will reliably defend the preference of the executive branch" (74). For other definitions and labels, see Melo and Pereira (2013), Amorim Neto (2006, 424), and Power (2010, 25–6).

[6] Scholars such as Chaisty, Cheeseman, and Power (2014) have emphasized that coalitional formation and cabinet inclusiveness are *political* choices (80).

TABLE 2 *Multiparty Presidentialism and Coalitions in Latin America*
(1979–2012)

Country	Effective number of parties in Lower House	Lower House seats held by the president's party (%)	Index of coalitional necessity – mean since democratization[a]
Brazil	7.36	21.78	59.29
Ecuador	6.86	18.07	57.52
Chile	5.17	17.63	42.59
Panama	3.7	31.32	25.41
Bolivia	3.95	37.19	24.78
Colombia	3.8	37.93	23.59
Guatemala	3.7	41.16	21.75
El Salvador	3.4	37.94	21.13
Venezuela	3.05	36.43	19.87
Peru	3.23	43.37	18.26
Uruguay	3.04	40.93	17.95
Paraguay	2.8	50.03	17.5
Argentina	3.18	46.29	17.05
Mexico	2.8	45.61	15.22
Dominican Republic	2.5	40.44	14.87
Costa Rica	2.79	47.12	14.78
Nicaragua	2.43	50.85	11.92
Honduras	2.22	50.83	10.92

[a] Index of coalitional necessity is obtained by multiplying the effective number of parties by the complement of the percentage of seats held by the president's own party, then dividing by ten for ease of interpretation (Power 2010b, 25). The figures shown here reflect a country's mean since democratization. These countries are: Argentina (1983–2012), Bolivia (1982–2012), Brazil (1985–2012), Chile (1990–2012), Colombia (1978–2012), Costa Rica (1978–2012), El Salvador (1994–2012), Ecuador (1979–95, 1997–2005), Guatemala (1996–2011), Honduras (1982–2008, 2010–12), Mexico (1988–2011), Nicaragua (1997–2006), Panama (1991–2008), Paraguay (1993–7, 1999–2011), Peru (1980–2008), Dominican Republic (1996–2009), Uruguay (1985–2012), and Venezuela (1979–2001).
Source: Calculated by author from data in Power (2010b, 25) and Meireles (2016).

scores highest on the index and has developed strong power-sharing practices. Like Brazil, Ecuador offers a case of extreme multiparty presidentialism; however, while scholars have highlighted the role of clandestine "ghost cabinets" (secret inter-party agreements for perks, power sharing, and political support that provide covert coalition building between parties) in coalitional management, these patterns of power sharing have not developed into enduring practices.[7] Moreover, given institutional design, we might expect single-party cabinets in Uruguay. Yet thanks to the important and enduring role of factions, Uruguay has developed patterns of power sharing (Altman 2000; Magar and Moraes 2012). This situation suggests that there is greater variation in governing patterns than formal electoral rules alone can explain.[8]

Entrenched governing patterns are shaped in large part by expectations about how a president will govern. Party (or group) A's monopolistic practices – eschewing compromise and negotiation with the opposition or even other factions of the party, stacking the bureaucracy and other institutions with loyalists, and reorienting the structure of institutions and the state to undermine the resources of would-be opponents – nearly guarantee that Party B's practices will be equally exclusionary toward Party A. In this way, a pattern of sequential exclusion is developed.

In Argentina, single-party cabinets date at least back to President Hipólito Yrigoyen (1916–22), who established the precedent of hegemonic exclusion by appointing a narrow rather than broad-based cabinet. During the turnover between President Yrigoyen and President Marcelo Alvear (1922–8), Alvear removed nearly all Yrigoyen's loyalists from the executive and installed his own supporters, rejecting notions of power sharing within the executive, even though both presidents were from the same party (Romero and Brennan 2013, 50–3). After over a decade of military rule, the election of Juan Perón and the subsequent purge of the public sector served to entrench the pattern of exclusion. Large numbers of bureaucratic personnel hired by previous governments were removed and Peronist loyalists installed (Buchanan 1985, 73; Kurtz 2013, 192), marking the beginning of a transformation of the state that involved the wholesale creation of institutions and sweeping changes to the economy. This pattern of gutting the bureaucracy with alternations in power

---

[7] Mejía Acosta (2009) shows that between 1979 and 1996, Ecuadorian presidents had developed clandestine mechanisms for managing coalitions, which he labels "ghost coalitions." Yet changes starting in 1996 disrupted practices of coalition building and undermined governability (Mejía Acosta and Polga-Hecimovich 2011). In the following years, three consecutive presidents were ousted before the end of their mandate.

[8] For instance, of all presidents without majority support in the legislature, 35 percent decided not to form coalitions (Martínez-Gallardo 2010, 126).

between Peronists and anti-Peronists only reinforced the exclusionary governing pattern.

By contrast, if a party (or group) includes other political parties in the governing coalition, appointing coalitional allies to ministries and agencies or providing pork, the next power holders are induced to include coalitional allies. Over time, smaller parties come to expect a certain level of participation in the executive; a pattern of inclusion is developed. In Brazil, wide-ranging coalitions date back to the Second Brazilian Republic (1946–64), when the typical cabinet included parties that represented 78 percent of the seats in Congress (Abranches 1988; Ames 2001, 160).

As a pattern of sequential exclusion or inclusion is developed, the costs of deviating from the regularized practices increase as political actors develop expectations about the spoils they will enjoy with a president in power. As Pierson (2000) highlights, such political-organizational arrangements "encourage individuals and organizations to invest in specialized skills, deepen relationships with other individuals and organizations, and develop particular political and social identities. These activities increase attractiveness of existing institutional arrangements relative to hypothetical alternatives. As social actors make commitments based on existing institutions and policies, their cost of exit from established arrangements rises dramatically" (259). Political actors thus develop expectations and skills based on the presumption that presidents will follow the fold. For instance, many Brazilian parties anticipate that, regardless of which party wins the presidency, they will receive a good share of executive appointments and a certain number of budget amendments. By contrast, Argentine political actors maintain the implicit assumption that the president will reward her own party or loyalists with discretionary appointments.

Deviation from these entrenched patterns come with high costs. Brazilian presidents who have governed in an exclusionary manner have been thrown out, whereas Argentine presidents who govern in an inclusionary fashion have been weakened and pushed out. For instance, since 1946 all formally democratic governments in Brazil have adopted the inclusionary governing style – with the exception of President Fernando Collor de Mello (1990–2) and, to a certain extent, Dilma Rousseff (2011–16). Collor's deviation demonstrates the costs of breaking with the established approach. Upon taking office, Collor's National Reconstruction Party (*Partido da Reconstrução Nacional,* PRN) comprised only 5.1 percent of the seats in the Chamber of Deputies. In spite of this minority status, President Collor reserved cabinet positions for a narrow group of cronies and technocrats instead of distributing discretionary appointments to form an oversized coalition in Congress (Amorim Neto 2002). Throughout his term, other parties were indeed included in his cabinet. Yet in contrast to the largesse of other Brazilian presidents, who doled out positions within the government, Collor narrowly allocated portfolios. This exclusionary approach was exacerbated by his extensive use of decree power: Collor issued thirty-six decrees during his first fifteen days in office (Amorim Neto 2002, 76). When Congress reacted to this by threatening to rein in executive decrees with a bill (Power 1998, 211), Collor backtracked, reducing the number of executive decrees and increasing the number of discretionary appointments to other parties. It was, however, too late: After a corruption scandal erupted, President Collor was impeached by his colleagues in Congress (Weyland 1998).

The circumstances that led to the impeachment of Dilma Rousseff are more complex, but her failure to build alliances was a crucial factor. Interviews with numerous political and bureaucratic actors suggest that, combined with her technocratic micromanaging, the corruption sweep at the beginning of Rousseff's first term removing numerous corrupt coalitional allies from heads of ministries and agencies left her isolated and vulnerable to impeachment.[9] Other Brazilian presidents have survived severe scandals without sanction from Congress,[10] but both Collor and Rousseff were different in that they neglected to realize the importance of coalition building.[11]

---

[9] See Chapters 5 and 7 on reforms of transport infrastructure and health care in Brazil.

[10] For instance, President Luiz Inácio "Lula" da Silva (2003–11) survived the Mensalão vote-buying scandal, one of the more prominent incidences of corruption involving some of the highest levels of government.

[11] Even the most programmatic and principled Brazilian parties have avoided Collor's mistake of attempting to govern alone. For instance, in 1994, President Fernando Henrique Cardoso (1995–2002) of the social-democratic PSDB party included the conservative PFL and the clientelistic PTB in his coalition. Such alliances ensured an oversized majority with which to pursue the president's policy goal. In his presidency, Lula was initially constrained by the PT's distinctive commitment to party discipline and expectations that the vast majority of available positions in the executive would be allocated to PT members (Hunter 2010, 159–67). However, as Hunter (2007) points out, the once-radical and programmatic PT ended up applying tactics that it had long condemned by forging alliances with partners on the other side of the ideological spectrum. For instance, the PT accepted a running mate from the PL, a small right-wing party of evangelicals and businessmen. Furthermore, once in power the PT allied with the opportunistic PMDB. In this way, the subsequent leaders adopted coalitional presidentialism and allied with

After the return to democracy in Argentina, presidents with slim majorities have consistently fashioned single-party cabinets, concentrating power within their party or party faction. President Fernando de la Rúa's (1999–2001) attempt to deviate from this well-established pattern, an experiment with coalition rule, failed miserably, shedding light on the costs of deviating from expectations (Llanos and Margheritis 2006). In 1997, two parties – the Radical Civic Union (*Unión Cívica Radical*, UCR) and Front for a Country in Solidarity (*Frente por un País Solidario*, FREPASO) – came together to form the *Alianza* coalition, with de la Rúa at the helm. After winning the presidency with a campaign to wipe out corruption, the UCR and FREPASO soon found themselves unable to share power within government agencies. Rather than fostering cooperation, shared governing responsibilities created turf battles, with each party answering to its own chain of command. Ultimately, this failed attempt at forming a coalition government exacerbated a deepening economic crisis; the situation – ungovernable – forced President de la Rúa to resign. Since then, subsequent presidents have maintained the custom of appointing members of their own party or faction in an exclusionary manner, perhaps most clearly under President Cristina Fernández de Kirchner, who ran the country with a narrow cabinet of personal advisors.

The fact that deviation from the entrenched pattern results in the ousting of presidents reinforces such practices over time and provides clear guidelines for what will and will not be tolerated by the political class. In this way, political learning contributes to the perpetuation of such patterns, reinforcing norms of executive power sharing and expectations regarding coalitional formation.

Exclusionary Governing Facilitates Powering

Cohesive Teams Facilitate Decisive Overhauls

In Argentina, exclusionary governing patterns have resulted in single-party cabinets that concentrate power within loyal and cohesive teams of technocrats. Identifying loyal technocrats is a key to the president achieving his or her governance objectives. Yet such individuals, although

---

large support parties, PMDB for Lula and the PFL for Cardoso. These provided a network of local elites and political machines but tended to be silent on programmatic issues. Smaller parties (e.g., PTB, PL, and PP) were also included in the coalition, allowing the PT and its partners to reach 65 to 90 percent of seats in Congress. In this way, even the least likely parties have adapted to inclusionary governing practices.

close to the president, are often outsiders who know that their time in office is limited. In Argentina, only one party or faction is in the government at a time; for instance, when a UCR president is inaugurated, the Peronists are not included in the governing coalition, and vice versa. Because presidents win by slim margins, the governing group has to worry that they will no longer be in power after the next election. Thus, the absence of coalitions means that the current governing party has short time horizons, which creates incentives to rapidly move policy toward their ideal point and to push through reforms as quickly as possible.[12] Election cycles are brief and political constellations often short-lived, creating time pressure to enact preferred policies and make an immediate difference.

Moreover, many interests often have a stranglehold over existing institutional arrangements. To undercut these forces, change is often imposed by driving rapid, far-reaching overhauls of the state before beneficiaries of the status quo can mount a defense. Reform teams often comprise likeminded individuals who are close to the president and committed to similar objectives. This sense of solidarity facilitates political cooperation within the government (Huber 1998; Spiller and Tommasi 2007; Martínez-Gallardo 2011). Cohesive, insulated teams are often able to swiftly pursue their objectives, unhindered by internal dissent and footdragging bureaucrats (Axelrod 1970; de Swann 1973). Presidents unconstrained by diverse cabinets are able to give these teams the power to impose reform. Thus, single-party cabinets, which engender short time horizons and access to the president, facilitate powering.

Loyal Technocrats Tighten Cognitive Constraints

Single-party cabinets – especially the appointment of loyal technocrats to key positions within the executive – also shape the collective capabilities of decision-makers. Because the Argentine president exerts his own discretion in appointments, the technocratic outsiders predominate rather than civil servants or long-standing state technocrats, who might slow down the executive's policy goals. Experts may possess impressive academic credentials (Dargent 2011), but their real appeal may rely on the

---

[12] As Levitsky and Murillo (2014) note, a broad governing coalition means that the ruling coalition at t+1 is likely to not be too far from the coalition that enacted the reforms, so policy stability ensues because of the continuity of preferences. By contrast, the absence of coalitions in Argentina means that the ruling party that creates a set of institutions may have a very different set of preferences than the ruling party that inherits the institutions. This instability of preferences is also a source of instability for institutions in Argentina.

alignment of their policy views with those of the president. Indeed, Bambaci, Spiller, and Tommasi (2007) demonstrate that "temporary bureaucrats" in Argentina tend to respond to the individual political patron who recruits them (cf. Grindle 2012).

Overreliance on such outsiders, though convenient, can reduce the quality of policymaking. Their personal selection means that the fate of these political technocrats is linked to the political actor who appointed them. The result is shorter time horizons and an absence of the type of expertise developed over time from experience in the public sector. This contextual knowledge is crucial for understanding the effects of change in new contexts. Moreover, hand-selected teams of like-minded individuals are prone to the problems of "groupthink" (Janis 1982). Instead of fostering debate and deliberation to cross-check inferences, and bringing to bear prior reform experiences on new problems, tight-knit groups suffer from severe distortions in judgment, with rash inferences reinforcing each other (McDermott 2004, 249–56; Schafer and Crichlow 2010). Indeed, policy reform processes led by outsiders or loyal technocrats often demonize bureaucrats, who might otherwise have good arguments to contribute, stereotyping them as the "out-group" and marginalizing civil servants from reforms designed in an exclusive manner, closing them off from debate (see also Janis 1982, Schafer and Crichlow 2010). Conformity and cohesiveness are good for rapid implementation but not for identifying problems in grand reform plans.

This extensive leeway in bureaucratic appointments has enduring effects on the quality of the public sector. All countries in Latin America have rules on the books mandating a meritocratic civil service (Grindle 2012). Yet governing patterns affect the extent to which presidents abide by such rules. In Argentina, where the civil service rules are often disregarded, a president might come in and appoint his cronies, only to have another dismiss them and appoint her own loyalists. This *individual-level* "serial replacement" engenders high rates of turnover within the executive. For instance, a president who decides to overhaul an agency might appoint a minister of his or her own party; such a minister is then often free to bring in his or her own team of bureaucratic outsiders (Zuvanic and Iacoviello 2010, 167–8). Resistance to reforms can be overcome by either dismissing existing employees or shifting them into irrelevant positions.[13] An exclusionary governing approach might increase expertise in the short

---

[13] Such an approach creates "parallel bureaucracies." See Zuvanic and Iacoviello (2010, 167–8).

term – at the expense of maintaining a neutral, meritocratically recruited civil service in the long term.

In sum, political-organizational patterns of governing in Argentina contribute to the selection of reform plans that are tremendously complex in attempting to solve all problems at once. Such radical changes are led by those in power, but small circles of outsiders often fall prey to groupthink and suffer tight cognitive constraints given their inexperience in the public sector. In all of these ways, exclusionary governing patterns reduce collective capabilities of the reformers and tighten bounds of rationality in both the short and long terms.

Inclusionary Governing Frustrates Powering and Facilitates Problem Solving

Broad Coalitions Moderate Reforms

By contrast, coalitional presidentialism, by inducing Brazilian presidents to share executive power, shapes decision-making and information processing by shifting the prerogative to transform the public administration from presidents and their tight-knit reform teams to a broader group of coalition allies. As a result of negotiation and compromise with numerous veto players (Tsebelis 1995), radical and comprehensive reforms are rarely executed as a coherent whole; instead, changes often advance slowly and haltingly.[14] Executive decision-making is bogged down by the slow plodding required to get changes past coalitional allies who represent a diverse set of interests.

Governing coalitions are less likely to push policy far to one extreme. Wide-ranging coalitions in Brazil mean that any party included has a high probability of being part of the next government. Parties such as the Brazilian Democratic Movement Party (*Partido do Movimento Democrático Brasileiro*, PMDB) have been included in governments of both the Brazilian Social Democracy Party (*Partido da Social Democracia Brasileira*, PSDB) and the Workers' Party (*Partido dos Trabalhadores*, PT). Furthermore, until President Luiz Inácio "Lula" da Silva (2003–11), the Liberal Front Party (*Partido da Frente Liberal*, PFL) had always governed – during the military dictatorship and in the administrations of

---

[14] This argument resonates with Mahoney and Thelen's (2010) emphasis on the importance of veto possibilities for either accelerating or hindering the pace of reform. In contexts of strong veto players and high levels of enforcement, layering is more common (19).

Presidents Sarney, Collor, Franco, and Cardoso. Everyone needed them. This dynamic has lengthened the time horizons of parties and has encouraged them to build gradually. Even if a party is finally removed from the governing coalition, as the PFL eventually was under Lula, policy decisions do not change drastically because coalitions are comprised of diverse interests; big ships take time to turn. Therefore, the next governing coalition is unlikely to feel an impulse to pull drastically back in the other direction.

In sum, broad governing coalitions not only affect the reform process, by slowing the pace and scale of reforms, but also affect its preferences. The inclusion of broad governing coalitions means that the policy positions of subsequent ruling coalition are likely not too far removed from the original reforms, resulting in greater continuity of preferences than in Argentina (Levitsky and Murillo 2014).

In the policymaking process, inclusive governments also afford a much greater role to insiders: experts from within the state like longtime technocrats and civil servants. Coalitional presidentialism blocks sweeping, comprehensive change, frustrating most attempts to gut bureaucratic agencies and offering a greater sense of stability to civil servants. Second, presidents, to achieve their policy objectives, often rely on neutral experts within the federal administration (Praça, Freitas, and Hoepers 2011). Coalitions compel Brazilian presidents to distribute positions in the cabinet and throughout the bureaucracy to allied parties, which means executives are limited in the extent to which they may replace ministry staff with handpicked loyalists. This creates a dilemma: Coalitional "allies" may not be interested in advancing the president's policy or governance objectives in any meaningful way; in fact, their primary objective may be rent seeking or party-directed corruption (Mistree 2015). As a partial antidote to rent seeking, however, Brazilian executives have often used experts within the state to serve as a counterweight to political appointments to achieve their governance objectives. For instance, Brazilian presidents often appoint neutral experts to the "number two" positions of the ministries controlled by coalitional allies to reduce "stealing for the team" – i.e., party-directed corruption (Praça, Freitas, and Hoepers 2011; Gingerich 2013). Moreover, a striking number of civil servants are appointed to discretionary positions in the public sector (Praça, Freitas, and Hoepers 2011). Interviews with elite government administrators suggest that the presidential calculus of appointments has placed increasing weight on having specialists within the state to advance governance objectives.[15] This relative stability extends neutral technocrats' time horizons for effecting change, with smaller, gradual changes often left in the hands of civil servants as opposed to political leaders or high-level technocrats.[16]

Finally, because the attention of political actors is limited – bombarded, as they are, by multiple issues and a constant stream of new information – the possibilities expand for actors with experience, longer time horizons, and expertise to fashion reforms. While politicians and bureaucratic appointees focus on high-level legislative changes and winning the next election, permanent technocrats and civil servants may wield a variety of tools that collectively transform policies over time. Thus, coalitional presidentialism, by blocking big, comprehensive changes, opens up space for smaller reforms that build on the longer time horizons of actors within the state.

Coalitional Presidentialism Loosens Cognitive Constraints

Coalitional presidentialism also increases the collective capabilities of reformers on two levels. First, it impels top-level decision-makers to subject policy proposals to the scrutiny of a diverse set of interests and experts and to adjust policies accordingly. Unlike policymakers in Argentina, who are part of cohesive groups that often suffer from groupthink (McDermott 2004; Schafer and Crichlow 2010), the numerous parties represented in the executive loosen the bounds of rationality by creating a deliberative environment that cross-checks inferences.

Second, and more importantly, because Brazilian presidents are limited in their ability to replace ministry staff with handpicked loyalists, they rely more on neutral experts within the federal administration to achieve their governance objectives.[17] Experts' institutional positions and significant

---

[15] Author interview with Aldino Graef (Assessor especial da Subchefia de Análise e Acompanhamento de Políticas Governamentais da Casa Civil da Presidência da República; Especialista em Políticas Públicas e Gestão Governamental, 1993–present), December 5, 2011; author interview with Dr. Luiz Alberto dos Santos (Subchefe da Casa Civil da Presidência da República, 2003–14; Especialista em Políticas Públicas e Gestão Governamental (1990–2002), December 8, 2011.

[16] For an in-depth analysis of the trade-offs of different forms of politicization, in addition to their relationship with capacity and governance outcomes, see Bersch, Praça, and Taylor (2017b).

[17] The appointments of neutral experts arise not only because of the constraints of veto players but also because these appointments advance the governance objectives of a president. Thus, while this argument does not deny the importance of veto players (see Chapter 2 for discussion of insurance arguments and veto player logic), it also recognizes the important positive governance function that such appointments play.

experience give these officials much better information, and a greater capacity for its processing, than high-level political leaders forced to rely on cognitive shortcuts to craft and implement complex reforms. Additionally, experts within the state benefit from learning over time. Civil servants who gain their positions meritocratically rather than through political appointment often serve longer terms, which allows them to build institutional memory based on what has worked previously and to build networks of support within the bureaucracy. Therefore, while such individuals still apply inferential heuristics, their judgments tend to be closer to the mark.

Thus, who reformers are and how they reach their positions have direct consequences for the dominant reform type. Outsiders with a short time horizon (e.g., party loyalists, coalitional allies, and other political appointees) face tight cognitive constraints. Yet technocratic insiders can advance problem-solving reforms because smaller-scale change often does not gain the attention of outsiders, who have only temporary positions in the executive. This provides space for the continuation of a sequential reform process and allows civil servants to increase their expertise over time. These patterns do not manifest uniformly or consistently, of course.[18] Particular political factors remain important for the quality of reforms. Reforms that require legislative approval may fall prey to the effects of fragmentation, or a deliberative policy-making environment may inadvertently open the door to political calculations. If coalitions are fractious and unstable, presidents may resort to illicit side payments to pass legislative agendas or insulate priority ministries from allies' patronage demands. Nonetheless, applying the insights from ideal types and examining the influence of broader macrofactors provides a powerful framework for understanding crucial components and conditions of successful reform.

In sum, the presence of various veto players in Brazilian coalitional presidentialism reduces the viable scale and speed of reform, thereby reducing complexity. Brazil for this reason has often been considered a reform laggard. Pension reform in Latin American countries, for example, has ranged from full privatization (Chile, Mexico, and El Salvador) to complementary private systems that do not replace public systems

---

For other studies that emphasize the importance of the governance logic, see Nunes (2010) and Brinks and Blass (2015).

[18] As the empirical chapters will show, even though coalitional presidentialism makes problem solving more likely, both approaches are applied in Brazil and Argentina.

(Colombia, Peru) and mixed systems (Uruguay, Argentina) (Madrid 2002). But Brazil implemented far more modest "parametric reforms," revising benefits without substantially altering the public system (Mesa-Lago and Müller 2002, 688; Huber and Stephens 2000). The opposition from numerous veto players in Brazil has led reformers to spread responsibility for reform and seek large majorities such that the pension reform process has been slower, more moderate, and more deliberative (see Taylor 2008, 132–50). Not only do such diverse perspectives enhance the quality of decision-making by cross-checking policy designs, "parametric reforms" tend to involve technocrats from within the state to a greater degree than high-level political actors, loosening the bounds of rationality of policy decision-makers. The emphasis on small changes does not mean that important reforms do not occur but rather that *time* is important in the reform process – transformations occur by sequencing changes over time that become *cumulatively transformative*. Instead of preventing much-needed change, the absence of drastic shifts creates possibilities for a more enduring and effective transformation of the state over time.

CONCLUSION

Exclusionary governing patterns, wherein presidents appoint single-party cabinets, result in greater reliance on the powering strategy, whereas inclusionary governing patterns, where presidents share executive power with a coalition, result in greater reliance on the problem-solving strategy. Therefore the organization of executive power mediates the impact of cognitive limitations on political decision-making, which is a collective process. The broader political-organizational context shapes both the scale and speed of the reforms pursued as well as the type of individuals involved.

The locus of policy decision-making in Argentina is concentrated in small, cohesive groups, which facilitates rapid and radical reorientations of the public sector. In such contexts, power is concentrated at the apex of the state: Presidents and their political appointees rely heavily on informational shortcuts in designing and implementing institutional transformations. Bounds of rationality are especially tight for such decision-makers, because election cycles are short and such high-level appointees usually come and go with the executive who appointed them. Accordingly, they rush to make reform decisions in order to make a difference before opposition has time to mount against the changes. They sacrifice careful planning, evaluation, and scrutiny for short-term outcomes, leading to ill-informed decisions. Where there are fewer constraints to hold back political leaders, they pursue their governance objectives by resorting to sweeping overhauls, using the policymaking process to overreact to problems. Yet, after the big push, powering often fails to achieve consolidation, which creates the next crisis.

In Brazil, the locus of policy decision-making is shifted to a broader set of actors. Coalitional presidentialism, which induces presidents to share executive power, slows sweeping overhauls through negotiation and compromise with coalitional partners. Policy proposals benefit from scrutiny and discussion since diverse perspectives lead to revisions and corrections. Such negotiations also often result in the downsizing of initial proposals. Consequently, dramatic overhauls and overreactions to problems are less common. The difficulty of wholesale reforms also privileges the search for infra-legislative change: changes to process or procedure, rather than to big-ticket legislation that must pass through Congress. In this context, neutral experts from within the state are afforded a much greater role in the policy-making process, as their relative job stability extends their time horizons; gradual, small-scale changes are often left in their hands, as opposed to those of political leaders or high-level technocrats. Moreover, the technical acumen and access to information of technocrats and civil servants, in addition to the more limited scope of reform, mean that these individuals are able to process information in a more balanced fashion. The bounds of rationality loosen when sweeping change is broken into smaller pieces and when these experts play a greater role in crafting reforms.

4

Transportation in Argentina: Powering (Re-)Creates Crisis

The return to democracy in Argentina has prompted recurring attempts to overhaul government institutions. In the 1990s, President Carlos Menem (1989–99) concentrated executive authority to push through a sweeping neoliberal transformation of the state, restructuring state-owned electricity, petroleum, natural gas, and telephone monopolies; privatizing postal services, water, and sewage; outsourcing the operation and maintenance of airports, roads, and railways to private companies; and reforming the civil service, health care, and pension systems. During this period, Argentina became the poster child of executing politically challenging reform, with the World Bank, the IMF, the US Treasury, and numerous other international agencies heaping praise on the efforts of the Menem government.[1] A decade later, however, corruption and performance problems plagued many of the same institutions Menem transformed, prompting Presidents Néstor Kirchner (2003–7) and Cristina Fernández de Kirchner (2007–15) to push through another set of comprehensive overhauls, many of which reversed Menem's changes. In both cases, however, the veneer of success quickly wore thin, revealing new issues. Thus, despite ideological differences, the same pattern of powering change

---

[1] For instance, in October 1998, Michel Camdessus, the managing director of the IMF, had only positive words for Argentina: "In many respects the experience of Argentina in recent years has been exemplary, including in particular the adoption of the proper strategy at the beginning of the 1990s and the very courageous adaptation of it when the tequila crisis put the overall sub-continent at risk of major turmoil. Notable, too, are the efforts of Argentina since that time to continue its excellent compliance with the performance criteria under our arrangements" (Blustein 2005, 58).

and failure has repeated itself during Menem's center-right and the Kirchners' center-left governments.

What explains reforms of different ideological orientations producing the same outcome? Why are promising efforts to improve service delivery abandoned? Why are the same institutions overhauled again and again without lasting success? Examining transportation reforms in Argentina over time offers some new answers.

Menem's overhaul of the sector in the 1990s illustrates two of powering's negative consequences. First, it reveals the insurmountable challenges of designing comprehensive reforms, which ultimately lead officials to rely on inferential shortcuts and best guesses in the face of uncertainty. To undercut the opposition, the privatization of the transportation sector was swift and deep-cutting, completed during the "window of opportunity" opened during the economic crisis. The rapid approach important for overcoming the opposition, however, made planning such extensive change a Herculean task. Instead of proactively seeking out alternatives and calculating their advantages and disadvantages, policymakers relied on international reform models and ad hoc calculations in the face of significant uncertainty. As a result, unanticipated outcomes appeared almost immediately, and grave performance problems plagued the transport sector for decades.

Second, Menem's transport reforms underscore the toll powering takes on institutional capacity. By concentrating power in the hands of outside experts and change teams in the Ministries of Economics and Public Works, Menem was able to overcome resistance, uproot the status quo, and establish new transport agencies. Although successful in demolishing existing agencies, reformers were less successful in creating the institutions crucial for the long-term success of privatized infrastructure, such as those responsible for monitoring and regulating transport. Such failures of consolidation had enduring effects. When Menem and his technocrats left office, few individuals with expertise in the reform effort or concession contracts more generally remained in the federal administration. The lessons learned from a decade of reform were essentially lost. Under subsequent presidents, control over transport remained centralized in the hands of political appointees, who lacked the time, experience, and attention to tackle the intractable problems that afflicted the sector. Consequently, all but the most serious policy problems were overlooked, and the transportation sector continued to deteriorate, failing to achieve the consolidation predicted by conventional historical institutionalism's path dependency.

The situation in transport deteriorated until 2012, when a massive train collision in downtown Buenos Aires killed 51 people and injured 700. This laid bare the depth of the problems in transportation and the failures of the government to ensure even the most basic standards of safety. This unprecedented event prompted President Cristina Fernández de Kirchner to dramatically reverse the transport policies of the 1990s and essentially recreate Ferrocarriles Argentinos, the state-run rail company that Menem demolished. While some technocrats attempted a more moderate problem-solving approach, these gradual efforts were thwarted by grander attempts at change.

Thus, the same institutions were overhauled again and again. When powering reform efforts predictably failed, changes were discarded as a partial solution that failed to strike at the root of the problem, and the search for another comprehensive model began anew. In this way, powering creates its own unhealthy dynamic: Not only do reforms fail to produce the expected results, but the recurring dramatic changes also make it very difficult for subsequent reformers to begin a process of successful problem solving. Powering (re-)creates crisis.

MENEM OVERHAULS TRANSPORTATION

Argentina once had one of the most impressive transportation systems in the world. In 1914, the Argentine rail network was the most extensive in Latin America, and the Buenos Aires metro rivaled those in Europe and the United States. Over the course of the twentieth century, Argentina also built one of the most expansive highway systems in Latin America.

By the late 1980s, however, the quality of the rail and highway infrastructure had declined, and the ever-increasing operation and maintenance costs had become a substantial drain on the national treasury (Gerchunoff and Coloma 1993, 276–7). In particular, the integrated national public enterprise responsible for railway services, Ferrocarriles Argentinos, consumed an estimated US$800 million to US$1.4 billion annually in the late 1980s (Sharp 2005, 15). By 1990, 54 percent of the total rail network track was in bad or fair condition, and only 49 percent of a total fleet of 992 locomotives was available for service (Estache, Carbajo, and de Rus 1999, 7). The highway system was also in need of improved management and substantial investment. In 1989, construction costs were twice what was considered best practice; thus, despite the millions poured into improvements, only 36 percent of the national highways were in fit condition (Natale 1993). Increasing dependence on automobiles and the poor quality of the rail network meant that the financial performance of the transport sector would continue its precipitous decline unless something were done.

Privatization provided a seemingly clear, comprehensive model for resolving numerous problems in the transportation sector. The neoliberal thinking of the Washington Consensus, which dominated the policy recommendations of the World Bank and other IFIs in the 1990s, linked issues in the transportation sector to a single underlying concern: overburdened, inefficient states. Consequently, the solution for both fiscal and administrative problems relied on privatizing state services and assets to reduce the size of the state. Such an approach aimed to reduce the deficit and improve the quality of services by increasing market competition. For transportation in particular, concession agreements – privatization of infrastructure services through long-term management and investment contracts – provided a rapid means of achieving such goals.[2]

It seemed an elegant solution: By auctioning off the right to charge tolls, the state expected to generate substantial revenue in the short term and improve quality in the long term by shifting the responsibility for modernization and maintenance to private companies (*concessionaires*). This approach would also make large state agencies redundant, facilitating reductions in public sector staff and public payroll by immediately transferring responsibility to private companies. In this way, the neoliberal approach provided a clear, off-the-shelf solution to the complex problems in the transport sector.

Despite his statist campaign promises, President Carlos Menem, who faced exploding inflation and depleted state coffers immediately following his 1989 election, embraced the neoliberal solution. Not only did his powering reform show decisive action on pressing issues to citizens suffering from the effects of hyperinflation and recession, the comprehensive reform model also provided a shortcut to the laborious process of assessing the numerous problems and carefully crafting solutions. A variety of problems were linked to the root cause of excessive state intervention and

---

[2] Concession agreements are a type of public–private partnership that give the company the right to use all utility assets conferred as well as the responsibility for operation and investment. Private companies pay a fee, or *canon*, for the right to use infrastructure for the life of the concession agreement, and assets revert to state authority at the end of the concession period. In a concession, the company/operator typically obtains its revenues directly from the consumer. Unlike with privatization, concessions are not transferred to private ownership and are contract-based, not regulator-based. In both privatizations and concessions, however, the staff is transferred to the private sector.

hyperinflation and were thus used to justify emergency measures (Murillo 2009, 240). This allowed reformers to act quickly to gain credibility with foreign investors, raise cash to finance the fiscal debt, and prevent the organization of anti-privatization lobbies (Manzetti 1999, 99).[3]

Outsider technocrats were deemed essential for this process. They seemed crucial given the nature of the reforms – novel, foreign models required specialized expertise – and the lack of highly trained technocrats within the state bureaucracy (Teichman 1997, 33–4; 2004, 60). Thus, when Minister of the Economy Domingo Cavallo (1991–6), a Harvard-trained economist and former consultant for the World Bank, assumed his position within the administration, he brought with him a team from the Fundación Mediterránea, a think tank with a history of strong connections to the Bank (N'haux 1993, 248, 267). Such tight-knit teams of experts and World Bank officials shared similar training and work experience; in the words of one bank official, "Argentine Economy officials are well known to us; we speak the same language, and there are no basic differences in our views."[4] Relying on technocrats and bureaucrats from within the state would have risked pushback from individuals with a vested interest in the status quo. Control over reforms became increasingly centralized in the hands of the economic minister and this core group of experts; their unified vision reduced internal opposition and allowed for rapid and far-reaching change. Cavallo surrounded himself with such a like-minded and intensely loyal team that consultation and discussion were considered secondary because "Cavallo's team knew him, and, therefore, knew what he wanted done" (Teichman 1997, 48). Moreover, Cavallo, his technocrats, and World Bank officials had few ties to the public sector so were in a better position to implement the comprehensive changes, especially the drastic reduction in public sector workers.

Cutting the number of public employees also weakened political rivals' access to patronage and the power of unions (Manzetti 1999, 91). By uprooting public officials appointed by Menem's predecessors, his administration further concentrated power in the apex of the ministries and agencies, mitigating bureaucratic antagonism toward the new policies. The National Highway Agency (DNV), deemed redundant because

---

[3] Two laws passed in 1989 – the Law for Reform of the State and the Economic Emergency Law – provided the legal framework that allowed the president to bypass Congress and institute changes by presidential decree.

[4] Senior bank official quoted in Teichman (2004, 62).

responsibility for highway construction and maintenance would be transferred to the provinces and to concessionaires, lost 1,300 employees by
1992 (World Bank 1993). In 1989, Ferrocarriles Argentinos had 94,800
employees; by 1996, Menem's reform teams had slashed the employees to
a mere 17,064, cutting 82 percent of its workforce (Kogan 1999; Gómez-
Ibáñez 2003, 96). By dismantling existing institutions deemed corrupt and
inefficient, Menem consolidated authority during this first phase of
reform, undercutting rivals and stifling internal dissent.

In addition to an upper-level concentration of power, achieved by
arrogating more extensive decree authority and packing the Supreme
Court,[5] such measures facilitated Menem's lightning-fast transformation
of the transport sector. By 1990, after twelve simultaneous bidding con-
tests, the government had auctioned off about one third of the intercity
highways (Estache and Carbajo 1996, 2).[6] Five months after the first set of
concession agreements were signed, the government initiated a second
wave of concessions, this time for Buenos Aires access roads. Meanwhile,
a similar privatization process began to break up Ferrocarriles Argentinos'
fully integrated and centralized network, dividing it into monopoly fran-
chises that combined track and service operations for both freight services
and metropolitan commuter rail. Between 1991 and 1993, five thirty-year
freight concessions were completed; within the next two years, seven
Buenos Aires commuter service lines were auctioned off for twenty-year
time periods.

The rapid-fire concession auctions of railways and highways had, by
the mid-1990s, seemed to accomplish what most observers thought
impossible; this generated considerable optimism, especially among international observers. The World Bank, the IMF, and foreign investors
praised reforms that had turned Argentina into a "miracle" by taming
inflation and restoring growth (Blustein 2005, 58; Manzetti 2009, 147).
The title of a World Bank article from 1996 declared that railway reforms
in Argentina were "Heading Down the Right Track" (Carbajo and
Estache 1996, 1), improving services while controlling costs (CEER
2001; Manzetti 2003, 346; Sharp 2005, 16). Indeed, advances seemed
promising: Assessments showed that the Menem administration had

---

[5] Between 1990 and 1994, Menem issued over 300 decrees of necessity and urgency
(Manzetti 1999, 92).

[6] Private companies paid US$890 million to the state for the use of the road infrastructure
during the life of the concession agreement. The road concessions initially appeared
competitive, with 147 bids submitted (Estache and Carbajo 1996).

bested an intransigent opposition in a wide variety of policy areas, allowing the government to reduce the fiscal drain of the public sector payroll by shrinking state agencies; raise substantial funds through auctioning off the rights to toll highways and operate railways; and inject competition, private management, and investment finance into Argentina's dilapidated transport infrastructure (FIEL 1999). Between Menem's powering and Argentina's 30 percent cumulative growth rate from 1990 to 1994, the country seemed to be on a roll.

The powering approach initially yielded political dividends for Menem as well. Positive evaluations of the changes in Menem's first term buoyed his approval ratings, facilitating the ratification of a series of constitutional reforms with the Olivos Pact of 1994. Menem had proven himself a resolute reformer, and, in May 1995, he won a second term by a landslide. Such glowing initial evaluations and the benefits of his approach indeed underscore the allure of powering for political leaders with only a few short years to make a difference before they are up for reelection.

Yet what contributed to quick success in the short term undermined the effectiveness and sustainability of sweeping new policies in the long term. The economic crisis opened a window of opportunity to rapidly push through changes, but it also meant that reform calculations were made in a moment of tremendous uncertainty. The time pressure was particularly problematic for concession contracts, because they offered a one-shot opportunity to craft deals for anywhere from twelve to thirty years. The whole idea of such a contract is to protect both the public and the concessionaire by specifying all the terms of the concession in advance. That is, Argentina's concession contracts, and especially those of railways, were intended to be very specific about the way in which tariffs, quality, investment, exclusivity, and so on would evolve over time (Campos-Méndez, Estache, and Trujillo 2001, 23). Yet former Secretary of Transportation Armando Canosa notes that at the time no one – neither IFI officials nor government officials – had a systematic way of estimating how much income concessionaires were expected to make or how demand would evolve given the fluidity of the economic situation and evolving regulatory framework.[7] As a result, projections wildly under- and over-estimated how much rail and road traffic could be expected. Without the

---

[7] Author interview with Armando Norberto Canosa (Secretario de Transporte de la Nación, Ministerio de Economía y Obras y Servicios Públicos de la Nación, 1996–1999), November 21, 2012.

necessary revenue, many concessionaires were unable to fulfill their investment promises. In other cases, increased usage meant that roads and rails required more maintenance and investment than anticipated (FIEL 1999, 188–90). Due to the flawed calculations, by the late 1990s none of the companies had paid the amount they owed to the government based on concession agreements, and few had made the promised investments to improve infrastructure (Estache, Carbajo, and de Rus 1999, 10).

The Menem administration could have waited until the economic situation stabilized before commencing the changes in transport. In fact, this option was proposed by some Argentine transport experts,[8] who suggested moderate changes that would alleviate the fiscal drain on public spending while targeting repairs in areas with critical deficiencies. This approach would have allowed policymakers to wait until the hyperinflation and macroeconomic adjustment volatility had subsided to advance changes. But proponents of radical reform argued that the window of opportunity was limited.[9] Narrowing the scope or slowing the speed of concession auctions would have also allowed decision-makers to make more modest changes and observe the effects. Powering advocates, however, aimed to prevent opponents, especially the powerful public sector unions linked to transportation, from organizing against the changes.[10] Menem and his team of reformers scheduled the first wave of transport auctions to occur just months after assuming office, during the height of the economic crisis.

Where transport was rapidly transformed, the most egregious problems occurred. For example, inaccurate models used to forecast profits for the concessionaires that won twelve simultaneous auctions in 1991, privatizing one third of highways, prompted the new owners to charge tolls 67 percent higher than the agreed-upon amount, violating the terms of the concession agreements (Gerchunoff and Coloma 1993, 280). Furthermore, agreements stipulated that the most serious deficiencies had to be repaired *before* collecting tolls (Estache and Carbajo 1996). Yet companies argued that the government relied on incomplete information to estimate profits and that the macro-adjustment plan had adversely affected their ability to collect revenue – a situation not

---

[8] Author interview with former civil servant in the transport sector, 2011.
[9] Author interview with former World Bank official, 2012.
[10] Canosa, interview; author interview with Eladio Sánchez (Director of Economic Management, Secretariat of Transportation, Ministry of the Interior and Transportation), November 27, 2012.

covered in concessions agreements. Thus, to complete promised repairs, owners imposed tolls and increased rates. Public outrage ensued. As a result, only five months after the contracts had been signed, the government forced private companies to reduce the tolls, both sides breaking with the terms of the newly signed concession agreements.

In contrast to highway privatizations, the rail concessions, though still executed rapidly, were staggered not simultaneous, and did not face the same immediate challenges (FIEL 1999; CEER 2001; Sharp 2005, 16). Problems occurred later, but initial estimates were closer to the mark because they were crafted based on existing concession agreements and reflected lessons learned during a more stable economic situation. The effectiveness of the reforms in this case was inversely related to their pace and depth.

The damage done by the first waves of concession agreements affected not only the initial contracts. By renegotiating, the government also set a dangerous precedent for the entire transport sector: Private companies could win contracts by underbidding then reap higher returns through renegotiation. This process reduced competition and transparency, undercutting the central idea of the reform. After a year and a half of renegotiations following the initial failure of the highway concessions, the government and concessionaires signed new contracts (Decree 1817/1992). The Menem administration was able to come to an agreement whereby the toll would be set at the initially agreed-upon rate but at a steep cost to the government: The private companies' US$890 million payment for the rights to charge tolls was eliminated, and tax relief and subsidies were granted to the concession holders at a cost to the treasury of about US$1,755 million (Gerchunoff and Coloma 1993, 280–1). Only three years later, renegotiation processes resumed for nearly all of the highway contracts and continued throughout the 1990s (Estache, Carbajo, and de Rus 1999, 16–17). Private companies operating railways followed suit. Thus, by 1998, the government was renegotiating all railway concessions, while spending US$400 million per year in subsidies, with a commitment from the state to pay for US$6 billion in investment over the following twenty years (ibid., 10). Given the data available, it is nearly impossible to know whether the root cause of railway renegotiations was the flawed initial agreements or whether private railway companies took advantage of the fact that the government could be compelled to renegotiate. In either case, by pushing through rapid and wholesale privatizations of the road network, the Menem administration exacerbated problems in the transport sector by crafting unsustainable agreements and undercutting its own authority to enforce contracts.

Finally, relying on outside experts undermined the quality of reform design in a variety of ways. Outsiders to the federal administration lacked the experience to adapt reform to the Argentine context. For instance, outside experts had assumed that companies would compete against each other in the bidding process (Gerchunoff and Coloma 1993), yet the main competitors, especially for the highway system, had agreed among themselves which routes they would claim.[11] Interviews with government contractors suggest that experts from the National Highway Agency (DNV), who had years of experience with private companies in the road sector, could have anticipated and prevented much of the cartel activity – had they been involved.[12] In order to push through the changes quickly and avoid resistance from public sector employees, reform teams had sidelined experts who possessed such foresight and nuanced understandings of local conditions.[13]

These outsiders created other problems as well. Instead of representing a variety of interests and perspectives, political technocrats were selected based on their commitment to a shared neoliberal reform objective. Such insular reform teams failed to engender the debate necessary for strong planning. Instead, they limited creativity and fostered groupthink by creating an overly optimistic belief that, despite problems in estimates and reform designs, market mechanisms would prevail (Teichman 1997, 48).[14] Additionally, incentives encouraged political technocrats and IFI experts to implement their reform plans on time, even if quality or sustainability were threatened. World Bank reports from the mid-1990s imply that they overlooked crucial problems and warning signs because they were already invested in the process (World Bank 1996a, 29).[15]

---

[11] Author interviews with government contractors, 2011 and 2012.

[12] Author interview with former employee of a highway concessionaire, 2012; author interview with Horacio Fischbarg (Government Contractor, 1982–2005), July 26, 2010; author interview with Dr. Luisa Maria Hynes (Directora de Control de Obras Públicas, Tribunal de Cuentas de la Nación, 1982–1991; Asesora de Gabinete, AGN, 1994–1995; Consultant, PNUD and UNDP, 2006–2009), August 28, 2012.

[13] Sánchez, interview; author interview with Beatriz López (Administrador Gubernamental and Engineer), November 14, 2012.

[14] Hynes, interview.

[15] Specifically, the World Bank's "OED [Operations Evaluation Department] concluded that the reform of public enterprises with the support of PERAL was among the most far-reaching ever carried out by any country, and that the alternative of delaying privatization until an adequate regulatory framework was in place would have threatened the implementation of the privatization program itself, indefinitely prolonging the burden of

Moreover, during the auction processes, domestic groups failed on a number of occasions to meet the financial and technical prerequisites imposed by the contracts; the government was faced with the choice either to postpone the auction or sign a long-term concession agreement with private sector partners who might not be able to maintain roads adequately (Manzetti 1999, 100). Under pressure to push the changes through, political technocrats chose to go ahead with the concessions even in the absence of bidders who met technical prerequisites.[16]

The timing, scope, and speed of reforms meant that decision-makers deviated significantly from the maxims of rational decision-making. Instead of careful assessments, Menem's reformers relied excessively on foreign models, rash inferences, and a near-religious belief that the neo-liberal approach would prevail. While some blame can be placed on the reformers themselves, an assessment of the depth and scope of the changes at a time of economic uncertainty meant that they faced an almost impossible task. At the heart of the failure was the decision to reject more moderated reforms for the powering approach.

Once the path of deep, precipitous reforms was taken, a cascade of new problems appeared. Unfortunately, reversing course or addressing problems became ever more difficult because, in the process of driving through deep changes, institutions were stripped of their capacity to identify and address problems in policymaking. Once power was centralized in the hands of political technocrats, it was very difficult to create new institutions, employ individuals with adequate expertise and experience, and devolve authority that had been concentrated in the upper echelons of ministries.

As a result, the regulatory agencies necessary for monitoring and enforcing compliance remained weak and ineffective. According to reform plans, the DNV was to serve as the agency responsible for the supervision of concessions.[17] By the late 1990s and increasingly in the early 2000s, analysts noted that the DNV lacked the independence, organization, and staffing to supervise the concessionaires (Estache, Carbajo, and de Rus 1999). Similar problems plagued railway institutions: From 1992 to 1996, there were at least four separate attempts to create different types of regulatory bodies (AGN 2004). In 1996, the National

---

the deficits of the privatized enterprises. Privatization provided substantial benefits to Argentina even if in a less-than-ideal competitive framework with the absence of a regulatory framework" (World Bank 1996a, 29).

[16] Former World Bank official, interview.   [17] López, interview.

Transportation Regulatory Commission (*Comisión Nacional de Regulación del Transporte*, CNRT) was finally created (Decree 660/1996). Yet this decentralized regulatory agency was not given the authority, capacity, or autonomy to modify contracts or collect accounting information from private firms, weakening its capacity for the crucial task of monitoring and enforcing concession agreements (Campos-Méndez, Estache, and Trujillo 2001).[18] Finally, after a number of different arrangements, the CNRT was placed under the direct control of the Ministry of Economy and Public Works, further weakening the independence of the regulatory body (Campos-Méndez, Estache, and Trujillo 2001, 6–7). High-level political technocrats thus retained exclusive oversight of the rapidly evolving transport sector.

The weak mechanisms for communication and oversight soon became evident. By the late 1990s, some concessionaires were distributing record profits despite receiving state subsidies and failing to pay the mandated *canon* (Baer and Montes-Rojas 2008, 332). At the same time, within a two-year period government officials renegotiated over 42 percent of infrastructure contracts in Argentina outside the mechanisms established in the contract, nearly 15 percent more than the regional average (Guasch 2004).

In sum, root-and-branch overhauls that were expected to create exemplary and irreversible changes to infrastructure development instead weakened institutions and led to a new set of problems. Contrary to what theories of historical institutionalism would predict, changes failed to consolidate.

Why did the powering reforms in transport, which seemed to hold so much promise for resolving the problems plaguing the sector, ultimately have such disappointing results? Are privatization and deregulation simply ineffective policy approaches for infrastructure development and maintenance? What role did corruption play in derailing the process? A comparison with other cases reveals that other Latin American countries, including Chile and Brazil, also privatized infrastructure in the 1990s, yet their reforms were not plagued by the same profound problems as in Argentina. Moreover, the United States deregulated the railroad industry in the 1980s with great success (Gallamore 1999; Winston 2005), demonstrating that privatization and deregulation are not bad policy choices per se. Nor did the failure of the reforms hinge on the corruption of policymakers. Because details of contract renegotiations

---

[18] Hynes, interview.

and subsidies were poorly recorded and tracked, the Menem administration, journalists, and watchdogs were all unable to make inferences from solid information.[19] Reports of shady deals between concessionaires and top-tier government officials soon emerged.[20] Indeed, there were clear cases of corruption: The Minister of Infrastructure Roberto José Dromi, who led the first set of reforms, was notoriously corrupt, though he was soon replaced. Allegations of corruptions swirled around Menem as well. In contrast, although transport institutions in Brazil were not immune to high-level corruption, reforms proved more successful. In the end, the failure of Argentina's transport overhaul cannot be blamed on corruption. Instead, the persistent problems stemmed from the very approach to reform, which heightened uncertainty, limited the foresight of reform designers, and weakened existing institutions. Thus, powering in the transport sector in the 1990s successfully altered the status quo but failed to create strong institutions that would ensure the continued vitality of reforms.

CONTINUED DETERIORATION OF TRANSPORTATION REFORMS (2000–2012)

Making the concession model functional would have required strengthening institutions and solving a number of problems created by the initial set of comprehensive reforms, but the mechanisms established by Menem's unilateral imposition of reform continued to hinder improvements in the transport model.

The lack of transparency and ongoing renegotiation of contracts with transport concessionaires cast a pall of corruption over Menem's administration. In 1999, President de la Rúa took office on a platform opposed to Menem's neoliberal reforms and alleged corruption.[21] The transition resulted in the extensive turnover of public sector employees, especially in the transport agencies, where Menem's political technocrats were replaced by technocrats loyal to one of the two political parties in de la Rúa's Alianza coalition.[22] When Menem's political technocrats left, few

---

[19] Daniel Santoro, personal communication, July 28, 2010.
[20] *Página12*, December 4, 1999. [21] *La Nación*, May 26, 1999.
[22] Alianza was an electoral coalition formed in order to defeat the PJ candidate; in it, the UCR joined with FREPASO (a party formed in the mid-1990s by eight deputies breaking away from the PJ, including Carlos "Chacho" Álvarez) and other small parties who opposed Menem's neoliberal policies.

who knew the history of reform remained in the administration.[23] Consequently, the de la Rúa administration spent the next year evaluating the concession agreements only to realize that they faced the same stark choices as the previous government (Gómez-Ibáñez 2003, 103). Instead of seeking to resolve the fundamental problems, they papered over the issues with subsidies to the sector and another string of renegotiations, pursuing the policies under Menem that de la Rúa had criticized.

Soon, however, the failing economic and political situation overshadowed concerns about the transport sector. Faced with deep political divisions in the ruling Alianza coalition, de la Rúa resorted to tactics that compromised his own anti-corruption agenda. In June 2000, *La Nación* published an article revealing that Peronist senators had received significant personal favors for passing a labor reform bill.[24] Shortly after the incident, FREPASO vice-president Chacho Álvarez resigned to protest the government's bribery of the opposition.[25] De la Rúa's subsequent appointment of Domingo Cavallo, who had led the neoliberal crusade under Menem, as minister of the economy only heightened the political crisis after Cavallo decided to freeze bank accounts so as to stop a run on banks. In the ensuing months, the deteriorating economic situation led to massive street protests and lootings, which were met by a strong government crackdown. Weakened and isolated, de la Rúa resigned in December 2001. After appointing five presidents in twelve days, the Legislative Assembly finally chose Eduardo Duhalde as a provisional president to complete de la Rúa's term (Katz 2006, 415–18). Finally, with the election of Néstor Kirchner in 2003, the political and economic crises seemed at last to abate.

While this unprecedented economic crisis intensified the challenges of Menem's transportation reforms in the short term, it was not the pivotal factor in their continued deterioration. The crisis of 2001 and 2002 reduced the concessionaires' revenue from tolls and rail tickets: Around 2000, growth plummeted, inflation skyrocketed, and use of rails and roads declined precipitously. Yet passenger traffic recovered quickly after 2002, and the Argentine economy made an impressive recovery in the decade that followed the crisis. Thus, while the economic crisis hurt the private companies responsible for transport services, it was not decisive for the long-term breakdown of the concession model.

---

[23] Author interview with high official in Menem Interior Ministry, 2012.
[24] *La Nación*, June 25, 2000.   [25] *La Nación*, October 7, 2000.

The continued deterioration of the concession model resulted largely from the weakening of transport institutions under Menem's powering reforms and during de la Rúa's clean sweep of personnel. Transportation policy under Menem and de la Rúa had been cobbled together by a few technocrats at the highest levels of government. As a result, Néstor Kirchner inherited a Highway Agency (DNV) that was a shadow of its former self, its roles and responsibilities indistinguishable from those of the Agency of Road Concessions (OCCOVI) created by Menem in 2001 to regulate highway concessions. The state-owned railway company, Ferrocarriles Argentinos, no longer existed. The CNRT had never been given any real power; it had twelve agents to monitor 240 stations, 900 km of roads, and 2,000 locomotives and railcars (Pérez 2014, 120), not nearly enough to adequately enforce standards specified in concession contracts. A National Audit Body (*Auditoría General de la Nación*, AGN) report completed just before Néstor Kirchner assumed office corroborates the deterioration of the regulatory agencies, stating that their inability to monitor and sanction concessionaires contributed to the owner's consistent failures to make promised investments (AGN 2004, 14–15).[26] In 2003, a total of 389 railway passengers in the Buenos Aires metropolitan area were killed in accidents, and many commuters lost limbs while riding the footboards or on top of packed trains after waiting hours upon hours for trains to arrive. If there had been stronger regulatory institutions and a core cadre of experts within the administration, they might have been able to supervise concessionaires and gradually improve the concession model. Without such continuity, however, the lessons learned from a decade of reform were essentially lost, and Kirchner inherited hollowed-out institutions.

Within this vacuum, authority became even more concentrated in the upper levels of government. In 2003, Kirchner created a new Ministry of Planning, Investment, and Public Services that absorbed competencies and resources from other ministries as well as the presidency. Kirchner appointed Julio de Vido, a trusted advisor and aide from Santa Cruz, as

---

[26] The inability of regulatory agencies to sanction concessionaires meant that private companies operating railways failed to make necessary investments or resume service. Alarming reports in 2003 showed that 70 percent of railway cars had problems with their brake systems, but the AGN showed that in only one case was a concessionaire sanctioned (AGN 2004). In February 2003, Judge Angel Di Mateo stated that he had found the railway cars and stations in the Roca line "in a calamitous state," with the passengers traveling "like cattle," and ordered the concessionaire, Transporte Metropolitano S.A., to provide "decent and efficient service."

minister; de Vido's new bureaucratic empire spanned transportation, communications, mining, energy, sewer systems, public works, housing, water, roads, and planning of public investments (Decree 1283/2003). Another long-time Santa Cruz connection, Ricardo Jaime, was appointed to the Transportation Secretariat within de Vido's ministry.

In this and other areas, the failure of Menem's reforms was used to justify sustained centralization of authority in the hands of political appointees. The weakness of institutions resulted in further usurpation of authority. Menem appropriated control of regulatory agencies, such as the CNRT and OCCOVI, by unilaterally appointing a "caretaker" or *interventor* to each agency (Decree 1388/1996), sidestepping legal requirements that require autonomous regulatory agencies to be run by a board of directors. Kirchner justified this control by pointing to the "failure of the management to meet its objectives for users, competitiveness of the market, and safe transport" (ACIJ 2008, 10–12). His actions undercut the autonomy of regulatory agencies, making them dependent on the de Vido–Jaime nexus, which retained de facto authority to sanction, renegotiate, and re-privatize concessions (Cipoletta Tomassian and Sánchez 2009, 56). Such centralization of authority extended well beyond transport: Kirchner also appointed *interventores* to agencies regulating public utilities (gas, electricity, communications, etc.), alleging "situations of exception" and a lack of time to undergo the selection process for these key positions (Scherlis 2010, 104).

Not only did such high-level officials lack experience in the federal government prior to appointment, but they were also bombarded with policy problems. Without the capacity to address small problems one by one, they focused solely on maintaining the semblance of a functioning transport system. For example, instead of seeking a sustainable means of financing the transport sector, the Kirchner administration papered over the problem again by relying on government subsidies from off-the-books *fondos fiduciarios*, which transferred public funds to private companies responsible for highways and railroads.[27] Despite the increase in government money to the transport sector, problems were largely ignored and

[27] These are fiduciary funds, trust funds originally created to allocate money for a specific purpose. During the crisis, such funds were first used to compensate concessionaires for freezing of tariffs. In 2001, there were only eight such fiduciary funds; by 2007, there were over sixteen, and expenditures from such trusts had increased by 6,000 percent, from US$96.9 million to US$5.9 trillion (Uña 2007, 4). Such funds are financed through the budget, revenues, and tariffs, as well as the profits from assets of privatized firms, and loans from international credit institutions (AGN 2004, 14–16). Most importantly,

violations of concession contracts overlooked. The case of ALL Central S.A., a Brazilian company that held one of the most important freight concessions, exemplifies this trend: The government failed to hold the company to account despite violations of the concession agreement and continued to provide substantial subsidies (AGN 2006; ACIJ 2007, 20). Similarly, concessionaires like Metropolitano faced no consequences when they failed again and again to make basic upgrades or ensure security on their lines, despite receiving substantial subsidies.

Given the overwhelming problems, high-level transport officials focused only on the most dramatic crises. In 2004, after a number of fatalities on Metropolitano's San Martín line, AGN released a scathing report on the precarious situation of transport in general and this line in particular. Instead of taking measures to monitor the concessionaire, the Kirchner administration terminated its San Martín concession (Decrees 798/2004 and 591/2007).[28] It placed the re-nationalized concession in the hands of the government-created Unidad de Gestión Operativa Ferroviaria de Emergencia (UGOFE), a consortium of Argentine companies formed in January 2005 by Ferrovías, Metrovías, and Trenes de Buenos Aires, the remaining companies operating the commuter rail services in Buenos Aires (Decree 789/2004, Secretaría de Transporte Resolution 408/2004). Metropolitano maintained control over two other concessions, Belgrano Norte and Roca, but the government ignored warning signs and failed to monitor the company. The situation came to a head in 2007, when hundreds of passengers stormed the Constitution Terminal in an hours-long confrontation with police after they had again been informed that service was suspended (Pérez and Rebón 2012). This dramatic incident prompted the government to transfer control of this line to the remaining concessionaires.

This haphazard approach was quite different from problem solving. Although changes were often incremental – a small subsidy increase here or there – they were not part of a plan, a sequence of modifications on

---

because such trusts are not governed by the same rules as other public expenditures, it is impossible to know how the money is used. These funds are not included in the annual public budget, even though by 2005 *fondo fiduciarios'* expenditures had surpassed the level authorized by Congress (Rinaldi et al. 2005, 4). Accounting and control standards are absent, and there are no external audit requirements (AGN 2004, 15; Lo Vuolo and Seppi 2006), and attempts by AGN to monitor these funds have been met with hostility. Legal requirements oblige the chief of cabinet to inform Congress on fiduciary funds (Law 25.827/04), but in practice this has not occurred (Rinaldi and Staffa 2006, 1).

[28] For the endless legal battles that ensued, see *La Nación*, June 26, 2004.

a particular path to address policy-making issues. Instead, they were reactive, addressing problems at the point of crisis, and focused only on restoring the status quo. In this way, the approach during the Kirchner years was in keeping with the type of change that occurs after a critical juncture or punctuated equilibrium: incremental, non-directional, and unproductive over time. Such an approach meant that problems became entrenched.

Facing mounting concerns, Kirchner blamed his predecessors' reforms and the private companies. Indeed, Menem's powering had weakened Kirchner's incentives to strengthen his predecessor's reforms. Why would Menem's successors want to make transport concessions successful, especially after changes had been discredited because of poor performance? Why champion improvements of a "failed" reform? Thus, instead of strengthening institutions important for transport, Kirchner continued to let them flounder. From 1995 to 2005, the number of civil servants in the Highway Agency (DNV) dropped by nearly 40 percent, and the number of agents per 1000 km of the highway network (non-concessioned) went from 129 to 78 agents during the same time period (Dirección Nacional de Vialidad 2007). Similarly, CNRT, the regulatory agency for railways, was the agency with the least budget growth between 2001 and 2007 (ACIJ 2008). Despite CNRT's bleak outlook, experts argue that the personnel situation was even more precarious in OCCOVI and the DNV.[29] Without enough funds or civil servants to monitor compliance and apply sanctions, the transport agencies had no chance of correcting the flaws in Menem's initial reforms.

The continuation of Néstor Kirchner's policies under the administration of his wife, Cristina Fernández de Kirchner, spurred further increases in subsidies even as the system deteriorated. Between 2005 and 2011, state subsidies to the railways tripled, going from 2.4 billion to 6.8 billion pesos (IDESA 2012).[30] Figure 1 shows that, despite this investment, the quality of services deteriorated: The number of seats was reduced from 2007 to 2010, and, as operators stopped collecting fares, the number of passengers who actually paid for tickets also declined (IDESA 2012). *La Nación* estimated that the subsidy was ten times the basic one-peso ticket price, while only 6 in every 100 metropolitan rail passengers purchased a valid ticket.[31]

[29] Author interview with high official in Kirchner's Ministry of the Interior, November 27, 2012; author interview with high official in Menem's Ministry of the Interior, October 22, 2012.

[30] Figures are measured in 2011 pesos.   [31] *La Nación*, October 5, 2013.

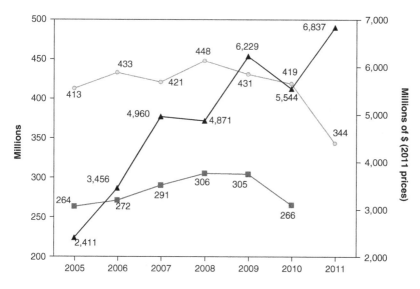

FIGURE 1 Subsidies, Available Seats, and Tickets Purchased
Source: IDESA 2012

Given the feeble institutions, centralized authority, and weak incentives to improve, it is hardly surprising that allegations of corruption abounded around those at the helm of transportation agencies. De Vido, Jaime, and Claudio Uberti, OCCOVI's interventor, along with contractors, were implicated in numerous scandals involving bribes, cartels, cost overruns in contracting, and work paid for but never completed (Cabot and Olivera 2008; Guillan-Montero 2011). In 2005, the World Bank discovered that 63 percent of highway works were awarded to four companies with ties to Santa Cruz, where they had obtained similar deals in the 1990s from de Vido, minister of the economy at the time under then-Governor Néstor Kirchner. The Minister of the Economy Roberto Lavagna denounced the "cartelization" of highway contracts (Cabot and Olivera 2008, 22–3; Manzetti 2014, 185).[32]

---

[32] Together with the Kirchner administration, the World Bank had funded CREMA, a program designed to maintain and modernize the highway system. Subsequently, officials began investigating problematic cost overruns. Later in 2006, the DNV found that such contracts had cost overruns that exceeded the budget by anywhere from 29 to 290 percent (Manzetti 2014, 185).

Such denunciations continued. In a criminal lawsuit against Kirchner and de Vido,[33] Elisa Carrió further detailed the cartel operation, which resulted in numerous other money-laundering investigations involving Santa Cruz entrepreneurs. These included the infamous Lázaro Báez, who earned public contracts worth US$1 billion and allegedly set up an intricate money-laundering scheme, in which over fifty ghost firms were used to transfer money abroad.[34] In 2007, Claudio Uberti, a close associate of de Vido responsible for the regulatory agency that controlled all tolls in the country, was dismissed after he was found with a group carrying undeclared bags containing US$800,000 from the Venezuelan government, allegedly destined to finance Cristina Fernández de Kirchner's electoral campaign (Cabot and Olivera 2008; Scherlis 2010, 156).[35] In 2009, Ricardo Jaime submitted his resignation after investigators accused him of accepting bribes from, among others, the Cirigliano Group, whose family company Cometrans controlled Trains of Buenos Aires (TBA), a company that received millions in state subsidies for railway concessions.[36] Jaime was also alleged to have illicitly collected millions for the Kirchner campaign by pressuring companies to contribute.[37] In sum, weak institutions and centralized control resulting from Menem's reforms in many ways facilitated siphoning money out of the transport sector to be used for the Kirchners' political ends.[38]

Throughout this period, officials ignored ominous reports that predicted catastrophe without corrective actions.[39] AGN released report

---

[33] For the full text of Carrió's allegations, see *Perfil*, November 27, 2008.

[34] On Báez, see *La Nación*, February 7, 2010; June 26, 2007; June 30, 2008; *Wall Street Journal*, July 29, 2014.

[35] Even after he was dismissed, Uberti allegedly served as a so-called "parallel ambassador" to Venezuela (*Perfil*, April 8, 2012).

[36] *Perfil*, February 24, 2009. Prosecutor of Administrative Investigations Manuel Garrido led the effort that denounced the secretary of transportation.

[37] *Clarín*, November 22, 2010. Jaime currently faces around twenty separate court cases of administrative fraud and overpricing of railway concession contracts.

[38] Author interview with Guillermo Jorge (Law Professor, San Andres University; IFI consultant on money laundering and corruption), August 22, 2012. Guillermo Jorge and legal counsel at the some of the largest governmental contractors suggest that corruption under the Kirchners does not follow the cartel model as it did under Menem, but, rather, the government selects which companies it will work with and provides extensive subsidies in return for kickbacks into political coffers.

[39] Complaints about investment and maintenance seemed to fall on deaf ears (*La Nación*, February 23, 2012). CNRT submitted several official reports to Secretary of Transport Juan Pablo Schiavi in 2010 and 2011, which emphasized the precarious state of the rails. In particular, the report from March 21, 2011, states that Línea Sarmiento, operated by TBA, was in a deplorable state. The tracks' "irreversible faults" meant that the trains

after report that revealed the calamitous state of the railways and the corruption in public works contracts. Several NGOs, labor unions, and government agencies denounced the critical state of several services and the failures of the government to hold concessionaires to account (ACIJ 2008; Baer and Montes-Rojas 2008, 331). The number of railway accidents steadily increased between 2007 and 2011; the average deaths in the Buenos Aires Metropolitan Area alone were 400 per year. In 2008, there were more than 3,200 accidents, resulting in 2,700 injuries (Pérez 2014, 126). Protests against poor quality services turned violent on numerous occasions.[40]

On February 22, 2012, tragedy stuck: A train on the busy Sarmiento line failed to stop at the *Once* station in downtown Buenos Aires and careened into the platform, killing 51 people and injuring 700.[41] Modern safety technology would have prevented the train cars, run by concessionaire TBA, from slamming into each other after a hard stop, but the carriages used on the Sarmiento line were more than fifty years old. Then, in June 2013, two passenger trains collided into each other, again on the Sarmiento line, killing 3 and injuring more than 100. Again in October of the same year, a train failed to stop and crashed into the buffers at *Once*, injuring ninety-nine people. The government cast blame on TBA, but the *Once* crash and subsequent collisions proved too momentous to ignore; finally, the administration of Cristina Fernández de Kirchner shifted its attention to the problems in transport.

In sum, the structural effects of Menem's powering continued to threaten the viability of the reforms. The exit of political technocrats after his departure and the resulting absence of experienced individuals meant that subsequent administrations were left without the capacity to identify and address problems. This lack of experience below allowed the

should reduce their speed; the report also states that "a pronounced maintenance deficit can be observed, with worrying faults from the security viewpoint, because of their gravity and recurrence." The report continues: "The infrastructure delivered from the [TBA] concession presents significant deficits regarding the contractually established requirements ... and both its routine maintenance such as human and material resources are insufficient to reverse a situation of steady decay." The report was issued by the manager of transportation safety of CNRT, Horacio Faggiani, and signed by the organization's intervenor, Antonio Sícaro (Nota CNRT 445/2011; *La Nación*, February 29, 2012). Yet according to AGN, CNRT took no meaningful corrective actions, despite the fact that AGN issued a report in 2008 (and continued to issue such reports) that highlighted failures of the TBA: trains had missing handles on emergency brakes and ineffective handbrakes, among other deficiencies (*La Nación*, February 23, 2012).

[40] *Página12*, May 16, 2007.

[41] Here, *once* refers to the Spanish word for eleven, rather than the English "once."

concentration of power above, paving the way for corruption. Moreover, the backlash against Menem's dramatic neoliberal reforms left few incentives for subsequent presidents to strengthen the concession model. Together, these factors meant that problems were heeded only when they became crises.

POWERING DÉJÀ VU: FERNÁNDEZ REVERSES MENEM'S REFORMS (2012–2015)

Following the *Once* crisis, executive attention shifted abruptly to problems in transportation. Instead of making medium or proportionate adjustments and improvements, however, such as monitoring concessionaires, enforcing concession contracts, or upgrading the most dilapidated trains, the Fernández administration embarked upon a sweeping overhaul of the transport sector. The new model rescinded concession contracts and centralized control of railway services in the state-owned rail company, Trenes Argentinos (also known as Sociedad Operadora Ferroviaria Sociedad del Estado, SOFSE), and its freight sister company, Belgrano Cargas y Logística Sociedad Anónima (hereafter, Belgrano Cargas). Under the Fernández administration, the structure of the transport sector became strikingly similar to what existed before Menem took office.

In an attempt to reverse Menem's changes, Fernández nevertheless drew upon his tactics: restructuring organizations, centralizing power in *interventores*, and issuing executive decrees (*Decretos de Necesidad y Urgencia*, DNUs) in the face of "crisis." Following the *Once* tragedies, the administration of transportation, including its control over ballooning subsidies, was moved from de Vido's empire in the Ministry of Planning to the Ministry of Interior, which henceforth became the Ministry of Interior and Transportation (Decree 874/2012). In March 2012, Florencio Randazzo, the minister of the newly created agency, "intervened" in TBA, taking over the company's management of the metro and appointing an *interventor* for the private company. Instead of delegating day-to-day operation to the ministry and its agencies, the president communicated directly with Randazzo on matters regarding transportation.[42]

Concessions fell like dominoes, with the Fernández administration canceling one contract after the other. Randazzo announced

---

[42] Author interview with Maria Eugenia Coutinho (Directora General Programas y Acción de Gobierno, Presidencia de la Nación), November 5, 2012; Author interview with high official in Fernández Interior Ministry, September 5, 2012.

in October 2013 that the Sarmiento line contract with TBA would be rescinded (Resolution 1083/2013). Operation of the Sarmiento line was placed in the hands of Trenes Argentinos, a nascent state-run company that ran a few minor lines in the interior of the country, while another newly created agency, Administración de Infraestructura Ferroviarias S.E. (ADIF), was put in charge of maintaining and modernizing the railway infrastructure (Resolution 1244/2013).[43] During the same period of time, state-run Trenes Argentinos and ADIF similarly assumed responsibility for the San Martín, Belgrano Sur, and Roca lines, which had been run by the UGOFE consortium, which had included TBA; the Mitre line, which had also been run by TBA; and the Tren de la Costa line, a concession with Sociedad Comercial del Plata.[44]

The transformation extended to freight as well.[45] In May 2013, the Fernández administration nationalized the Belgrano Cargas freight line, which covered fourteen provinces and connected Argentina to Bolivia until it was concessioned in 1997. In 1998, the Belgrano Cargas had transported 3,287,515 tons per year; when the agreement was revoked in 2006, the annual cargo was just over 500,000 tons.[46] The operation of the line was handed over to newly created, state-owned Belgrano Cargas, comprised of Trenes Argentinos, the General Port Administration (Administración General de Puertos, AGP), and ADIF (Decree 566/2013). On June 4, 2013, the state revoked the contract with the Brazilian logistics company América Latina Logística (ALL), which ran the San Martín and General Urquiza freight lines. The Fernández administration struck a deal with China

---

[43] *Página12*, October 26, 2013.   [44] *La Nación*, June 5, 2013.

[45] At the same time, after a back-and-forth with the president, Buenos Aires Mayor Mauricio Macri finally announced that he would take over responsibility for the Metro (*Subte*) from the Fernández administration (*La Nación*, December 20, 2012; *Latin American Weekly Report*, July 4, 2013).

[46] The history of this concession is complicated. Initially, Unión Ferroviaria, a union of railway workers, and Laguan Paiva, an industrial cooperative, were granted the concession. The union, however, allegedly siphoned off subsidies that were meant for rail investment, and the government rescinded the contract. During Néstor Kirchner's presidency, Franco Macri presented an investment plan with Shima, a Chinese company. Yet the government demanded that the unions and Emepa and Grupo Roggio, the major passenger rail operators in Buenos Aires, be part of the operator holding, at which time the consortium withdrew (*La Nación*, May 23, 2014).

to help rebuild Belgrano Cargas' rail networks and to modernize the line's rail-car fleet.[47]

The recreation of Ferrocarriles Argentinos was complete when the government announced that it would take over operation of long-distance passenger rail services in July 2014[48] and rescinded contracts with the two remaining concessionaires, Grupo Roggio's Urquiza line and Emepa's Belgrano Norte line, a year later (Resolution 171/2015). With this move, the Ministry of Interior and Transportation became responsible for operating and maintaining railways and freight services in Buenos Aires and to other cities. The Kirchner administration named the new state-owned agency Ferrocarriles Argentinos Sociedad del Estado, known as Ferrocarriles Argentinos, just like its predecessor.

As time would reveal, rescinding contract after contract was a disproportionate response to the problems. The Fernández administration cited noncompliance to renege on its contractual agreements. The government argued that the Brazilian company ALL, for example, had repeatedly failed to meet conditions set forth in the concession contract. These serious breaches, the government argued, resulted in over 30 percent of ALL's fleet being disabled. Yet according to reports by AGN, such failures were not adequately sanctioned; in only one of the cases did CNRT effectively apply the appropriate penalty (AGN 2013).[49] The failure to monitor contracts with concessionaires, experts argued, should have called into question the government's ability to tackle the more formidable challenges of operating rail lines.[50] Instead of taking a more moderate approach – monitoring concessionaires and applying sanctions – policymakers overreacted to the problems, causing a major shift in transport policy.

The timing of this overhaul also suggests that political motivations may have influenced the decision to adopt a powering approach. From 2003 to 2011, the Kirchners found a key ally in Hugo Moyano, leader of the General Confederation of Labor (*Confederación General del Trabajo*, or CGT), the truck drivers' union and the largest trade union in the country. His interests clashed with those of freight operators: Whereas the deterioration of freight increased the power of the CGT to shut down transport in Argentina, efficient and extended freight lines would diminish the truck drivers' control over shipping. Moyano's alliance with the

---

[47] *Financial Times,* July 14, 2014.   [48] *Clarín,* July 11, 2014.
[49] *ElAuditor.Info,* May 29, 2013.
[50] Author interview with World Bank official, September 28, 2012; López, interview.

Fernández administration effectively ended with a series of truckers' strikes in 2012. The 2013 decision to invest in improvements to freight was thus intended to weaken the power of the truckers' unions and their ability to halt transport.

Surprisingly, the Fernández administration's takeover of transportation faced little resistance. Perhaps the rail system was in such a state of crisis that consensus had been forged. Something needed to be done. Yet the crisis was of the administration's making; numerous groups had anticipated such a tragedy given the state of rail infrastructure. Concessionaires did not put up a fight because they had nothing to lose. They had already benefited from the extravagant subsidies, and the cancellation of their concession agreements now meant that they could return the dilapidated tracks, train cars, and locomotives to the state, washing their hands of responsibility. The continued poor performance had discredited the privatization model, and so citizens were in favor of dramatic reform after years of underinvestment and neglect. The civil service was not going to stand in the way of change, since the Kirchner administrations had transformed the civil service system constructed under Menem.[51] Finally, most agencies related to transport had been gutted, first by Menem and then the Kirchners. Accordingly, institutional weakness resulting from powering reforms that purged experienced civil servants and decision-makers meant that the Fernández administration faced few barriers to change once again deemed necessary given the problems that had precipitated a "crisis."

PROBLEM SOLVING TRAMPLED

Powering's frequent and massive overhauls of the state also disrupted problem-solving processes. In the midst of the powering highlighted above, a variety of attempts at gradual problem-solving reforms made fleeting advances: Eduardo Salas, the director of the National Office of Public Employment, worked to maintain meritocratic standards for the civil service and bolstered training for public employees (Coutinho 2007, 5);[52] Oscar Luna of the National Office of Contracting enhanced

---

[51] Author interview with Guillermo Schweinheim (Former Director of Training and Development, Tribunal de Cuentas de la Nación, 1984–92; Director of the Center of Studies of the Association of Personnel of the Audit Institutions (APOC), 2006–present), August 22, 2012.

[52] Schweinheim, interview; author interview with Hugo Dalbosco (Administrador Gubernamental, 2001–present), November 6, 2012; author interview with Graciela

government contracting transparency (Volosin 2010);[53] Nicolás Raigorodsky, head of transparency policy in the Anticorruption Office, advanced standards for monitoring contracts (Raigorodsky 2007); and Guillermo Bellingi, the head of the National Office of Contracting, introduced legislation to clarify ambiguities in the legal framework for procurement.[54] These and many similar efforts may have stalled or thwarted some of the most deleterious effects of powering. Ultimately, however, the dramatic changes in the service model in the 1990s – swinging from state to private provision of services – trampled most of these problem-solving attempts.

As a result of the frequent overhauls, the process of building expertise was consistently interrupted. By the late 1990s, powering tactics – organizational restructuring, concentrating power, and dismissing civil servants – reduced the number of public sector employees experienced in different approaches to infrastructure contracting and halted the accumulation of expertise. Powering left few individuals with the institutional knowledge crucial for anything other than supporting the concession model, and even these efforts lacked capacity. Administrative capabilities for long-term planning, procurement, project management, and oversight were abandoned. Private concessionaires, not government officials, became responsible for buying materials to lay track or purchase train cars, meaning procurement procedures for public works were largely unused for over a decade.

The same pattern repeated itself under the Kirchner and the first part of the Fernández administrations. Attempts to improve the neglected procurement model of contracting and address the long-standing issues – lack of transparency, rigidity of rules, inefficient procedures, corruption, and collusion[55] – provide a poignant example of how sweeping overhauls wipe out smaller-scale problem-solving efforts. As the director of the ONC, Oscar Luna, a civil servant and engineer, led numerous incremental, moderate attempts to increase transparency in public procurement by automating contracting procedures and placing information online.

Silva (Coordinator for Management of Training and Quality, National Institute of Public Administration (INAP)), November 5, 2010.

[53] Author interview with Guillermo Bellingi (Director of the National Office of Contracting, 2010–12), November 14, 2012.

[54] Author interview with Vanesa del Boca (Anticorruption Office employee), September 12, 2012; author interview with Oscar Luna (Director of the National Office of Contracting, 1996–2006), September 12, 2012.

[55] Bellingi, interview.

Such efforts initially flew under the radar of political attention. In 2002, when President Duhalde and the country were still focused on the aftermath of the 2001 political and economic crises, procurement reform was far down on the agenda, but Luna took this moment of national preoccupation with larger crises as an opportunity to slowly begin enhancing transparency and efficiency. Luna sought assistance from the international financial community and, in 2002, acquired a technology solution from the Government of Australia that automated procurement procedures and published them online. The system was essentially free, the source code allowed Argentine officials to adapt the system to their own requirements, and the flexible process facilitated incremental changes to the project (Trotta 2008, 9).

The quiet, gradual efforts of Luna's team held promise but were soon upended by powering reforms at a higher level. Indeed, the ONC team initially employed an approach similar to successful problem-solving efforts in Brazil; however, the intentionally low-key, piecemeal efforts were stymied by instability. Luna's team was so often "reorganized" from above as part of broader powering reforms that he sought expertise from outside the public sector, relying increasingly on consultants from IFIs or college interns as developers.[56] While such individuals were often quite skilled, they held only brief stints working in the Argentine public administration, and efforts at reform suffered as a result. The adaptation of the Australian model to the Argentine context should have been simple, quick, and cost-effective. Without personnel continuity, however, there was no one to manage the project from start to finish. Consultants and interns responsible for modifications to the original source code each adapted it on their own and rarely left clear documentation of what had been changed or why. This incoherent patchwork of adaptations were modified again with each wave of interns and consultants until the challenges became insurmountable.[57]

Despite growing problems, in December 2005 Secretary of Public Management Juan Abal Medina finally introduced the electronic system Sistema Electrónico de Contrataciones Públicas (SECOP) and its internet platform "ArgentinaCompra" in a presentation that included various public authorities. Days later, Luna again lost the key technical members of his team to "organizational restructuring" (Volosin 2010, 172).

---

[56] Luna, interview.
[57] Author interview with Hernan Clerc (SECOP team lead and contracting expert, the National Office of Contracting, 2009–12), July 16, 2010.

SECOP was obsolete before it was even introduced and became what is known in many parts of Latin America as a project *para inglês ver* (for the English to see), a shiny façade that conceals a significantly different reality on the ground. In 2007, the ONC finally abandoned the idea of resuscitating a system that had become a labyrinth of jumbled code,[58] and Luna's problem-solving initiatives were shelved. Luna, one of the few civil servants with detailed knowledge of procurement, the budget, and past attempts to increase transparency and accountability in contracting, resigned in 2006.[59]

The reasons for Luna's failure, however, extend beyond this particular attempt at change. After Luna left, Fernando Díaz and Guillermo Bellingi, the subsequent directors of the ONC, attempted to implement two different e-government procurement systems and failed. Experts argue that today Argentina lags far behind most countries in Latin America in terms of transparency of government procurement and a sound institutional framework for government contracting.[60] The powering approach can be held responsible for such failures. Each time, just as an initiative looked promising, employee turnover or organizational restructuring resulting from either reform initiatives or patronage appointments displaced the new team.[61] The trampling of reforms in these areas is particularly problematic now that the state has again assumed responsibility for the transport sector.

To cope with the lack of capable personnel, problem solvers often rely on expertise or human capital from outside of the public sector. Under Néstor Kirchner and Cristina Fernández de Kirchner, the number of agreements with universities skyrocketed as did the off-the-books funds directed to such entities.[62] This pattern seems to follow a political logic: The federal administration's unprecedented connection to universities has been correlated to the rise of La Cámpora, the youth movement led by the Kirchners' son Máximo. Foreign consultants and interns also serve as an important source of expertise.

---

[58] Bellingi, interview.   [59] Luna, interview.

[60] Author interview with Dr. Guillermo Rozenwurcel (Coordinador of the Inter-American Network on Government Procurement), August 22, 2012.

[61] Author interview with Bellingi.

[62] Author interviews with Guillermo Schweinheim, Director of the Center of Studies of the Association of Personnel of the Audit Institutions, August 22, 2012; Hugo Dalbosco, Administrador Gubernamental, Ministry of Economy, Civil Service Secretariat, November 6, 2012.

Relying on temporary consultants may have resolved short-term capacity issues but has had deleterious long-term costs for the public administration. When interns and consultants leave, their knowledge goes with them, inhibiting the accumulation of expertise and frustrating gradual attempts to increase transparency, reduce corruption, and strengthen institutions. This individual-level serial replacement has meant that the private companies that serve as the counterparts to short-term employees are able to take advantage of an asymmetry of information and expertise. Employees of large construction companies readily admit that, as they work with new government officials with each shift in power, they can count on their public sector counterparts not to understand the contractual details and technical requirements, giving the private sector the upper hand.[63] The learning process starts from scratch with each administration or turnover of personnel, eroding institutional capacity over time.

CONCLUSION

The same factors facilitating rapid transformations of the public sector threatened the effectiveness and durability of powering reforms in the long run. Faced with crisis situations in the early 1990s, President Menem and his political technocrats initiated wholesale changes to wipe out corruption and improve basic service delivery before opposition could slow reforms. The moment of crisis opened a window of opportunity but also meant reforms were designed at the height of economic uncertainty. The speed of the changes prevented organized opposition but left little time for careful calculations. The depth of the reforms allowed Menem's team to undercut the status quo but reduced opportunities for testing approaches or sequencing changes. Tight-knit teams of outside experts enhanced the government's ability to move quickly and institute ideal-typical models of change but meant that reform designers were unfamiliar with the particularities of the Argentine public sector. Finally, the concentration of authority in Menem's technocrats allowed for decisive decision-making and rapid implementation of deep cuts to the public sector but left few permanent technocrats left in the public sector to consolidate the dramatic reforms.

---

[63] Author interview with government contractors, November 15, 2012, and December 5, 2012; author interview with Claudia Maskin (Regional Compliance Officer, Siemens), November 22, 2012.

As a result, the success of the reforms was inversely related to the scope and speed of the changes. Highway privatization, which occurred at the height of the economic crisis, was an almost immediate disaster. Econometric models used to forecast profits were based on foreign models and relied on assumptions about private companies as well as the economic situation that many later admitted were wild guesses. While freight concessions, which were implemented a few years after the economic crisis, did not create the same immediate crisis that afflicted highway concessions, the speed and scope of the changes still meant that they failed to account for changing conditions and unforeseen circumstances. Thus, by the end of the 1990s, the powering reform to slow the transport sector's drain on the budget and to improve the quality of services had achieved neither of those objectives.

Most problematic, however, was that the very process of powering – destroying the status quo and autocratically imposing changes – weakened transport institutions, leaving very few public servants with the expertise and experience to deal with all of the new challenges. Menem concentrated power in the hands of political technocrats and dramatically reduced the number of public sector employees with experience and expertise in the transport sector. The idea was that transport institutions would be rebuilt, but this takes time and requires individuals to assume authority relinquished by high-level officials. Neither condition was met. Consequently, when President de la Rúa took office, nearly all of the political technocrats responsible for transportation changed. The same occurred once more when the Kirchners came to power.

Menem's reforms continued to deteriorate during subsequent administrations, underscoring the deleterious and enduring effects of the powering approach. The Kirchners inherited institutions lacking the capacity to identify and resolve problems in the policy process. Moreover, they had few incentives to strengthen Menem's reforms, which had unleashed a public backlash against privatization. In this context, problems were overlooked, meaning reforms never consolidated the way that theories of historical institutionalism would predict. Instead, the 1990s policies that weakened the public sector shaped the civil service for years to come, and thus the subsequent reformers.[64] Without adequate attention, problems in transportation continued to fester until they reached crisis levels again.

---

[64] Some scholars have highlighted that previous policies shape subsequent reform efforts by empowering some organizations while weakening others (Pribble 2013). This is true not only of interest groups but also of the civil service.

The devastating railway collision at *Once* finally prompted President Fernández de Kirchner to act. Yet instead of taking more modest measures to address the problem, Kirchner embarked upon a fresh set of radical reforms that reversed those of the 1990s.

Thus, powering begets powering, with presidents of completely different ideological orientations using the same reform approach. Such an approach, while alluring in the short run for its air of resolute decisiveness, exacerbates the situation, creating new unintended consequences and weakening state institutions. Bulldozing existing institutions to wipe out corruption hindered the consolidation of reforms and has had pernicious effects on bureaucratic stability over the long run. As time revealed, corruption and inefficiency proliferated in the new institutions, which perversely led to new attempts at wholesale reform.

5

Transportation in Brazil: Powering Curtailed, Problem Solving Inches Forward

Although Brazil's return to democracy was initially marked by ambitious attempts to overhaul the state, the country's political trajectory soon took a different turn. At first, presidents in both Argentina and Brazil sought to push through sweeping neoliberal reforms that would shift responsibility for highways and railways from the state to the private sector. The powering attempt by Brazilian President Collor, like that of President Menem in Argentina, swiftly reduced the size of the public sector in transport. Yet Brazil's powering efforts were dramatically halted with Collor's impeachment in 1992.[1] Most radical transformations of the state were halted; reforms that advanced did so much more slowly than in Argentina and were later subject to change, sequenced incrementally over time.

Although the abrupt shift in 1992 made Brazil appear at first a sluggish reformer, especially when compared to repeated powering reforms in Argentina, the more gradual, problem-solving approach has slowly strengthened Brazil's institutions. Both countries were subject to profound transformation in the early 1990s, but Brazil has slowly rebuilt its capabilities in transportation: assessments of its transport infrastructure have improved in many areas. By contrast, Argentina has been plagued by metro car collisions and increasingly dangerous highway conditions.

---

[1] While this cannot be considered a true natural experiment, it is close. "As-if" random assignment (Dunning 2012) is a very high bar for comparing powering to problem solving. After all, powering is so sweeping in nature and occurrences so rare that identifying instances of as-if random assignment are quite unlikely. Thus, my assessment exploits this natural variation but also recognizes the limits of such comparisons and emphasizes that important confounds – namely political-organizational background factors – do indeed come into play here.

What explains Brazil's progress in so many areas and persistent challenges in others? Why has Brazil consistently failed to implement comprehensive reforms in a timely manner, and what then accounts for the eventual advances in state building?

Answers highlight how political-organizational context affects the adoption of the powering approach. While Argentine government executives concentrated power in small, loyal, and coherent teams of technocrats to bring about rapid and sweeping changes, Brazil's coalitional presidentialism, by inducing presidents to share executive power, has disrupted most attempts to transform the country's public sector and reshaped the bounds of rationality. Specifically, the prerogative to transform the state does not rest with presidents and their tight-knit reform teams but is instead placed in the hands of a broader group of coalition allies. Reforms are subject to the scrutiny of a diverse set of interests and experts, slowing the process considerably while promoting negotiation, compromise, and revision. As a result, radical and comprehensive reforms have rarely been executed as a coherent whole; instead, they are often implemented piece by piece, which has allowed for a learning process to develop.

The presence of coalitional allies has also resulted in presidents relying on existing experts within the federal administration. Brazilian presidents may wish to appoint handpicked technocrats or party members who share their policy views to the executive, but, in order to build broad-based coalitions, they share control over appointments with allies. To achieve their policy goals in this context, they often delegate greater responsibility to less partisan actors – politically neutral civil servants and state technocrats. With institutional positions and extensive experience, these officials have had much better information and greater capacity for its processing than high-level political leaders, who, as in Argentina, were forced to rely on cognitive shortcuts and outsider expertise to craft and implement complex reforms. Therefore, in the Brazilian context, although individual rationality was still subject to limits, individual judgments were much closer to the mark. Accordingly, reforms in Brazil since the 1990s have been less radical, more gradual, and comparatively successful.

In other areas of government, the same dynamic plays out, as presidents constrained by coalitional demands cede greater authority to experts within the state and limit the scope of their original reforms. Indeed, although this chapter focuses on Brazilian transportation, institutions of accountability play a crucial role throughout this chapter. Such institutions, along with the bureaucracy and courts, made significant gains over the course of the past generation – between the transition to democracy and today (Bill Chavez 2004; Power and Taylor 2011; Melo and Pereira 2013; Praça and Taylor 2014). Executive constraints in Brazil have weakened governments but strengthened the state over time. Here, reform approach serves as the mechanism through which executive constraints strengthen the capacity and autonomy of the state. At the same time, the a priori level of state capacity can also condition the choice of reform approach. In this sense, structure and choice are linked as part of an endogenous explanation for the strengthening of state institutions over time.

The role of political-organizational context in shaping reform choice helps explain how President Fernando Collor's (1990–2) powering attempt resulted in his impeachment and what lesson subsequent presidents learned about the perils of powering and importance of coalitions. Subsequently, transportation overhauls during the presidency of Fernando Henrique Cardoso (1995–2002) were subjected to compromise, revision, and negotiation with coalitional allies; the details of such plans were delegated to experts within the state, resulting in slow, limited changes that were ultimately more effective than those pushed through in Argentina. During the presidencies of Luiz Inacio Lula da Silva (2003–10) and Dilma Rousseff (2011–16), in the absence of dramatic overhauls the transport sector has undergone a marked problem-solving transformation, illustrating how experts within the state have played a crucial role in advancing individually small but cumulatively substantial changes. At the same time, the deleterious and enduring effects of previous powering reforms endure. Restoring capacity in agencies overhauled by Collor has been a slow and arduous process.

THE NATURE AND CHARACTERISTICS OF TRANSPORTATION REFORM

Although Brazil and Argentina had once led Latin America in the development of infrastructure, by the early 1990s both countries faced similar challenges. Between 1945 and 1980, the highway network in Brazil had expanded rapidly under the direction of the highly capable and fiscally autonomous Transport Planning Agency (*Grupo Executivo de Integração da Política de Transporte*, GEIPOT).[2] Although Brazil placed greater emphasis on the

---

[2] GEIPOT maintained high levels of autonomy during this time and employed impressive engineering and planning teams. During this period, the National Department of Roads

highway network than on railways, which were far more developed in Argentina (Summerhill 1998; De Castro 1999, 4), by the 1980s Argentina and Brazil had developed some of the most expansive transport infrastructure networks in the region (Barat 2007). During the "lost decade" of the 1980s, however, sluggish growth in Latin America resulted in fiscal crises, and public spending on infrastructure plummeted to less than 1 percent of GDP, resulting in the rapid deterioration of roads, bridges, and railways.[3]

In response to such challenges, and facing an escalating economic crisis and international pressure to implement neoliberal reforms, President Collor initiated a sweeping neoliberal overhaul of the transport sector aimed at shifting the responsibility for transport from large public agencies to private companies via concessional agreements. Like Menem in Argentina, Collor precipitously reduced the number of public employees and was thus successful in the first phase of reform: pushing changes past resistance. Collor's ambitious powering attempt resulted in the near-complete destruction of transportation agencies. Yet his efforts were halted just before infrastructure was privatized. Whereas Argentina's reforms later failed, owing to patterns of powering that continually weakened state institutions, changes in Brazil under Collor were never fully implemented. He eliminated most of the institutions that supported the existing model of transport infrastructure provision but never switched the model itself. Thus, the institutions, though stripped of expertise, retained responsibility for roads, bridges, and railways.[4] Collor dramatically weakened transport institutions and the sector without a cohesive approach, seeming to precipitate disaster.

Yet over the next twenty years, Brazil made slow but considerable progress in advancing transport infrastructure capacity. Table 3 presents the various types of infrastructure provision and the degree to which they emphasize public/private provision. Whereas the reform pendulum in Argentina swung from privatization to re-nationalization, a variety of different transport models in Brazil have been strengthened over time. President Cardoso continued traditional, state-led infrastructure projects while enhancing the institutional framework for privatization, which advanced at a slow but steady pace. President Lula, a self-declared socialist who might have been expected to

---

and Highways (*Departamento Nacional de Estradas de Rodagem*, DNER) was granted administrative and fiscal autonomy with the creation of the National Road Fund (*Fundo Rodoviário Nacional*, FRN) (World Bank 2003).

[3] Public investments in transport reached 3.3 percent of GNP in 1975, only to drop far below 1 percent in the 1980s (World Bank 1996b, 7).

[4] It also included responsibility for ports and airports, but, for the purposes of the comparison with Argentina, I compare only roads and railways transportation infrastructure.

TABLE 3   *Types of Infrastructure Contracts, Private/Public*

Private   Public

←——————————————————————————————————————→

	Privatization/ Concessions	Public–Private Partnerships (PPPs)	Procurement	State-Led/ Direct Execution
Funding	Private sector funding in exchange for right to charge tolls	Mixture of government and private funds	Government funds	Government funds
Execution	Private sector	Private sector	Private sector contracted to execute projects	Government employees
Example	Concession Law of 1995	PPP Law of 2004	Law 8666 of 1993, Pregão, RDC	Army Corps of Engineers

reverse privatization, instead took an eclectic approach, slightly increasing the level of privatized infrastructure, continuing the procurement model, expanding state-led provision of infrastructure through the use of the Army Corps of Engineers, and introducing a new model of transport infrastructure service provision: public–private partnerships, which mixed the private and state-led approaches. President Rousseff continued Lula's polices but expanded privatizations, accelerated the use of public–private partnerships, and sought to substantially increase the capacity of transport agencies. In sum, despite their different ideological backgrounds, these presidents created and strengthened a variety of options and institutions for enhancing infrastructure in Brazil.

The slow but steady advances over the last twenty-five years appear in various indicators. In 2001, over 80 percent of Brazil's transport network was in bad or terrible condition, and only 20 percent was deemed in good condition; by 2011, this latter figure had jumped to over 60 percent (CNT 2014). These advances reflect gradual, problem-solving reforms that slowly improved Brazil's ability to develop transport infrastructure by strengthening existing capabilities. This homegrown and heterogeneous approach enhanced the capacity of transport agencies, expanded the role

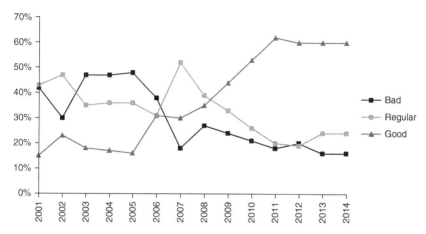

FIGURE 2 Quality of Paved Federal Roads in Brazil
Source: Confederação Nacional do Transporte (CNT) 2014

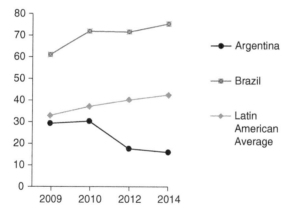

FIGURE 3 Institutional Framework for Private Investment in Infrastructure
Source: EIU (2014)

of the Army Corps of Engineers in infrastructure development, and continued efforts to privatize viable sections of roads and rails and to strengthen the regulatory framework that governed such concessions. Figure 2 shows improvements in the quality of federal roads, and Figure 3 shows the evolution of Brazil's composite scores on *The Economist*'s Infrascope Index, which measures a country's ability to mobilize private investment through concessions and PPPs. By 2014, Brazil ranked second only to Chile in Latin America in terms of its regulatory and institutional framework, project experience and success, investment climate, and financial facilities (*Economist* 2014). After delays and, by many accounts, underutilization of private investment, concessions and PPPs slowly but surely accounted for more of the transport sector (Martin, Sirtaine, and Briceno-Garmendia 2014). Today, Brazil's privatized road network is second only to China's (World Bank 2013, 25). This is especially significant given that leftist presidents governed from 2002 to 2016.

Despite advances, many analysts would argue that Brazil's progress in transport infrastructure has been disappointing (Armijo and Rhodes 2017), especially compared to the rapid improvements made from 1950 to 1980. Indeed, transport infrastructure remains a serious bottleneck for development in Brazil[5] and remains vulnerable to cartel behavior.[6] Yet the legacy of underinvestment and the near-destruction of transport agencies takes time to undo.

The comparison with Argentina sets the advances of Brazil at the federal level into starker relief.[7] While Brazil has made incremental improvements in many areas, Argentina's transport infrastructure is rated at a lower level than in the early 1990s when the powering approach was applied.[8] Thereafter, Brazilian executives (having learned from Collor's failure) moderated extreme policy changes, which they saw as courting backlash from political allies. Changes were advanced piece by

---

[5] *The Economist*, September 28, 2013.

[6] Author interview with Rodolpho Tourinho Neto (Senator and Minister of Mines and Energy, 1999–2001; President, Sindicato Nacional da Indústria da Construção Pesada), April 18, 2012; author interview with Beatriz Nunes (Confederação Nacional da Indústria), December 12, 2011; author interview with Claudio Weber Abramo (Consultant, Sindicato da Indústria da Construção Civil do Estado de São Paulo, 1990–5; Founder and Executive Director, Transparência Brasil, 2000–15), March 12, 2012; author interview with Carlos Alvares da Silva Campos Neto (Coordenador de Infraestrutura Econômica, IPEA), April 24, 2012.

[7] It is also important to note that this analysis focuses on the development of federal-level transport infrastructure. Many additional challenges remain at the state and municipal level.

[8] In a comparison of Latin American countries, Cerra et. al (2016) show that Brazil has improved the quality of its roads from 2006 to 2015, whereas the quality of Argentina's roads has declined (8–9). The most significant changes in both countries occurred in the railway sector. Brazil has not made substantial comparative gains in railway quality, but it has still outperformed Argentina (ibid.). Thus, the differences between countries and between sectors both support my argument.

piece as opportunities arose. Sequences of policy changes advanced slowly, and so proved more durable than comprehensive reforms.

Expectations of power sharing among the Brazilian political elite made a crucial difference by shifting the locus of decision-making. Instead of a small group of homogenous loyalists implementing changes, high-level reform decisions were vetted by diverse organizations of political allies. Moreover, the details of change were delegated to state organizations that retained neutral experts.[9] As a result, responses to policy problems became less dramatic and more restricted, less expeditious and more methodical, less decisive and more sustainable.

POLITICAL LEARNING FROM COLLOR'S HALTED POWERING

When President Collor was inaugurated, Brazil faced a situation similar to Argentina's: The state could no longer afford substantial public investment in infrastructure – nor the salaries of all employees in the transport sector. At the same time, the neglect of rails and roads since the 1980s meant that transport infrastructure needed repair.

The predominant neoliberal thinking at the time provided a seemingly clear solution to the complex problem of ensuring both economic stability and providing sound infrastructure: Eliminate large agencies responsible for infrastructure by privatizing roads, rails, and ports (World Bank 1996b). Such an approach promised to reduce state expenditures and provide sorely needed infrastructure investment, unburdening the state by drawing upon private investment. Once this solution was identified, achieving such change became primarily a question of political will to break down resistance.

President Collor seemed a promising reformer. Like his counterpart in Argentina, Collor was a political outsider, unencumbered by the need to pay off political cronies. He appealed to popular frustration with the political class and promised a "housecleaning." Once in office, Collor used executive decrees to rapidly overhaul the state apparatus, shifting control to a small team of loyalists led by his campaign treasurer, Paulo César Farias (Loureiro and Abrúcio 1999;

---

[9] It is important to note, however, that many transport agencies had been stripped of internal expertise by Collor's overhaul. Thus, advances were very slow until some of the capabilities of transport institutions were recreated.

Gomide 2011, 87). Just as Collor had promised in his campaign, he refused to comply with the bureaucratic nominations of other political parties (Weyland 1997, 76). Thus, he seized control over the state apparatus and embarked on a drastic adjustment plan – a fundamental restructuring of the state that entailed implementing austerity packages, reorganizing the state to cut payroll, and privatizing public enterprises and services (PR 1990, 20).

Some of the most dramatic changes in transportation occurred within the once-autonomous National Department of Roads and Highways (*Departamento Nacional de Estradas de Rodagem*, DNER) that had transformed Brazil in the 1960s and 1970s (Barat 2007). The Collor administration reasoned that if the majority of the highway network were either auctioned off in concessions or transferred to states and municipalities, then a large federal agency would no longer be necessary (Ribeiro 1990). As a result, DNER was dismantled: The number of employees was slashed from 19,000 to 8,000 by 1991, a 58 percent reduction in one year; within ninety days, its functions were transferred from Rio de Janeiro to Brasília; the planning unit within the agency was eliminated; and over 86 percent of planning staff was cut (MT 1994). As Cavalcanti (1995) highlights, the effects on the institution were profound. "Retirement and dismissal of personnel resulted in intense consequences for the technical-organizational world within DNER," Cavalcanti writes, "because it resulted in a great loss of the accumulated institutional memory, experience, and technical competence that left with the individuals that left the agency" (86–7).

The Collor administration successfully pushed sweeping overhauls past opposition, but the reforms that were to follow – concession auctions and transferring the highway network to the states – were soon halted as Collor's powering approach encountered serious political challenges. At first, Congress supported Collor's draconian initiatives, but because Collor failed to craft a coalitional government (in which executive power is shared among allies in rough proportion to their seats in Congress) his unilateral imposition of drastic reforms soon generated widespread disgust among the political class. Instead of seeking to negotiate and compromise on adjustments to his reform program, Collor stood intransigent (Weyland 1997). When evidence of corruption emerged, political leaders were only too willing to capitalize on the scandal. Farias, Collor's former campaign manager and political operative, was found to have solicited millions of dollars in bribes in return for government contracts. A transport program for repairing highways was revealed to have used non-competitive bidding procedures and required companies to make kickbacks for contracts.[10] One scandal led to another, resulting in massive protests against Collor and his impeachment in 1992.[11]

Whereas Menem's powering failed because performance problems and political backlash arose after the reforms were complete, Collor's attempt was halted by the Brazilian political class before it was ever finished. Like Collor, Menem had also been implicated in shady dealings and corruption (Verbitsky 1993), but this was not enough to bring him down. This difference highlights how political-organizational context shapes the extent to which the powering approach can succeed. Whereas Argentine executives are able to concentrate power by filling positions in the executive with loyalists, facilitating dramatic reforms, Brazilian executives are expected to share executive authority with political allies, making the powering approach far more difficult.

Collor's demise also provided a powerful example to subsequent presidents. Evidence suggests that each president had a strong powering impulse – a desire to push through sweeping changes to bring the institutional framework in line with his policy preferences.[12] When successive presidents ran up against resistance, however, each of them could have attempted to impose reform as Collor had in Brazil and Menem and the Kirchners had in Argentina. Collor's failure inspired political learning: When subsequent presidents ran up against resistance, they moderated their reforms and relied on an inclusionary approach to achieve their objectives.[13] Thus, political-organizational context has important implications for reform approaches.

---

[10] *Veja*, June 1992.

[11] The ensuing breakdown in political order, in conjunction with another major contract corruption scandal in Congress, opened up space for another powering attempt. This culminated in the enactment of sweeping new procurement legislation that would plague the public sector for years to come, Law 8666 of 1993.

[12] See previous section, "The Nature and Characteristics of Transportation Reform."

[13] Rousseff is a partial exception here. While she did not attempt a powering reform, interviews with anonymous sources close to the president in 2012 suggested that she often eschewed negotiation and an inclusionary approach. Interviewees also suggested that she used her technocratic prowess to keep a tight rein on coalitional allies in the executive, which may have ultimately contributed to her impeachment.

REDUCING REFORM PACE, DEPTH: WIDENING BOUNDS
OF RATIONALITY

Cardoso's Inclusion of Coalitional Allies Slows and Dilutes State Reform and Privatization

President Cardoso assumed the presidency in 1995, riding a wave of support generated from his success in stabilizing the economy as interim President Franco's finance minister. His ability to use his political capital to push through sweeping reforms was attenuated, however, by his broad-based governing coalition. By this time, Menem had already successfully privatized many sectors and advanced administrative reform in Argentina. In contrast, World Bank experts saw Brazil as a reform laggard.[14] Chronic underinvestment in transport meant that infrastructure was in dire need of funds, but previous fiscal crises put the state in no position to finance such expenditures. Moreover, in the political vacuum created by Collor's 1992 impeachment, politicians pushed through Law 8666, which established demanding procedures meant to reduce the discretion of contracting officials and make bidding and award procedures impervious to corruption. This sweeping new procurement legislation resulted in endless delays and cost overruns, frustrating government attempts to improve and expand transport infrastructure.[15] To address these problems, Cardoso's minister of state reform, Luiz Carlos Bresser-Pereira, called for a sweeping overhaul of the public sector to reform procurement and creating a smaller state with a stronger civil service. Cardoso began his term intent on privatizing infrastructure while relying on Bresser-Pereira to overhaul civil service and procurement policies. Yet unlike Collor and Menem, who concentrated control of reform design and implementation in insular teams of loyalists, Cardoso appointed a wide array of political actors. This power sharing substantially reduced Cardoso's ability to impose his preferred reforms unilaterally.

Indeed, attempts to power through state reforms were quickly halted or diminished. Cardoso initially supported Bresser-Pereira's bold state reform plan. When resistance to the changes mounted from other ministers in the diverse cabinet, however, Cardoso was willing to support Bresser-Pereira only insofar as his coalition would

---

[14] Interview with former World Bank official, March 15, 2012.
[15] As subsequent sections will show, the new procurement rules tilted the legal framework in favor of construction companies, and other unintended consequences of the law entrenched a new set of corrupt practices.

back the reforms, emphasizing that it was up to him "to convince the executive branch that it is a good proposal" (Gaetani 2003, 233). The ensuing negotiation and transaction shifted the center of decision-making from a cohesive team to a broader set of diverse actors within the executive. As a result, Bresser-Pereira's powering attempt ended up looking less like the wholesale reconfiguration of the public sector and more like a partial reform. A replacement to Law 8666 was diluted then halted by Congress (Fernandes 2010, 165), and although Bresser-Pereira passed a constitutional amendment that made civil servant dismissal more flexible (Constitutional Amendment 19 of 1998), most of the amendment was never regulated. According to many experts, little changed (Rezende 2008).

Cardoso's efforts to revitalize the transport sector with private funding advanced slowly and unevenly,[16] following a problem-solving rather than a powering strategy. External conditions favored this approach: The hyperinflationary crisis had abated by the time Brazil resumed concessions, reducing uncertainty in planning long-term concessions. The absence of an "exceptional" crisis meant less latitude for forcing radical change. If Cardoso were to impose dramatic reforms, it would require extensive use of his political capital to press changes past resistance. And he had learned from past experience: His problem-solving approach rested on building broad consensus and advancing changes that built on his predecessor Collor's reform blueprints and the cautionary tale of previous privatization attempts (Cardoso 1994). His strategy included passing a Concession Law developed by leading jurists during the Collor and Franco presidencies.[17] Plans were subject to a broad array of conflicting political and ideological views from the start; members of the council responsible for privatization of transportation included coalitional allies in addition to key ministers from the president's party, the PSDB. To achieve consensus in this contentious environment, privatization plans were significantly moderated, and the most significant changes targeted areas of consensus, namely railways (World Bank 1996b).[18] Yet the challenges in taking even this modest step toward privatization remained formidable.

---

[16] For an analysis of the broader set of privatization reforms, see Manzetti (1999).

[17] Author interview with Vera Monteiro (Sundfeld Advogados), November 27, 2011. The Concession Law was Law 8987 of 1995.

[18] In contrast to Argentina's vast rail network, railways in Brazil were much less important than the highway system, and they were not tied to the national identity in the same way as those in Argentina.

Embedded Experts within Dense Organizations: Carefully Crafted Reforms

Non-partisan experts within the federal administration were charged with designing and implementing the concession program so as to insulate many of the technical decisions from political influence. A privatization council took responsibility for setting policy guidelines, but the powerful Development Bank (BNDES) was to manage much of the reform process (World Bank 1996b; Manzetti 1999, 187). Cardoso may have preferred technocrats of confidence from his own party to steer the reform process, but conferring authority to experts within the state allowed him to achieve his policy objectives and circumvent incessant coalitional in-fighting while including coalitional allies in the broader process.[19] Imposing executive constraints resulted in strengthening the authority and autonomy of experts within state institutions.

Experts tasked with designing privatizations enjoyed considerable information-processing advantages over political leaders or technocratic outsiders. BNDES technocrats had access to richer and more reliable information on Brazil derived from analyzing reform examples.[20] Highway concession plans drew on earlier experiences with toll roads, for example, and the institutional framework set up under previous presidents.[21] Not only had they learned from Collor's reforms and Franco's efforts at change; they also paid close attention to the privatization efforts in other countries and had been experimenting with and working on privatization plans for decades. Instead of relying on rash inferences, reformers crafted plans that were better grounded and tested than they were in Argentina. Experts often halted counterproductive, off-the-shelf plans that would have disregarded context, moving forward only after reform blueprints addressed challenges particular to Brazil.

Moreover, throughout their careers in BNDES and other government agencies, civil servants had faced debate and scrutiny of their reform ideas. Whereas in Argentina reform efforts were staffed with

---

[19] Author interview with Rodolpho Tourinho Neto (President, Sindicato Nacional da Indústria da Construção Pesada, 2011–15; Senator and Minister of Mines and Energy, 1999–2001), April 18, 2012.

[20] Tourinho, interview. See also Willis (1995).

[21] In the 1970s, DNER had experimented with the use of tolls for five sections of highway, and in the 1980s there were a number of attempts to concession railways. For more on how these efforts built on earlier reforms, see Gomide (2011, 87–91).

individuals who had been selected based on their commitment to privatization, in Brazil civil servants in such key agencies as the Development Bank and the external audit body were primarily chosen based on competitive exams that test technical capabilities instead of their commitment to a particular ideological model (Willis 1995; Pereira 2016). Individuals might have differed in their perspectives and proposals, but esprit de corps was often strong, with individuals united in terms of broad objectives (e.g., improving transport infrastructure or ensuring transparent, accountable procedures). Debate and deliberation abounded under both neoliberal leadership and presidents with a developmental approach. Because recruitment and promotion were based on merit instead of presidential loyalty or academic credentials (Willis 1995), the resulting diversity protected against the groupthink (Page 2008) so common in Menem's tight-knit technocratic teams (Teichman 1997, 48). In this way, these pluralistic and dense organizational structures allowed for scrutiny of a wide range of ideas, broadened the bounds of rationality for reform designers, and provided internal safeguards against hasty inferences.

Thanks to the organizational structure of reform groups, their information advantages, and the smaller-scale plans, Brazilian reform blueprints avoided the mistakes that doomed Argentine planners. Consider that Argentina charged high canons that concessionaires were later unable to pay. In contrast, Brazil's canon rates were much lower and charged up-front (Estashe 2001, 224). Whereas Argentina transferred a substantial amount of debt to concessionaires that they ultimately could not repay, Brazil transferred much less, and its predictions were more realistic and sustainable (De Castro 1999). The Argentine reform plans assumed that strong regulatory institutions would monitor concessionaires and market mechanisms would correct problems in the sector, but Brazilian planners foresaw the challenges of creating a strong regulatory environment so sought to address these challenges by including regulatory clauses in the contracts (Pinheiro 2011, 268) along with preliminary regulatory guidelines established by executive decree.[22] As a result, the reforms that ultimately advanced in Brazil were quite limited in comparison to the changes in Argentina.

---

[22] Regulation of railway transportation was established by Decree 1832 of March 1996, which created the Federal Railway Transport Commission under the Ministry of Transportation (De Castro 1999, 11; Gomide 2011, 85). Subsequent sections address the establishment of the regulatory agencies, which would occur only years later.

The most extensive privatization occurred in Brazil's railway sector: Between 1996 and 1999, seven railway concession auctions granted the operation and maintenance of lines to concessionaires for thirty years.[23] This may seem substantial, but railways constitute a very small portion of transport infrastructure in Brazil. Additionally, while highway privatizations started during this time, with five sections of federal roads offered to concessionaires for twenty to twenty-five years, this accounted for only 2 percent of the federal highway system, a fraction of what Argentina had privatized in a few short years (OECD 2008, 178).

Although many in the Cardoso administration sought to extend the privatization program, powerful political constraints (Cardoso's coalition) would only allow changes to be taken so far. Soon the highway privatization program was halted, mired in endless delays based on objections from the variety of political actors involved in the process.[24] In the end, highway concessions only affected a small portion of the network, and demands by coalitional allies meant that a state-owned agency would continue playing an important role in the development and maintenance of rail lines.[25]

Sustainable Reforms

Despite the small scale of reforms, privatizations that did advance were far more effective than those pushed through in Argentina. Brazil's labor productivity in transportation increased; performance substantially improved; the railway agency's debts were rescheduled or settled through revenues from the sale of concessions as well as non-rail assets; and the cost of freight transport decreased by approximately 31 percent from 1996 to 2000 (World Bank 2003, 3). Argentina faced severe problems in

---

[23] This included not only the six lines of federal state-owned railway company but also São Paulo's state-owned rail company, known as the Malha Paulista, which was transferred to the federal government in 1997 as part of the financial agreement between the federal government and the state of São Paulo (Decreto 2.502/1998). The iron ore company Companhia Vale do Rio Doce owned two additional freight lines, Estrada de Ferro Vitória-Minas and Estrada de Ferro Carajás, which were auctioned off as a part of the Vale privatization process.

[24] Some delays were the result of regulatory negotiations in congress, court cases, audit authority questioning, and opposition from the small and medium-sized construction companies (OECD 2008, 181).

[25] An agency known as Valec continued maintaining the remaining rail lines, and the liquidation process of the state-owned rail company, Rede Ferroviária Federal S.A. (RFFSA), dragged on until 2007 (CGU 2011).

the long run,[26] but the design of Brazil's concession agreements meant that later problems were minor (De Castro 1999).

The wide range of political actors involved in the process, which slowed and diluted reforms, also had a propitious byproduct: Problem-solving reforms allowed decision-makers to work out the existing concessions rather than renegotiate across the sector. Brazil staggered highway concessions, addressing particular problems before moving on to bigger changes. These stop-and-start efforts allowed time to implement changes, assess them, and apply lessons learned to the next set of reforms (De Castro 1999).[27] The first concession contracts lacked crucial details, for example, such as captive shipper stipulations[28] and requirements for providing accounting data, but these were resolved with amendments instead of full-scale renegotiations (World Bank 2003, 3). Technocrats then knew how to prevent similar problems from occurring in subsequent concessions. Thus, the process in Brazil allowed reformers to learn over time.

Smaller-scale changes phased in over time also forged greater political consensus at the outset. In Brazil, privatization was not associated with one administration or one political party. Many of the parties in Franco's – and even Collor's – coalition were also in Cardoso's cabinet, and subsequent presidents would include parties such as the PMDB in their coalitions as well. The inclusion of a broad set of actors slowed reforms while fostering the political support crucial for sustaining change. Moreover, the scrutiny from a diverse set of actors also ensured a higher degree of transparency and subjected the reform plans to a wider range of perspectives. Compared with other Latin American countries, Brazil pursued a remarkably transparent process of privatization (Lora 2007).

In sum, Brazil's privatization process under Cardoso was much more limited than Argentina's under Menem, but it was far more successful and enduring. At the same time, the relative success of problem-solving reform in Brazil raises a number of questions. To what extent was the reform approach itself more successful? Or was Cardoso simply more skilled and less corrupt than rent-seeking Menem? Can Brazil's privatizations be

---

[26] See Chapter 4.

[27] Unexpected economic downturns, in particular the devaluation of the *real*, which accelerated in 1999, had negative repercussions that resulted in serious problems for concessions. Yet these were short-lived, in large part because Brazilian contracts were designed with an eye toward such possibilities (World Bank 2003, 3).

[28] Captive shippers are producers of grain or steel, for example, who are dependent upon a single railroad to move their freight. For more on the challenges of addressing such monopoly conditions see Estache, Goldstein, and Pittman (2001, 230–1).

clearly characterized as problem-solving reforms, or did they contain elements of powering as well? Could Collor's powering efforts have been crucial for breaking resistance to Cardoso's later privatizations? Given the enduring transport challenges in Brazil, was Cardoso's privatization successful? Or, in backing away from resistance and moderating reform plans, was the attempt just less ambitious?

Although Cardoso's skill and commitment to anticorruption were important in many instances, they were not decisive for the success of the reforms. After all, Cardoso did not ultimately play a central role in elaborating the changes. To propel the complicated process past coalitional resistance, his core team left the design to BNDES. Therefore, Cardoso's decision to delegate reform to a team of experts was crucial. But Menem had sought to do the same in Argentina: What was the difference? Consider that Cardoso conferred authority to a team of "neutral" experts embedded within the state to get reforms past coalitional partners, whereas Menem charged experts from outside the state to push changes past resistance. The key factor was not the level of presidential skill but rather the choice to negotiate smaller-scale changes with insiders rather than decree sweeping changes from outside.

Nor were the different outcomes simply the result of Cardoso's commitment to clean government. After all, Cardoso was not above making difficult compromises that sullied his administration with rent seeking and corruption. During Cardoso's tenure, the transport agencies were filled from "top to bottom" with members of the PMDB in exchange for the party's tacit support of other reforms.[29] This was in large part facilitated by the vacuum left in the wake of Collor's powering reform, which made such political dominance of the agency possible. Reform progress was not driven by one leader's commitment to good governance; progress in enhancing transparency, accountability, and strengthening institutions was uneven.

Halting advances also reflect the fact that during Cardoso's tenure a variety of reform techniques were employed, some of which hew closer to problem solving and others closer to powering. For instance, in a knee-jerk reaction to the politicization and corruption scandals within the highway agency during the late 1990s, Congress voted to abolish the agency. The law eliminated both DNER and the planning agency GEIPOT, both previously lauded as "islands of excellence" (Barat

---

[29] *Veja*, December 17, 1997, 42. Indeed, this further weakened the highways agency that had recently been gutted by Collor.

2007). DNER was to be replaced by a new agency responsible for federal infrastructure (waterways, railways, and highways), the National Department of Transport Infrastructure (*Departamento Nacional de Infraestrutura de Transportes*, DNIT). No replacement was developed for the planning agency. Congress further weakened the same agency that Collor had gutted, recreating it under a new name with half the employees (Barat 2007).

Although this action was not the president's, it had many of the hallmarks of the powering approach, and it further derogated an already-weak agency, creating enduring challenges for transport infrastructure. At the same time, however, Congress finally passed legislation that created regulatory agencies for transportation. While some analyses highlight a number of shortcomings in the late passage of regulatory institutions, the buy-in of political actors meant that a stronger consensus had been formed and that such agencies were more resilient to being overturned in the future (ANT, PL-1615 of 1999). Ultimately, not all reforms in transport under Cardoso can be characterized as clear cases of problem solving, but those closest to the powering side of the reform spectrum were some of the least effective and generated the greatest problems for subsequent presidents.

The mixture of powering and problem-solving strategies raises another question: Were Collor's powering efforts crucial for breaking resistance and paving the way for Cardoso's later privatizations? True, demolishing the technical core of DNER reduced some opposition to reforms, but the technical core did not pose the staunchest opposition; rather, the greatest threat came from members of the political elite who benefited from the status quo. Cardoso still faced considerable resistance, which he reduced not by forcing through changes but by sequencing them over time, using transaction and negotiation to appease his opponents. Cardoso could also build on Collor and Franco's plans instead of starting from scratch. By building on the institutions and strategies he inherited from Collor, Cardoso could make progress.

To be sure, the slow introduction of privatization was far from perfect. Yet it showed clear progress in improving transport infrastructure in Brazil, and the comparison with Argentina brings advances in Brazil into sharp relief. By the late 1990s, privatization in Argentina had failed to such an extent that the government was again pouring money into transport. Worse, there was no one left in government with expertise in the transport sector. By contrast, while the changes in Brazil might seem unambitious, they established a model that for the most part was functioning as planned. Problems to be worked out required minor tweaks, not major overhauls. Perhaps most importantly, there remained a cadre of civil servants in some key agencies with the ability to make such changes. Finally, the new model for transport infrastructure did not replace the procurement or state-led models, giving presidents the option to rely on one approach or another, rather than radically eliminating one model and creating a second from scratch. Such flexibility and incrementalism was important in building institutions crucial for transport infrastructure in the years to come.

PROBLEM SOLVING INCHES FORWARD UNDER LULA AND ROUSSEFF

In the past, President Lula, like other leftists in Latin America, criticized privatization, and so might have been expected to overhaul the transportation institutions and policies of his predecessor. Indeed, in his first term, he took steps toward powering: He crafted a narrow coalition and attempted to push through an "emergency" program that sidestepped competitive bidding procedures.[30] But Congress and coalitional allies underrepresented in executive appointments stymied the Lulu administration's use of exceptional measures (Correia 2011).[31] Lula later broadened the coalition, which ameliorated some of the executive-legislative conflicts, and the inclusion of allied parties further reduced the executive's ability to institute sweeping change. Moreover, Lula moderated his leftist politics considerably to win the election (Hunter 2010). He recognized that breaking privatization contracts, which would require the state to finance maintenance and construction of transport infrastructure, would effectively reverse electoral commitments like maintaining the primary surplus. Neither governing alone nor overhauling institutions to reverse privatization was a viable option. Instead, to achieve their goals, the PT governments of Lula and Rousseff were induced to share executive appointments with

[30] With this move, the Lula administration sought to address problems created by the legacy of previous powering reforms, such as delays caused by Law 8666 and weakness of transport agencies to follow the strict procurement procedures. By 2003, as a result of these problems and years of underinvestment, the condition of over 50 percent of roads was considered "terrible" (CNT 2014).

[31] For more on Lula's narrow first cabinet and later efforts to craft a broad coalition, see Hunter (2010, 159–67).

coalitional allies and work within the system to address the problems that made institutions weak in the first place.

Reform choices were influenced by the political-organizational context as well as the policy legacies of their predecessors.[32] Cardoso had left his successor a set of weak institutions, but he had not wiped them out entirely as Menem had in Argentina. Thus, while Lula certainly could have attempted to power through a massive overhaul of infrastructure, it would have taken an extraordinary expenditure of his political capital. Not only were concessions working quite well, but many of the political actors involved in Cardoso's changes also made up Lula's coalition. Consequently, Lula opted for a more modest approach and sought to improve the various transport models he inherited.

The Enduring Effects of Powering

The destruction of transport agencies in favor of regulatory agencies that supervised privatized infrastructure reduced the capacity of the remaining transport institutions. Many of the most capable civil servants, with years of expertise, exited either during the Collor purge of transport agencies or in 2000, when Congress replaced DNER with the weaker DNIT.[33] In sharp contrast to Cardoso, who relied on experts within BNDES to craft complex reform plans, Lula was left with very few transport experts to tackle the planning, contracting, engineering, and auditing required to build and maintain bridges, roads, and railways. While the transport agency had 19,000 public servants in 1990, DNIT was introduced in 2002 with just 1,300 (Correia 2011, 116, 186). The organization was a shadow of its former self, before powering, when the best and brightest were able to crosscheck inferences and craft complex solutions.

Insufficient personnel increased the complexity of tasks and time pressure each employee faced. Rather than having a pipeline of viable infrastructure projects, the DNIT started bidding processes with engineering blueprints of very low quality, many of them dating back to DNER

---

[32] See Pribble (2013) for another analysis that emphasizes the importance of policy legacies in constraining reform options.

[33] Author interview with André Pachioni Baeta (Diretor da Secretaria de Obras, TCU), May 25, 2011.

(Correia 2011, 220).[34] Even the brightest, most capable engineers and lawyers could not effectively manage the mountains of blueprints to be completed and contracts to be monitored. This resulted in cost overruns, contract modifications, and delays; without a clear engineering plan, especially for complex projects, it was impossible to estimate how much a project should cost and how long it should take. The TCU – the audit agency, which had amassed considerable expertise and power to audit infrastructure after a series of public works scandals in the 1990s – soon began to highlight grave irregularities in DNIT contracts.[35] The highway agency was increasingly villainized as corrupt, despite the presence of talented engineers committed to increasing transparency and rooting out corruption. There were notable exceptions to the weak capacity in the transport institutions, such as Secretary Executive of Transportation Paulo Sérgio Passos, an experienced engineer and civil servant who would later prove one of the most capable reformers. But such project managers had to fight fires while begging for backup, as they tried to convince the new Lula administration that the sector's most pressing issue was the lack of qualified personnel. The asymmetry between the number of qualified employees and the work they were expected to complete tightened the bounds of rationality, making it nearly impossible to get all the calculations right to ensure that roads, bridges, and railways were designed carefully, contracted fairly, and monitored appropriately.

Construction companies that were contracted to execute projects designed by DNIT were not subject to the same distortions in judgment. The construction giants – Odebrecht, Camargo Corrêa, and Andrade Gutierrez – deployed legions of engineers and lawyers to handle procurement requirements. In fact, many of DNER's most talented employees had migrated to such private sector companies after the downsizing of the transport agency.[36] This asymmetry in information, resources, and capabilities meant that DNIT was at a

---

34 Instead of using more detailed "executive" projects, DNIT relied on what are known as "basic projects" in Brazil. Such designs often lack essential details necessary for contractors to execute projects successfully and for DNIT employees to hold them accountable.

35 Author interview with Cláudio Cruz (Auditor Analista de Controle Externo, Tribunal de Contas da União, 1995–present), May 8, 2012; author interview with Henrique Ziller (Auditor Federal de Controle Externo, Tribunal de Contas da União, 2001–14; Founder and President, Instituto de Fiscalização e Controle, 2004–present), October 31, 2011. Since 1997, the budget laws have stipulated that the TCU send an annual recommendation to Congress of public works projects that ought to be halted due to grave irregularities. The number of halted projects jumped from thirty-eight in 2004 to fifty-six in 2006 (TCU 2005).

36 Tourinho, interview.

severe disadvantage. Despite the construction giants' positive track record – successfully completing private sector projects and winning contracts in Europe, the United States, and China – their state projects in Brazil have often remained incomplete. This has been in part due to the DNIT's inability to plan, obtain environmental licenses for,[37] contract, and monitor projects, but it has also been partly due to the companies' ability to use legal, informational, and resource advantage to reap government outlays with minimal risk.[38]

The new Lula administration initially failed to pick up on signals of distress in the transport sector; instead, following the reports by leading international institutions, they attributed the problem to years of under-investment in infrastructure. Brazil had indeed fallen behind in maintaining and upgrading infrastructure for years, but far more consequential was the failure of transport agencies to spend effectively.[39] This problem, however, was overlooked by Lula's administration, which had just entered the executive. They focused on increasing funds for transportation by launching an investment program known as the Growth Acceleration Program (*Programa de Aceleração do Crescimento*, PAC), a multi-sector development project focused on medium- to long-term strategic planning and increased infrastructure spending. Over R$28.6 billion was allocated to investments in the highway system alone, which was complemented by private investment (PAC 2009).[40] PAC represented a major initiative, but it was very different from the sweeping powering reforms imposed in

---

[37] Expensive environmental studies are required at various stages of development of large construction projects, often delaying near-completed projects (*Estado de São Paulo*, July 1, 2009).

[38] Graef, interview; author interview with DNIT employee, May 25, 2012. Some of this has been due to politicization of transport agencies, which facilitated the operation of cartels and corruption. Indeed, most interviewees acknowledged off the record that *caixa dois*, off-the-books campaign contributions, and cartels were common practice. Inside experts argue that corruption and cartel activity in the transport sector are capped at specific rates, which construction giants consider a political tax of doing business with the government. What prevents the completion of infrastructure projects is rather the inability of the government to adequately plan and monitor construction contracts.

[39] Author interview with André Pachioni Baeta (Diretor da Secretaria de Obras, TCU), May 25, 2011; author interview with Marcelo Correia (Director of Highways and Railroads, Secretariat of the Growth Acceleration Program, Ministry of Planning, Budget and Management, 2007–15), December 9, 2011; Tourinho, interview.

[40] In responding to concerns about the lack of coordination, PAC addressed some of the challenges of coalitional presidentialism. Building on the PPI model, instead of allowing the PR – the allied party with the most appointments to the Ministry of Transport and DNIT – to use investment funds for pork, the PAC sought to ensure that infrastructure spending was in line with the president's objectives (Correia, interview).

Argentina and those initiated by Collor. Instead of relying on a tight-knit team to overhaul institutions and create a fully public or private infrastructure model, PAC relied on existing agencies, included a wide-ranging group of officials, and built on the experiences and lessons learned from an earlier Pilot Project for Investment (*Projecto Piloto de Investimento,* PPI).[41] Moreover, PAC included provisions for relying on both the public and private sectors to address infrastructure logjams. In this way, PAC worked within inherited policy frameworks and institutions, and thus its approach was more similar to problem solving than powering.

Nonetheless, the massive infusion of funds into infrastructure as part of PAC only widened the gap between the weak transport agencies and their powerful counterparts in the private sector. Although the state poured more money into PAC contracts, it did not enhance the staff responsible for such contracts. Even DNIT's director acknowledged the agency's lack of expertise and experience.[42] In 2010 alone, 79 percent of active PAC contracts were modified, with the additional costs averaging 32 percent of the original contracts (Correia 2011, 220). Overages ballooned, allegations of corruption emerged, and projects were left incomplete.[43]

Re-creating Embedded Expertise

The Lula administration had misidentified the core problem as underinvestment in infrastructure, and only after infrastructure spending had reached near-crisis levels did the administration pinpoint underlying issues. By the end of Lula's first year in office, the TCU had halted over 60 percent of transport disbursements (Correia 2011). This caught the attention of Dilma Rousseff, Lula's chief of staff, who would later go on to become president. She came into contact with Secretary Executive of Transport Passos, an experienced engineer and civil servant, who explained the problems at the heart of the highway agency failures: the lack of capabilities and experience of DNIT staff and the challenges created by Law 8666, which had been put in place to stymie corruption in procurement but had numerous negative consequences.[44] Thus began the painstakingly slow process of re-creating

---

[41] The PPI among other changes permitted the government to reduce the primary surplus by an equivalent amount to an increase in infrastructure expenditure (Azzoni et al. 2009, 260).

[42] *Estado de São Paulo*, July 5, 2009.

[43] *Estado de São Paulo*, July 1, 2009. By 2009, reports showed that most projects in DNIT were stalled or halted in the contracting process.

[44] Author interview with Ministry of Transport official, 2012.

embedded expertise in the transport sector and addressing the problems that prevented the completion of transport infrastructure projects.

In a first step, the Passos team sought to draw on the expertise of the TCU.[45] Spared the cuts in personnel in the 1990s, the audit body had developed extensive expertise and experience in transport infrastructure. After corruption scandals, Congress had increasingly conferred autonomy to the audit body to investigate and halt suspicious projects (Praça and Taylor 2014).[46] Initially, however, the relationship between TCU and the Lula administration was antagonistic, with the TCU halting ever more projects because of irregularities.[47] Indeed, DNIT was viewed as corrupt and incompetent by many, but over time – especially after Passos requested the TCU's help – auditors realized there was no way for DNIT to improve without assistance.[48] This turning point changed the relationship between the two organizations. DNIT began to adopt a new methodology based on TCU recommendations, requiring detailed engineering blueprints before the contracting process, for example, and using standardized bidding documents (Instrução Normativa 04/2007).[49] In these and many other ways, DNIT absorbed the guidance of the audit body, and by 2009 experts began to recognize its increasing professionalism.

Other measures were taken to recreate expertise and monitor the political appointees in the transport ministries and agencies. Passos persuaded the Lula administration to increase the number of engineers inside DNIT, developed blueprints for recreating a transport-planning agency, and talked with the administration about legislation to replace Law 8666. At the same time, the Casa Civil, led by the increasingly powerful chief of staff Rousseff, developed a team that used sophisticated "situation rooms" to monitor spending and identify potential bottlenecks in DNIT (Lameirão 2011).[50] Such oversight sought to check the power of political appointees within the transport agencies; in particular, it reined in the PR, the political party that dominated the agencies' leadership positions.

---

[45] For more on Brazil's web of accountability and the TCU, see Power and Taylor (2011).
[46] Cruz, interview.   [47] *Folha de São Paulo*, October 23, 2010; Graef, interview.
[48] Author interview with André Pachioni Baeta (Diretor da Secretaria de Obras, TCU), May 25, 2011. Passos asked the TCU for assistance in improving the capabilities and training of DNIT staff, explaining that many DNIT employees simply lacked the training and time to use "best practices" and to meet all the requirements of the onerous Law 8666.
[49] *Revista Construção e Mercado*, October 2009.
[50] Author interview with Miriam Barbuda Fernandes Chaves (Diretora de Programa da Secretaria-Executiva, Ministério do Planejamento, Orçamento e Gestão, 2007–present), November 8, 2011.

Transport officials also turned to three options to reduce DNIT's crushing workload and circumvent Law 8666: concessions, public–private partnerships (PPPs), and the Army Corps of Engineers.[51] Brazil's Army Corps had been spared the severe cuts to personnel in the 1990s; it was one of the few areas of the federal government that had retained its engineering capacity to design complex projects despite almost twenty years of underinvestment in infrastructure.[52] Shifting some of DNIT's projects allowed the agency to focus on design while the Army Corps executed the maintenance or construction, providing a way around Law 8666's procurement procedures and DNIT's limited capacity. In the meantime, launching concession and PPP agreements did not require following the procurement procedures of Law 8666, nor did it fall under the jurisdiction of the highway agency. Accordingly, these options shifted the engineering and construction burden away from DNIT to the Army Corps and the private sector.

At the same time, an abrupt shift to any of the alternative models of transport infrastructure provision would have generated serious opposition. After all, Lula had railed against privatizations; dramatically expanding the number of concessions would have been an about-face. Likewise, an abrupt expansion of PPPs, an idea developed under Cardoso and another means to increase the role of the private sector (Sundfeld 2007), would have been challenged by not only Lula's party but also other leftist parties in the coalition that had criticized the privatizations of the 1990s. Finally, relying heavily on the Army Corps of Engineers would have generated resistance from the right-wing opposition parties and coalitional allies, as it signaled the growing role of the state.

Given the potential for resistance, starting small was crucial. With privatization, reformers began concessions slowly and quietly, targeting only a small portion of the highway system. It was not until the end of 2006 that the government released an official invitation to bid.[53] The TCU audits stalled a second wave of concessions; auctions would only resume much later under the next administration (Portugal and Prado 2007). Although Congress passed the Public–Private Partnership Law (PPP,

---

[51] Author interview with former Ministry of Transport official; Tourinho, interview.
[52] *Valor Econômico*, July 12, 2012. Historically, the military has maintained twelve Engineering Battalions in the Department of Engineering and Construction (*Departamento de Engenharia e Construção*, DEC), responsible for executing small infrastructure projects for the army, which before 2005 accounted for approximately 3 percent of federal investments in infrastructure.
[53] *Folha de São Paulo*, November 8, 2006.

No. 11079) in 2004, the new model that seemed to hold so much promise would be implemented only years later, after states had experimented with the new approach.[54] The first transportation projects tackled by the Army Corps of Engineers were minor and in remote locations, often of little commercial interest to the private sector. Expanding the Army Corps's role gained more supporters as the military units completed projects ahead of schedule and at a cost 20 percent less than those contracted out by DNIT.[55] By 2010, the Army had become the largest contractor in the country, with 11,000 soldiers and other employees working on about eighty different projects, and was responsible for 16 percent of DNIT's budget.[56] By moving gradually in all of these directions at once, the Passos team lightened DNIT's burden without attracting attention of political opposition and expanded each of these alternative options over time.

Policy Experimentation: Trial and Error

At first failures seemed to outweigh successes. Attempts to reform Law 8666 were consistently blocked,[57] plans to create a planning agency were stalled, and cost overruns and bottlenecks abounded. Faced with such challenges, key policymakers seized the opportunity to adjust and implement an improved approach in the next iteration of reform.

---

[54] Tourinho, interview. PPPs generated criticism from a number of different parties: those who wanted to continue with the concession model, the segments of the private sector that wanted to see a fund that guaranteed payments established before they committed to the new model, and civil servants wary of the new approach (CNI 2005).

[55] *Folha de São Paulo*, November 6, 2005; *O Globo*, July 16, 2006; *Estado de São Paulo*, July 16, 2012.

[56] *Isto É Dinheiro*, August 2, 2010.

[57] One attempt at corrective legislation passed in the House (PL 7709/2007 – Câmara), but it stalled in the Senate (renamed PLC no. 32/2007), largely because of opposition from private construction contractors and political leaders who benefited from exploiting the legislation's loopholes. Interviews suggest that despite *public* support from large *empreiteiras* and many others (CNI 2008), substantial resistance remained (author interview with Beatriz Nunes, Confederação Nacional da Indústria, December 12, 2011). Some in the public administration opposed the bill because a rapid shift away from Law 8666 would reduce the ability of the TCU to carefully audit such funds. Many of the small and medium-sized businesses worried that a change in Law 8666 would push them out of the market entirely and back into subcontracting for the construction giants, the role they had filled prior to 1993. Finally, a shift implied uncertainty for the large *empreiteiras* who had learned how to reap massive profits from the Law (author interviews with private contractors, October 8, 2011). PLC 32 was the most notable attempt to change Law 8666 during Lula's presidency, although there were two other attempts to change Law 8666 (Nunes, interview).

Passos was afforded a number of opportunities at key junctures to test different approaches to reform and sequence changes over time. He served as interim minister of transport three different times when the PR ministers stepped down to campaign;[58] each time he returned to his executive secretary position after the appointment of one of the president's political allies to the position. During his time in office, Passos increased the number of civil servants in the transport sector, created the new position of infrastructure analyst (Correia 2011, 229),[59] and restructured salaries to make the transport sector more competitive. To address the absence of a planning body, the result of the destruction of GEIPOT, Passos and his team initiated discussions with transportation experts and the Army's transport planning body about creating a foundation or public company that would specialize in research and strategic planning to provide a forum for federal, state, and municipal coordination (Correia 2011, 211). In 2007, the body Passos advocated for, the National Logistics and Transport Plan (*Plano Nacional de Logística de Transportes*, PNLT), was created to provide long-term strategic plans (MT 2007).[60] All of these reforms meant that when later opportunities to make change arose, options had been proven, tested, negotiated, and discussed.

TECHNOCRATS AT THE HELM OF TRANSPORT: ADVANCES ACCELERATE

In 2011, Passos had the chance to sequence changes planned for almost a decade in a more sustained fashion. After the election of President Dilma Rousseff, a major scandal erupted that laid bare the political problems in DNIT.[61] The minister of transport, who was at the center of the scandal, was forced to step down, and Rousseff sacked twenty-seven of her party's top-level managers in the Ministry of Transport and associated

---

[58] April 2006–March 2007; April 2010–December 2010; July 2011–April 2013.

[59] Law Number 11.539 of November 8, 2007.

[60] While this was an achievement, the planning body developed in increments. In no way did it immediately fill the void left by GEIPOT.

[61] In 2011, scandal enveloped the sector as media reports revealed corruption and mismanagement of transportation contracts by PR appointees. Reports revealed that a PR operative (Valdemar Costa Neto) in conjunction with the National Highway Construction Association ran an intricate scheme to divide highway construction contracts among contractors, who would pay a 5 percent fee to the PR operative to "win" contracts (*Veja*, July 2, 2011). The allegations of illicit enrichment spiraled after the *Veja* report, confirming reports that PR's main campaign contributors all had construction contracts with the transport sector (*O Globo*, July 6, 2011; July 11, 2011).

agencies.[62] Passos was appointed as minister of transport and recommended the selection of long-time technocrats from within the state to the other top positions in transportation. For instance, the general responsible for the Army Corps of Engineers was appointed to DNIT, with a transportation auditor from the CGU as his second in command. With embedded experts at the helm of transport, the changes that had only inched forward as funds had poured in to improve infrastructure now gained momentum under PAC II, which continued and expanded on the changes under Lula. The transportation budget more than doubled, with projected investments totaling over US$100 billion (Biedermann and Galal 2013, 3).

Reform attempts during this time built on learning about what was politically feasible. For instance, after the failure to overturn Law 8666 in 2007 and subsequent attempts at change,[63] the reformers took a new, unorthodox approach. In 2011, Rousseff issued an executive decree to establish a Secretariat of Civil Aviation. This decree had nothing to do with contracting, but, when the measure was about to be approved by Congress, a deputy linked to the reforms proposed an amendment that would provide an alternative to Law 8666, known as the Differential Contracting Regime (*Regime Diferenciado de Contratações Públicas*, RDC). This amendment created the option to apply the auction logic of concessions to public works projects. By 2011, the positive evaluations of concessions and another alternative to Law 8666, known as *pregão*,[64] had attracted interest in other areas of the federal administration. The amendment was limited in a number of important ways. Among other restrictions, it could be applied only to World Cup and Olympics projects and only when "convenient" (Rosilho 2013). In this way, opponents of Law 8666 sought to introduce changes to procurement legislation for public works contracts without attracting the attention – or ire – of political actors on the other side of the issue.[65]

This change showed promise for reducing delays and cost overruns,[66] and it was soon extended. In July 2012, Congress made RDC applicable to

---

[62] *Estado de São Paulo*, September 25, 2011.

[63] For an analysis of all attempts to pass RDC see de Rezende (2011, 7–8).

[64] Pregão, however, was limited only to goods and services; that is, the law specifically forbade the application of the alternative procedures to construction contracts or public works projects (see Chapter 7).

[65] *Valor Econômico*, June 27, 2012; November 5, 2012; and November 20, 2012.

[66] The federal government has estimated that RDC reduces by 50 percent the amount of time required for procurement (PAC 2014, 29). For other benefits, see *Folha de São Paulo*, January 29, 2014.

PAC (Law 12688 of July 2012),[67] and in October 2012 RDC was authorized for public school construction. Its expansion has continued, and the approach can now be applied in almost all areas of the federal administration. RDC is not a panacea for all of Brazil's transport infrastructure issues, but the expectation among many is that as the new approach is more widely applied and refined, the repeal of Law 8666 will be a mere formality (Rosilho 2013, 8). Such a possibility was unthinkable in 2000. Yet these problem-solving changes, spearheaded by a reform coalition of civil servants and other public administrators with experience in Law 8666, slowly transformed rigid procedures and eroded resistance to change.

Passos and his team also took advantage of scandals to advance reforms that they had been planning for years. In particular, an internal report exposed the alarming lack of capacity in DNIT (MT 2011). In 1987, DNER was responsible for 51,000 km of roads with 19,000 civil servants; by 2011, although DNIT was managing an annual portfolio of investments to the order of R$15 billion, it had just over 2,600 employees, fewer than the highway department of the State of São Paulo.[68] The problems were particularly acute in some areas; the agency had only nine accountants (the three in Brasília alone were responsible for 597 delayed processes), and although the agency had 800 engineers, they needed 3,000 to design, evaluate, and supervise PAC projects. The report concluded that the biggest problem was not corruption per se but the waste created by the low capacity of the agency (MT 2011; Motta 2010), precisely what reformers had been trying to address for years.

In response, the Rousseff administration authorized a competitive exam for 1,200 DNIT civil servants (Edital ESAF 2012). In the meantime, to increase engineering capacity and experience with contracting, the Army Corps general, now at the head of DNIT, began appointing engineers from the Military Institute of Engineering to build capacity in DNIT's projects unit. In 2012, as minister of transport, Passos mandated that important posts within DNIT be reserved for career civil servants of

---

[67] *Valor Econômico*, April 26, 2012. The government highlighted the fact that the new procedures offered a 15 percent discount in relation to the reference price for six Infraero contracts and reduced contracting time from 250 days to 80 days.

[68] By 2016, one third of employees were scheduled to retire (*Estado de São Paulo*, February 18, 2012). Despite recent competitive exams for positions in DNIT (300 positions were opened in 2009), those who pass the exams are often poached by other federal ministries and agencies that provide higher salaries, less work, and more prestigious roles (e.g., the audit bodies or the Public Prosecutors' Office) or by the private sector (MT 2011, 11).

the agency.[69] His efforts to recreate a planning body similar to GEIPOT, which he began back in 2007, also came to fruition during this time with the creation of the Empresa de Planejamento e Logística in August 2012.

As embedded expertise was recreated in the transport sector, improvements began to accelerate. In 2003, approximately 20 percent of the network was classified in good condition; by 2011, that figure had risen to 60 percent (CNT 2014). Concession and PPP agreements began to offset extensive investments by the public sector (World Bank 2014). By the end of Rousseff's first term, in 2014, Brazil's problem-solving efforts had over time developed one of the strongest institutional frameworks for private investment in infrastructure in Latin America (EIU 2014). By the time Passos stepped down and the leadership of the Ministry of Transport was handed over to Rousseff's political allies, substantial improvements had been made, making it difficult for a political party to dominate the agency as in the late 1990s and early 2000s. Indeed, much remains to be done: The long task of building institutions is far from complete, and problems regarding private investment in infrastructure remain.[70] And scandals have been used to create new opportunities for reform. The Lava Jato investigation starting in 2014, for example, revealed how much remains to be done in terms of reducing corruption in Brazil yet also demonstrates just how far incremental efforts to enhance accountability have come.[71] Problem-solving modifications have charted a path forward.

CONCLUSION

Brazil's 1990s transportation reforms began, like Argentina's, with a powering attempt to privatize roads and rails and eliminate transport's heavy financial burden on the state, but the two countries quickly diverged. Expectations that Brazilian presidents would distribute bureaucratic positions to a broad base of coalitional allies meant that President Collor's attempt to impose reform intransigently met resistance from the Brazilian political class, resulting in his impeachment. President Cardoso learned from Collor's failure – governing alone was not an option – and

---

[69] *Grandes Construções*, May 8, 2012.
[70] Much remains to be done to strengthen regulatory agencies, especially those at the state level (Correa et al. 2006; Amann et al. 2014).
[71] While advances in accountability may mark a sea change, the dramatic events have also introduced increased uncertainty, and may yet usher in the type of dramatic powering overhauls that have been so detrimental to Argentina. These points are addressed further in Chapter 8.

returned to the inclusionary governing pattern. In his first term, President Lula da Silva sought to placate the PT's demand for executive positions by limiting the number of appointments allocated to allied parties; as a result, Congress halted some of his signature policies, including infrastructure projects. Consequently, Lula included a broader coalition in the executive in his second term. In all of these cases, the obstacles to concentrating power in small loyal teams close to the president tended to impede powering attempts.

After Collor's powering failure, political-organizational macro factors contributed to the adoption of a problem-solving approach in Brazil. The broad array of political actors in the policymaking process often stalled rapid attempts at change and reduced the depth as well as scope of proposed changes. This check proved crucial in designing concession contracts, as the delays allowed policymakers to learn from experiences of earlier privatizations. Reforms were also scrutinized by a diverse set of individuals, instead of likeminded reform teams prone to groupthink, enhancing the transparency of the process.

Certain underlying political-organizational macrofactors also strengthened key institutions. Executive constraints placed on Brazilian presidents by coalitional allies contributed to a weak executive but fueled a strong state (Bill Chavez 2004). Because Brazilian executives needed to appoint coalitional allies to key ministries and agencies within the executive to secure the support of Congress, they often conferred greater authority to technical experts. Under Cardoso, BNDES provided an antidote to coalitional allies' attempts to use privatization to their advantage. Lula turned to the Army to enhance capacity and limit rent-seeking in DNIT, while Rousseff turned over the top positions in transportation to a long-time civil servant and an Army general to reduce the agency's politicization and advance her policy objectives.[72] Argentine executives have tended to rely on individuals who are both technical experts and partisan loyalists to the executive, but Brazilian presidents, induced to distribute executive appointments among coalitional allies, have often relied on neutral technical experts.

---

[72] Interviews with high-level officials in the Rousseff administration suggest, however, that while she included a broad coalition, the tight leash she kept on political appointees countered expectations in Brazil and ultimately contributed to her impeachment. Thus, while Cardoso and Lula relied on neutral experts within the state and quiet changes, many of the reforms under Rousseff concentrated authority in the executive to a greater degree than inclusionary expectations of the Brazilian political elite would permit.

Such technical experts and civil servants, with greater expertise and experience, enjoy wider bounds of rationality than their political counterparts. Problem solvers such as Sérgio Passos pursued broad goals of improving transportation in Brazil and strengthening the capacity of transportation institutions step by step, focusing on big principles and moving persistently forward while making adjustments and corrections along the way. Such adjustments concern not only instruments and tactics but also bigger strategies and the very goal itself. The incremental, stop-and-start process in Brazil meant that complex problems were divided into smaller steps. Instead of relying on comprehensive planning to get reforms right in one shot, policymakers experimented with improving various approaches.

When powering did occur, it left negative and enduring repercussions. The destruction of transport agencies under Collor in the 1990s left few individuals with experience in the transport agencies. In the absence of a capable highway agency, one DNIT leader sought to recreate embedded expertise by drawing on other areas of the state that retained engineering and legal expertise, namely the military. That the process of problem-solving has advanced very slowly[73] underscores the importance of a minimal level of bureaucratic capacity and autonomy for smaller-scale improvements to advance.

Indeed, nearly all of the problems in the transport sector in Brazil today are in some way related to the challenges of rebuilding institutions stripped of capacity and autonomy. Weak institutions allow for the concentration of authority in the hands of political appointees and "political dominance" of transport agencies by particular parties (Bersch, Praça, and Taylor 2017b). The lack of capacity within transport agencies and simultaneous politicization made them particularly vulnerable to high-level corruption.

Protests in 2013 and 2014 over the quality of urban transport in Brazil occurred for good reasons. Earlier in the twentieth century, GEIPOT planned and coordinated urban transport development with states and municipalities. In the absence of a planning and coordination agency – or even a forum for discussion – municipalities have been left to hash out the complex engineering designs, jurisdictional questions, and investment issues on their own. Despite efforts to rebuild such institutions, reconstructing institutional memory, experience, expertise, and political autonomy is a long and arduous process.

---

[73] For a more clear-cut case of problem solving, see Chapter 7, on Brazilian health care.

Perhaps powering may fail yet still be more effective? Could powering miss the target but, by crushing resistance, still bring more improvements than less ambitious strategies? In theory, maybe. But theory must be validated by experience, and the examples of health-care reform in Argentina and Brazil provide another telling study in the value of incremental reform over powering strategies.

6

Health in Argentina: Impeded Powering Fosters Problem Solving

The swift and deep-cutting changes effected by Argentina's transportation reforms allowed Menem to undercut opposition, but the insurmountable challenges of rapidly planning such extensive change led to unintended consequences and new performance problems. Moreover, the weak institutions left in the wake of restructuring struggled to make improvements in the sector long after the initial reforms. Service provision deteriorated until it reached crisis levels, prompting a fresh set of powering reforms.

What if reforms had been crafted and implemented under more typical circumstances, not at the height of the hyperinflationary crisis? What effect did the depth and speed of reform have on the outcomes? Would powering have been more successful if reforms had been crafted by Argentine experts with greater experience than IFI teams and political technocrats? To what extent do insights about the reforms in transportation apply to changes in other policy areas, particularly the health sector?

Beginning in the 1990s, Argentine executives attempted to transform the health sector using the same powering approach applied to transportation. Like reforms in transportation, failures in comprehensive planning for the health transformations in the 1990s yielded disappointing outcomes. Reforms in health, especially Néstor Kirchner's powering reform in the Program of Integrated Medical Assistance (*Programa de Atención Médica Integral*, PAMI), which provides health services for pensioners, illustrate another aspect of the problems with powering: the credibility issue.

The credibility issue arises when relevant actors doubt the staying power of change, which diminishes the probability of enduring, consolidated reforms. The powering thesis assumes that comprehensive changes generate benefits such that a new set of beneficiaries will make changes viable in the long term by opposing attempts to weaken, abandon, or reverse reforms. The problem, as the case of PAMI under Néstor Kirchner demonstrates, is that reforms do not automatically inspire beneficiaries to defend changes. In fact, the process of powering undermines their commitment. Once the political will that sustained the changes dries up, defenders of the new program (diffuse benefits) are weaker than the *prior* defenders of the status quo (concentrated benefits). Furthermore, given the dismantling of institutions and disrupting of bureaucracy, few internal defenders of changes remain after technocratic reform teams have moved on. Potential beneficiaries, then, have many reasons to question the endurance of radical change and are less likely to support the changes.

In some areas of health, reforms did not cut as deeply or as far as they did in transport but instead fostered gradual improvements. Yet in others, the legacy of the most ambitious reforms of the 1990s continued to have detrimental effects. PAMI, the area in which the most drastic changes were made, ultimately had the most disappointing outcomes. Thus, reform speed and depth again proves to be negatively correlated with success, whereas delayed and stalled reforms gave rise to gradual, problem-solving efforts in some key areas.

HEALTH REFORM IN THE 1990S

When Argentina first instigated its health reforms, the international development community offered effusive praise. The Inter-American Development Bank (IDB) described Argentina's health sector reform as "the greatest transformation of a health care system in Latin America in the 1990s" (IDB 1998), and the World Bank lauded Argentina's ability to implement all the "key elements of reform ... in a very short period of time" (World Bank 1999, iii). Despite such accolades, however, the following analysis will show that changes fell far short of achieving their goals.

In the mid-1990s, the Menem government turned its attention from macroeconomic stabilization and privatization to increasing competition within Argentina's health-care system.[1] Deepening deficits and a steady stream of corruption scandals fueled the perception that the health sector

---

[1] This was one of a number of "second stage" reforms, which placed greater emphasis on improving social conditions and strengthening institutions (Naím 1994).

was in a state of crisis.[2] Among specialists, the problem was clear: Health insurance funds, known as *obras sociales*, functioned as monopolies.[3] In 1996, there were about 310 *obras sociales*, which covered 18 million individuals, or about 55 percent of the population. *Obras* comprised three different types of funds: national *obras sociales* (9 million members), province-based *obras sociales* (5 million members), and PAMI, a special *obra* serving the elderly and disabled (4 million members) (World Bank 1996c, 13).[4] Trade unions administered most of the national and province-based *obras*, which meant that employees in the formal sector in Argentina had compulsory health insurance with an *obra social* operated by their trade union. For many workers, this created a monopoly situation wherein they had only one choice for health insurance.

Funds differed considerably in terms of size, benefits, and financial stability. The absence of effective state regulation meant that there was no obligation to offer a minimum service package, and the system had become a complex labyrinth of contracting and subcontracting. Yet because the arrangement generated a significant revenue stream for many labor unions, opposition to change was fierce (Murillo 2001; Torres 2004). Specialists argued, however, that the solution for improving care while eliminating deficits required challenging the unions and changing the regulations to increase competition among *obras sociales*[5] as well as private insurance providers.[6]

The mid-1990s seemed a propitious time to attempt such a feat. If nothing were done, the large operating deficits and growing arrears of PAMI and the *obras sociales* would endanger economic stability (World Bank 1996c, 7). Moreover, Menem had proven himself a reform champion to IFIs with his fiscal reforms and complex, politically challenging infrastructure transformation; thus, pushing ahead with the formidable task of overhauling the health sector would seem to make use of Menem's

---

[2] See, for instance, the AGN report on corruption and the fiscal crisis in PAMI (1994). Moreover, two of PAMI's previous directors, Miguel Nazur and Matilde Menéndez, had been charged with corruption.

[3] Author interview with Hernán Charosky (Chief Health Analyst, Anticorruption Office, 2000–5; Executive Director, Poder Ciudadadano, Argentine Chapter of Transparency International, 2010–12), October 3, 2012.

[4] For the long history of *obras sociales*, see Belmartino (2005) and McGuire (2010, 131–43).

[5] PAMI was considered to be one of the *obras sociales*. The idea was to increase competition between all *obras*, including the health insurance fund for pensioners.

[6] Author interview with Dr. Mariana Chudnovsky (Professor, Universidad de San Andrés), October 25, 2012.

and his team's reform acumen. Furthermore, tackling the deteriorating health services, marked by rising mortality levels of hospitalized PAMI pensioners,[7] would address the electorate's concerns about the quality of health care. The crucial question seemed not to be how to design and implement reforms but rather how to overcome the opposition of potent unions and political forces that benefited from the status quo (Acuña and Chudnovsky 2002, 48).[8] The powering approach – using political will to drive through a clear reform project in a moment of crisis – seemed promising.

The task of crafting complex reforms was left to World Bank experts. They brought extensive expertise to bear on developing and supporting the implementation of health reform thanks to their earlier work in the Argentine health sector (World Bank 2002, 3). The Bank also provided financing for the ambitious mission, with loans totaling over US$350 million (World Bank 2002, 4),[9] and a clear, coherent model, which significantly reduced the challenges of designing reforms from scratch.[10] Acting alongside the Menem government, World Bank personnel undertook a sectoral analysis in the second half of the 1990s that established clear milestones for "revolutionary and irreversible changes in the mandatory health insurance system" (World Bank 1999, iii). Together, the milestones focused on increasing competition by allowing beneficiaries of *obras sociales* and PAMI to choose another health insurance provider, either public or private, and transfer their membership and financial contributions.[11]

In order to execute the new measures swiftly, government officials at the highest level – the president, ministers of labor and health, and, perhaps most importantly, the powerful minister of the economy, Domingo Cavallo – adopted a tight alliance with the World Bank, taking a unified position on the reform strategy (World Bank 2002). To bypass potential congressional obstacles that would delay and diminish the plan, the Menem administration approved initiatives as decrees (Montoya and

---

[7] AGN 1999; *Clarín Digital*, November 24, 1996.

[8] Author interview with José Priegue (Coordinator, International Finance Unit, Ministry of Health, 2002–7, 2009–present), November 29, 2012.

[9] On the extensive role of the IFIs in the reform process of the 1990s, see Teichman (2004). A separate loan of US$25 million funded technical experts to assist in the execution of the changes (World Bank 2002, 4).

[10] Reforms were developed using World Bank econometric models and estimations of expected growth. Priegue, interview.

[11] On reform plans, see World Bank (1996c).

Colina 1998).[12] In PAMI, Menem appointed an *interventor-normalizador,* Alejandro Bramer Markovic, to take the reins, carry out changes with the World Bank team, then "normalize" management by handing control back over to an elected board, restoring its autonomy.[13] Working with the minister of health and the heads of other regulatory agencies, Markovic brought in a new cadre of Argentine managers, lawyers, and technical specialists to build the capacity of the health sector (World Bank 2002, 3). Finally, the government subcontracted private firms to address the especially complex tasks of designing a new organizational structure for PAMI and carrying out financial analyses of the *obras sociales.* Together, these efforts concentrated power in a reform team of outsiders.

That the team was not beholden to the status quo was crucial for pushing changes past the unions. By using a policy of "divide and rule" and providing fiscal rewards to *obras* that signed on early and performed well, the health team eroded union opposition (World Bank 2002, 3). Many unions took advantage of the changes as a means of attracting members from rivals, and, because unions were engaged in more than one battle with the administration, reform teams leveraged threats in one area to force concessions in another (Acuña and Tuozzo 2000).[14]

Many aspects of the project initially appeared quite successful. Competition opened up among *obras sociales* and between *obras* and PAMI. By 1999, nearly 300,000 workers had switched funds (World Bank 1999, iii). For the first time, even the poorest funds offered a basic package of services (approximately $40 per member per month).[15] Moreover, many of the *obras* had been restructured to improve financial indicators, increase internal efficiency, and develop adequate systems to comply with new regulations (World Bank 1999, iii). The Solidarity Redistribution Fund (*Fondo Solidario de Redistribución,* FSR) was redesigned so that if an *obra* were unable to meet its commitments, the fund would supply resources. A unified regulatory agency, the Superintendency of Health (*Superintendencia de Servicios de Salud,* SSS), was established.

---

[12] Decrees 292 and 492 of 1995. See also MS 492/95 and MS 247/96.

[13] *La Nación,* August 1, 1996. Markovic seemed an ideal choice; as executive director of the National Social Security Administration, he had uncovered many of the problems in PAMI, and he was hailed for this health credentials and his close personal connection to the president.

[14] Chudnovsky, interview.

[15] In 1994 average revenue per beneficiary varied from US$5 to US$80 (Lloyd-Sherlock 2006, 357).

Furthermore, PAMI officials restructured internal controls and regulation, cut staff, eliminated its debt, and restructured the contracting system (Lloyd-Sherlock 2006, 360). These pioneering advances prompted the IDB to call Argentina's reform the greatest transformation of the health-care system in Latin America in the 1990s (IDB 1998; World Bank 1999, iii). A few years later, however, analysts declared that "overall, the reforms of the 1990s did almost nothing to improve the performance of the SHI [social health insurance] sector; indeed, in many ways they made matters worse" (Lloyd-Sherlock 2006, 359). Why did such promising reforms result in such disappointing outcomes?

Comprehensive Plans Generate New Performance Problems

Developing a coherent and wide-ranging program of change requires extensive computing capacity to evaluate complex problems, seek alternative solutions, and calculate advantages and disadvantages. Yet if any country could surmount these challenges, it should have been Argentina. The World Bank brought some of the top experts on health reform and poured millions into the sectoral analysis and design of the program. As a result, after key changes were implemented, many expected success.

Reform assumptions did not hold, however, and changes had unintended consequences. As a scholar of health reforms explained, "It was assumed that a 'rational and responsible' private insurance sector would seek to compete against the *obras sociales* [and] that new public management would revolutionize hospitals" (Lloyd-Sherlock 2005, 1899). Such expectations were not borne out. Econometric models that justified cutting contributions assumed continued growth, but when those assumptions faltered in 1998 and 1999, the health institutions such as the PAMI went even deeper into debt than before the reforms. With the 2001 economic crash, the situation became increasingly dire.

Despite increasing competition and transparency in some areas, the health overhaul exacerbated, rather than reduced, inequality and segmentation in health care (Pribble 2013, 146–7). The appearance of *gerenciadoras de salud* (health management agencies) was "not imagined at the time of initial design of the legal framework," but such agencies ended up running the plans for *obras* (World Bank 2002, 6), which further tangled the web of contracting and subcontracting.[16] In addition, analysts did not

---

[16] While the crucial role of the World Bank in the planning may have contributed to the adoption of faulty assumptions, the complexity of the changes attempted meant that even

anticipate that some *obras sociales* would go along with the changes yet seize the opportunity to gain members from rivals. By 2002, one of the key achievements in the 1990s reform – the limited allowance for movement between *obras* – became one of its most important problems. A growing number of affiliates, mostly high-income earners, moved to richer *obras* that had contracts with private insurers.[17] In May 2002, there were 21,000 transfers to richer *obras*, forcing thirty-eight of the poorer funds into semi-bankruptcy (Maceira 2009).

Many scholars of the 1990s health reform argue that the overhaul did not go far enough. The real problem, they claim, was the resistance of the labor unions to the changes (Pribble 2013; Niedzwiecki 2014, 41–2). Indeed, union resistance posed serious challenges to implementation of the project plan. But the main features of the intended reform were put in place: Competition was opened up among the *obras sociales* as well as between PAMI and the *obras*. Such changes were expected to propel other necessary steps. Given the faulty assumptions at the core of reform plans, however, it is questionable whether reforms would have had the intended effect even if all changes had been implemented.[18]

The powering approach contributed to flawed fundamental assumptions, but the implementation through powering was also problematic. The *paradox of powering* can be seen especially in terms of personnel. For instance, following the direction of the World Bank proposal, Markovic, the interventor, quickly sought to institute professional management in PAMI. Four days after his appointment, he fired over fifty individuals who sat in many of the most important positions, justifying the measure by declaring that it would allow "qualified personnel," selected in clean, transparent, and public proceedings, to change the profile of PAMI.[19] He offered other employees very attractive voluntary retirement packages, cutting the PAMI workforce by 30 percent.[20] These changes came at a steep cost: The employees who accepted the terms of retirement tended

---

health experts who had spent years in the Ministry of Health did not foresee the appearance of *gerenciadoras*.

[17] Author interview Hernán Charosky, Chief Analyst, Anticorruption Office (2000–5); Executive Director, Poder Ciudadano, Argentine Chapter of Transparency International (2010–12), October 3, 2012.

[18] Author interview with high official in Menem Ministry of Health, October 3, 2012; Charosky, interview. For lasting repercussions, see section *Powering Halted, Gradual Advancements*.

[19] *Clarín*, August 4, 1996.   [20] *La Nación*, March 26, 1997.

to be the most capable employees,[21] so after reform teams and consultants left PAMI, the institute had less capacity than it did at the start.[22]

The effects of the powering paradox were all the more damaging because the radical changes occurred under normal conditions. By the late 1990s, the hyperinflation crisis had long passed, hence blame could not be attributed to circumstances outside of the government's control. Had resistance to the plan been weakened by a serious crisis, perhaps the changes would not have been as deleterious for institutional development. As it was, the appointment of interventores in PAMI, use of decree power, and various ways in which Menem and his administration sought to bend or break institutional constraints – often with the blessing of the World Bank and others in favor of the reform – weakened the executive constraints for the next administration as well.

Health sector reform in the 1990s fell far short of advancing "revolutionary and irreversible changes." Despite the extraordinary time, expertise, and resources poured into comprehensive planning, the core assumptions of the ambitious reform program turned out to be faulty. Meanwhile, modest efforts to improve the situation were overlooked, which meant that many initially minor issues were ignored until they became such acute problems that another radical reform was necessary. The obvious performance problems in the agencies the comprehensive plan had sought to solve (e.g., by 2000, the arrears of PAMI alone ranged from an estimated US$1.8 to US$4 billion[23]) only contributed to the 2001 fiscal catastrophe in Argentina.

THE CREDIBILITY PROBLEM: INITIALLY IMPRESSIVE, YET UNSUSTAINABLE, PAMI REFORMS (2003–2007)

The economic crisis had subsided by the time Néstor Kirchner assumed the presidency in 2003, but corruption and fiscal troubles still plagued PAMI. The institute's previous directors had been charged with numerous counts of malfeasance, yet corruption schemes remained in place: The lion's share of PAMI's budget was going to sixty-three politically connected contracting middlemen, who reaped billions of pesos annually

---

[21] Author interview with Mercedes Iacoviello (Administrador Gubernamental; Public Sector Human Resource Management Consultant, IDB, 2002–present), November 23, 2012.

[22] Author interview with former PAMI official, November 25, 2012; Charosky, interview.

[23] Figures depend on interpretations of contractual obligations at the time (see below).

in PAMI outlays but often failed to provide the elderly with necessary services.[24] By 2000, PAMI's fiscal problems were exacerbated by the extraordinary economic crisis, which resulted in deficits equal to 75 percent of PAMI's previous annual budget.[25] In 2004, after a new spate of corruption scandals and an incriminating report by the National Audit Body (*Auditoría General de la Nación*, AGN), President Kirchner threw his full support behind comprehensive PAMI reform, appointing a new interventor to head PAMI and thereby sidestepping the legal procedures that demanded a board with participation of the affiliate representatives.[26] His choice of interventor indicated his commitment to transforming the agency: Graciela Ocaña, a representative from the Lower House of Congress who was well known for her unrelenting commitment to investigating money laundering and corruption. Kirchner assured her of his full backing in rooting out corruption in PAMI.[27]

Ocaña was an elected official with little experience working in the Argentine federal administration, and most of the tight-knit team she brought in had little to no experience in PAMI or the federal bureaucracies. That is not to say that the team lacked expertise entirely. Anti-Corruption Office and AGN personnel were crucial for developing and implementing the reform strategy,[28] and, in this way, PAMI reform under Néstor Kirchner differed substantially from earlier changes promoted by IFIs. Even so, the reformers were political technocrats in the sense that their appointments were sustained by the political will that supported Ocaña.

Instead of a gradual approach that built on their predecessors' efforts to improve the institute, the new strategy involved a fundamental restructuring of PAMI. Focused on rooting out corruption, Ocaña used her power as interventor to eliminate the intermediary system, taking contracts out of the hands of the powerful sixty-three middlemen and contracting directly with clinics and doctors.[29] She appointed members of her team to key

---

[24] Author interview with Santiago Nardelli (Executive Coordinator, PAMI, 2004–2007), October 17, 2012.
[25] Estimates vary widely (see Lloyd-Sherlock, 2006; *Wall Street Journal*, August 31, 2004).
[26] *La Nación*, June 22, 2003.
[27] Author interview with Graciela Ocaña (Director, PAMI, 2004–7), October 26, 2012.
[28] Author interview with Leandro Despouy (President, Auditoría General de la Nación, 2002–present), November 19, 2012; author interview with Nicolás Raigorodsky (Director of Transparency Policies, Anti-Corruption Office, 2002–7), November 13, 2012.
[29] Ocaña, interview.

positions with central control over personnel, contracting, and finances.[30] Within the first months, her team began rapidly implementing the changes – rewriting contracting laws and rationalizing and retraining personnel. Plans were implemented on a number of fronts rapidly and simultaneously, with team members often working around the clock.

Resistance came from all sides: the unions, the Ministry of Health, pharmaceutical companies, PAMI employees, and especially the insidious "Mafia of Medicines" (Charosky 2009).[31] Implementing the new contracting system involved the Herculean task of pushing reforms past the opposition of powerful and politically connected contracting intermediaries, who had benefited from skimming money off contracts. Ocaña and her team received ominous threats and grew exhausted racing against the clock to make changes. President Kirchner's support of Ocaña held firm. Moreover, because Ocaña had concentrated control over the institute in her handpicked team, there was little that the opposition within PAMI could do to halt the new policies.

Within three short years, the Ocaña team radically reconfigured PAMI. They completely restructured the provision of PAMI services; created an auditing body that specialized in PAMI contracting and appointed a respected federal prosecutor, Carlos Stornelli, to lead it; published contracting information online; reduced personnel by 10 percent;[32] set up training systems; and reduced deficits.[33] PAMI was no longer in the headlines for corruption scandals; instead, Ocaña was lauded for taking control and pushing through much-needed reform. Yet the glowing evaluations and effects of these bold reforms would be short-lived.

EPISODIC POLITICAL WILL, SHORT-LIVED PAMI REFORMS (2007–2014)

When Cristina Fernández de Kirchner was elected president in 2007, she might have been expected to continue the policies of her husband. This was not the case. After a row with the agricultural sector, Fernández's approval ratings plummeted, and she began to shift power to a new group within the Peronist party: La Cámpora, a student movement led by her

---

[30] Nardelli, interview.   [31] Ocaña, interview.
[32] Nardelli, interview. Reductions were result of retirements and dismissals for just cause.
[33] Author interview with Leandro Despouy (President, Auditoría General de la Nación, 2002–present), November 19, 2012.

son, Máximo.[34] This shift was reflected in PAMI and the changes under Ocaña's replacement as interventor, Luciano Di Cesare.

Di Cesare, a close Kirchner ally, placed his own team members in all of the key positions Ocaña's people had occupied then set about unraveling, or reversing entirely, many of her reforms. While Ocaña had purchased all PAMI ambulances to reduce corruption in ambulance service contracts, Di Cesare reprivatized these services. Ocaña had reduced PAMI staff, whereas Di Cesare filled PAMI ranks with new employees linked to La Cámpora; from 2007 to 2012, PAMI expanded from 10,800 to 16,000 employees.[35] Ocaña had sought to make the new auditing body independent; De Cesare replaced Stornelli.[36] After Ocaña had placed PAMI on sound fiscal footing, under Di Cesare PAMI's resources became an important campaign finance source.[37] Despite Ocaña's efforts, by 2012 PAMI was again making headlines for corruption.[38]

Where were the new vested interests in PAMI that powering theorists assumed would defend Ocaña's policies? Radical reforms had created new opponents but left few defenders. During the Ocaña years, political will and the power of Ocaña's political technocrats were enough to forestall reversal; when she and her team left, the will to stick to the new procedures left with them. Career administrators did not defend the reforms. The decision-making authority of career administrators was eclipsed by political technocrats (the so-

---

[34] Cristina Fernández de Kirchner's problems with the agricultural sector began in March 2008, shortly after assuming office in December 2007. In the midst of a commodity boom, the Fernández government changed agricultural export taxes from a fixed rate to one that fluctuated based on the international price of commodities, which effectively increased export taxes on soybeans by over 35 percent at the time of announcement (*Bloomberg*, March 9, 2009). Farmers and landowners launched an unprecedented mobilization that included highway blockades and massive public demonstrations. The conflict dragged on for months, but in April the government organized pro-government demonstrations that were attended by thousands of protesters, many of whom belonged to a youth organization supporting the Kirchners, La Cámpora. After the death of Néstor Kirchner, the La Cámpora movement became even more influential, with very young ministers replacing the close-knit advisors Néstor had brought into the government from Santa Cruz.

[35] Ocaña, interview.

[36] Author interview with Gastón Blanchetiere (Manager of Legal Affairs, PAMI, 2006–7; Subsecretary of Coordination, Ministry of Health, 2007–9), October 17, 2012.

[37] *El Día*, December 3, 2012.

[38] *El Clarín*, December 2, 2012; author interview with Ezequiel Nino (Co-director, Civil Association for Equality and Justice), October 10, 2012. In particular, corruption occurred in many areas reformed by Ocaña, such as ambulance services contracts and the provision of hearing aids.

called "parallel" bureaucracy) under both Ocaña and Di Cesare.[39] In other cases, civil servants were offered "voluntary" severance packages, which the most capable – those with career prospects out-side of the federal administration – often accepted. The remaining individuals within PAMI had little reason to believe that Ocaña's changes would stick after she left, and therefore, no reason to come out and support them.[40] In all of these ways, then, powering elimi-nated potential defenders of the changes within PAMI.

The main beneficiaries of Ocaña's policies were pensioners who rely on PAMI for hearing aids or ambulances, for example. Information deficits and collective action problems prevented pen-sioners from defending the reforms. Indeed, the reversal of reforms caught many pensioners' attention only after reports began to high-light the return of old problems, in particular after the media revealed that newly privatized ambulance services often failed to arrive.[41] Yet by then it was too late – another reform had already swept away Ocaña's changes. The initiators of powering, Ocaña and her team, did not remain in their positions to defend the changes against fresh attacks. Thus, the example of PAMI demonstrates the paradox of powering and in particular the credibility issue: Eliminating existing arrangements casts doubt on whether new rules will have staying power after reformers leave or whether the next powering reform will sweep changes away.

Initial versions of the powering thesis would argue that powering is only possible during crisis situations. Yet the reliance on political will instead of crisis often occurs under normal conditions. Accordingly, the more typical the circumstances under which powering is used, the more susceptible reforms are to being overturned by a subsequent administra-tion. Menem carried out a sweeping reform of PAMI in the mid-1990s, and then Kirchner did the same. Kirchner did not "intervene" in PAMI because of crisis; every president has intervened in PAMI (Scherlis 2013, 70). Political constellations change; political will falters. Powering reforms are not self-enforcing.

---

[39] The parallel bureaucracy is the cadre of appointed professionals with flexible and fixed-term contracts that form areas that are differentiated and not complementary to the regular administrative apparatus (Martínez Nogueira 2002).

[40] Author interview with PAMI official, October 15, 2012.

[41] *El Clarín*, December 2, 2012.

POWERING HALTED, GRADUAL ADVANCEMENTS IN THE MINISTRY OF HEALTH

Political Support Wanes, Powering Fails

In 2007, Ocaña's powering crusade shifted its focus from PAMI to the broader health sector when President Fernández de Kirchner appointed Ocaña as minister of health.[42] Using the same approach and strategies as in PAMI, Ocaña began to drive changes through the Ministry of Health, dismissing employees and replacing them with members of her team from PAMI: Gastón Blanchetiere, the former manager of legal affairs, was placed as head of national contracting; Nicolás Raigorodsky, the former head of transparency policies who had assisted Ocaña in designing the PAMI reforms, was placed as head of international contracting; and so on.[43] In the words of Blanchetiere, "We refused to be incrementalists ... it was all or nothing. We would either work with complete political backing or we would leave."[44] The team suspected that two key agencies – the SSS, which is responsible for monitoring the over 300 *obras sociales*, and the Administration of Special Programs (*Administración de Programas Especiales*, APE), which provides certain high-cost services and medicines (e.g., organ transplants and HIV/AIDS medication) – were involved in siphoning funds out of the health sector.[45] To combat corruption, the team sought to create a centralized database of health procurement information and increase information regarding SSS and APE funds.[46]

Such efforts were quickly stymied. The reform team had faced fierce opposition in the past from pharmaceutical companies, unions, PAMI employees, and medical associations. This was different. Instead of offering firm and unyielding presidential support as had her husband, Cristina Fernández de Kirchner failed to back Ocaña as she took on the *obras sociales* and the unions that managed them.[47] Without strong support from the top, Ocaña's powering strategy was inoperable.[48] Two years after assuming the position, frustrated by the lack of political support, she resigned.

[42] Ocaña, interview.
[43] Author interview with Ana Paula Herrera Viana (Coordinator, Procurement Operations Unit, Ministry of Health, 2002–present), November 2, 2012.
[44] Blanchetiere, interview.
[45] Charosky, interview; Nardelli, interview. For instance, they suspected fraud in the SSS to the tune of US$70 million, and in the APE they uncovered a number of ghost companies siphoning money to relatives of those who signed the contracts.
[46] Raigorodsky, interview.   [47] Ibid.; Blanchetierre, interview.   [48] Ocaña, interview.

Absence of Powering, Opportunities for Problem Solving

From the perspective of Ocaña, her team, and many health experts who wanted the president to take on the powerful unions, the lackluster support from Fernández was disappointing. Yet an analysis of some of the most successful programs in subsequent years shows that Ocaña's failure to upend the health sector allowed for gradual improvements to accumulate over time. Ministry of Health officials and civil servants, in addition to academics and health experts, suggest that, despite Ocaña's best intentions, she had thrown out a number of good apples, employees with extensive expertise and experience, along with the bad, namely those employees involved in corrupt schemes.[49] Individuals at the National Office of Employment (*Instituto Nacional de la Administración Pública*, INAP) and civil servants corroborate the fact that Ocaña interfered to a much greater extent than her predecessor, Minister Ginés González García, with the civil servants' positions.[50]

Ocaña's replacement, Juan Luis Manzur, reappointed a number of individuals with extensive experience, undoing some of the most deleterious effects of her powering attempt.[51] This relative continuity of personnel has been crucial for the success of health programs such as Remediar and Plan Nacer. For those living below the poverty line and the uninsured, Remediar provides free access to a group of essential prescription drugs (Tobar 2004, 15). Plan Nacer provides insurance for maternal and child health care (Gertler, Giovagnoli, and Martínez 2014, 1). These social emergency programs, started in 2002 with World Bank financing, made use of existing systems and personnel plus applied lessons learned from reform attempts in the 1990s in advancing targeted experimental programs.[52] They are widely recognized as successful examples of health service provision and results-based financing programs (McGuire 2010, 143; Gertler, Giovagnoli, and Martínez 2014).[53]

---

[49] Author interview with Paola Bergallo (Consultant, Ministry of Health; Law Professor, Universidad de Palermo), October 16, 2012; Herrera Viana, interview; Preigue, interview.

[50] Author interview with employees of the Ministry of Health, 2011 and 2012; Herrera Viana, interview. In the words of one Ministry of Health interviewee, "Ella [Ocaña] tocó mas la línea."

[51] *La Nación*, August 6, 2009.   [52] Priegue, interview.

[53] Author interview with Dr. Mariana Chudnovsky (Professor, Universidad de San Andrés), October 25, 2012; author interview with Paula Ferro (Coordinator, Program Remediar, Ministry of Health, 2008–12), November 16, 2012; Nino, interview.

Individuals such as José Priegue, head of international finance at the Ministry of Health, played a central role in the continued development and expansion of these programs over time. Ocaña had dismissed Priegue, along with a number of other individuals crucial for the continued success of such programs. If she had overhauled the Ministry of Health, Plan Nacer and Remediar would likely not have continued to receive the same support and expanded. Indeed, many attribute the achievements of these key programs to the relative continuity of personnel secured by Manzur's reappointment of former staff. For instance, the Center for Global Development, a think tank based in Washington, DC, hosted an event in 2013 that featured the successes of Plan Nacer. Keith Hansen, vice president of global practices at the World Bank, noted that since 2002 the same core group of twenty to thirty individuals from the Ministry of Health, provincial agencies, and the World Bank had been working together. He noted that the "sheer accumulated tacit knowledge developed through continuous improvements" was responsible for their success.[54] This would not have been possible had powering been successful.

Powering's Legacy

While capacity has flourished in some areas of the Ministry of Health, in particular those with international involvement, the deleterious effects of powering in the 1990s are ever-present in others. Menem's health reforms dramatically reduced the workforce in the Ministry of Health in general but bolstered capacity in particular areas that interacted with IFIs.[55] Disparities have only widened over time and are evident between the units responsible for contracting: The domestic contracting office has seven employees (three technicians, two secretaries, and one director, of whom four are civil servants; three have university degrees, and none has specialized training). By contrast, the international department has well over 100 employees, many with specialized training and degrees from elite universities.[56] Ministry of Health officials, pharmaceutical employees, and AGN auditors suggest that standards of transparency are high and no detail is overlooked in the international office.[57]

---

[54] Keynote address by Keith Hansen, World Bank at the Center for Global Development, September 18, 2013.

[55] Charosky, interview; Herrera Viana, interview; Raigorodsky, interview.

[56] Blanchetiere, interview; Priegue, interview.

[57] For instance, see the Procurement Plan Execution System (SEPA Argentina), which provides access to data on all contracts for works, goods, and services that implement

At the domestic office, however, it is simply not possible to ensure that procurement rules are adequately followed, given the limited training of the staff and the volume of contracts processed. The domestic office tends to rely on procurement "shortcuts," like the use of "revolving funds" called *fondos rotatorios* and "emergency contracting" to bypass procurement and accounting rules.[58] A number of agreements with the Pan American Health Organization and the World Health Organization allow for the procuring of goods and services without going through the domestic contracting system.[59] Thus, two parallel systems have developed: one relying on exceptional capacity and transparency; the other opaque and without the resources to adequately follow contracting standards. Here again the role of outsiders in developing changes, while leading to advancements in some areas, has crippled the development of domestic institutions (see Davis 2010).

In general, sweeping attempts to transform the health sector have had long-lasting effects on the structure of employment in the Ministry of Health. Many ministry positions have experience high turnover; units frequently experience complete turnover of personnel with shifts in political constellations, and employees often labor under the fear of being fired. The perception of short time horizons for public sector employees decreases their likelihood of making changes over the long haul and can encourage a rush to make changes before the next wave of turnover. Moreover, numerous ministerial employees have multiple jobs to supplement their meager hours and income.[60] Thus, public employment proves generally unattractive.[61] The lingering effects of prior choices highlight the challenges of building capacity in the areas hit hardest by powering reforms.

projects funded by the World Bank in Argentina: http://www.iniciativasepa.org/bm/sitio/argentina/index_ing.htm.

[58]   Herrera Viana, interview. A revolving fund is a pot of money that is used to pay for goods and services after the fact, but it violates the important accounting standard of reserving money (budget check) for a purchase before the contract is signed. These funds are important to maintain for cases of true emergency. Therefore, the health sector in particular frequently uses revolving funds for important purchases. However, *very* often in Argentina these funds are abused by organizations that do not plan ahead and realize that, for example, a security contract is running out and they extend the contract (without going through the appropriate channels).

[59]   Raigorodsky, interview.

[60]   Herrera Viana, interview; author interview with high officials in Kirchner and Fernández Ministry of Health, July 21, 2010, and December 3, 2012.

[61]   Bergallo, interview.

ANALYSIS OF COMPARATIVE CASES

An analysis of powering reforms in Argentina over twenty-five years reveals that radical overhauls of the state in both transportation and health resulted in disappointing outcomes. A dramatic restructuring of transportation produced unintended negative consequences and weak institutions that ushered in a period of significant decline, ultimately prompting a fresh powering attempt. In health, powering attempts also generated unexpected outcomes, and the deepest-cutting reform, that of PAMI under Kirchner, yielded initially promising but ultimately disappointing results as advancements were either abandoned or reversed soon after reformers left PAMI. In a variety of ways, then, these cases illustrate the problems with powering and document the failure of swift, comprehensive reforms.

What can be learned from the comparison between health and transportation? The overhaul of transportation in the 1990s was far more radical than the health sector, and its effects far more deleterious for institutional development. There are two reasons for this inverse relationship of depth and speed to reform success.

First, swifter and deeper changes imply more challenges for reform designers. Consider transport reforms under Menem that were crafted to be swift, comprehensive, and implemented during the "window of opportunity" provided by the economic crisis. Each of the reform characteristics – speed, scope, and timing – made efforts at comprehensive planning nearly impossible. Time pressures left little opportunity for carefully evaluating advantages and disadvantages. The sheer complexity of crafting a radical overhaul made proactively seeking out alternatives and evenhandedly assessing costs and benefits an impossible task. Moreover, instituting changes in the midst of an economic crisis only heightened ambiguity and uncertainty for reform designers. For these reasons, reform designers were forced to rely on inferential shortcuts instead of solid information and careful calculations. In particular, ideology (e.g., neoliberalism or nationalization) served as a mental shortcut, providing a clear-cut solution to circumvent more difficult, time-consuming endeavors to solve complex problems.

The designers of the health reforms also faced challenges in planning comprehensive changes, but reforms in the health sector were less radical. Implementation was swift but not nearly as instantaneous as the transport reforms. Reformers claimed that the health system was in a state of crisis, but the level of crisis was nowhere near what it had been earlier in the decade. So while health reformers were also forced to rely on cognitive shortcuts, which resulted in unintended consequences, the slower, more limited reforms allowed experts to make estimates that were closer to the mark than the wild guesses used to design transportation reforms. It is unsurprising, then, that the problems in the health sector were far less dire than those in transport.

Case comparisons, especially PAMI under Néstor Kirchner, highlight the linkage of speed and depth to another factor important for comprehensive planning: the capabilities of the reformers. In almost every case of powering considered here, reform teams were made up of individuals appointed from outside – technocrats or those with the will or capacity to rapidly push through deep restructurings that, once implemented, would undercut the status quo. Both Menem and Fernández relied on small, coherent teams to overhaul transportation. Such teams lacked the type of contextual expertise important for understanding the effects of change in a new environment.[62] By contrast, the greater diversity of individuals involved in the health sector changes under Menem slowed the process, but this ultimately resulted in a more deliberative method for crafting changes.

The importance of contextual experience in designing reforms is underscored by Ocaña's PAMI reforms under Kirchner. While Ocaña's overhaul resulted in some unintended consequences, they were far less severe than those in other sectors thanks in large part to the capabilities of the reformers. While Ocaña was an "outsider" to the bureaucracy, she brought with her to PAMI a group of AGN auditors who had been responsible for monitoring the institute for a number of years.[63] Ocaña's reform plan had essentially been crafted over a much longer period of time by a cadre of experts who also had extensive experience with PAMI and within the federal administration. Such organizational structures as AGN and PAMI enhanced information processing and loosened the bounds of rationality. As a result, the changes that such permanent technocrats fashioned were much more successful than the transportation overhauls, which were designed at breakneck speed by outsiders.

---

[62] Although not illustrated in the case examples, such tight-knit groups are also more prone to groupthink, which keeps dissenting views from being weighed and debated (Schafer and Crichlow 2010).

[63] Despouy, interview.

Second, the swifter and the deeper the reforms, the more damaging they tend to be for institutional capacity in the long run. During Menem's radical transformation of transport, government agencies and state-run companies were eliminated at a lightning pace as responsibility for roads and railways was transferred all at once to the private sector. The transformation was so draconian and so complete that few individuals were left in the state to follow up the changes with the long struggle to correct problems in the radical new models or to strengthen the capacity and autonomy of new institutions. Once power was concentrated, it remained concentrated, which in turn limited the ability of officials to craft solutions. By contrast, the health changes were significant but did not completely overhaul the Ministry of Health. Years later, when attention shifted away from powering in health, a core of experts with lengthy experience remained.[64]

The relative success of health programs like Remediar and Plan Nacer owes to the more stable conditions of the health sector. Greater continuity provided more favorable conditions for institutional learning. Indeed, the health reforms that cut most deeply, for instance in PAMI under Néstor Kirchner, ultimately resulted in the most disappointing outcomes over time. Changes pushed through by a small group of reformers during the Kirchner administration had little support among other PAMI employees, and powering reforms weakened the civil service structure over time. In this way, reform type significantly affects institutional capacity and bureaucratic quality by further weakening the institutional controls and civil service protections that existed before the powering attempt.

CONCLUSION

The analysis of the Argentine health sector reveals the same pattern as the previous chapter on transportation. Over and over again new governments in Argentina have argued that the state is so dysfunctional that dramatic sweeping reform is necessary. Reformers come in with their technocratic teams to institute a new approach, replacing previous reform teams that leave once political will to sustain their efforts dries up. This constant purging of decision-makers and implementers often involves throwing the baby out with the bathwater – throwing out positive aspects of prior reforms and capable public servants who have institutional knowledge of previous attempts. Incremental reform is thwarted by

---

[64] In some cases, experts were dismissed but then rehired by the subsequent administration.

grander transformations that usher in "modernization" and "flexibility."
The memory of what has been tried, what worked, and what failed is lost
with each new attempt. Years later, things are so bad that a dramatic
reform becomes necessary once again. Over time such a vicious cycle
erodes institutions and intensifies the need to do something radical to
break the cycle.

Powering fails for two primary reasons. The first concerns the extraordinary challenges it creates for comprehensive planning. Even though
extensive resources and expertise were poured into comprehensive plans
for health reform in the 1990s, getting the institutions right in one shot
proved a task too complex for planners and resulted in unintended negative consequences. The crucial components of the reform meant to ameliorate problems plaguing the Argentine health sector generated new
performance problems by 2003.

Second, powering can fail because of the paradox of powering:
Eliminating the status quo hinders the probability of enduring, consolidated reforms. The powering thesis assumes that comprehensive changes
generate benefits along with a new set of beneficiaries who will make
changes viable in the long term by opposing attempts to weaken, abandon, or reverse reforms. Yet reforms do not automatically engender
beneficiaries with the motivation and capacity to defend changes, as the
case of PAMI under Néstor Kirchner demonstrates. Relying on political
will to impose draconian reforms breeds opposition, dismantles existing
institutions, and disrupts bureaucratic continuity. Why, then, right after
an entirely new policy framework is installed would relevant actors
believe it has staying power? As the case of PAMI under the Kirchners
reveals, wiping out existing arrangements casts doubt about whether new
rules will simply be swept away. The swifter and more profound the
changes, the less successful they tend to be over time – precisely the
opposite of what the powering thesis would predict.

7

Health in Brazil: Problem-Solving Success

In the 1980s, health indicators in many areas of Brazil, particularly the northeast, lagged far behind those in other countries at a similar level of development (McGuire 2010). Health-care coverage reached only a limited percent of the population and was highly centralized, leaving many areas underserved. Since the return of democracy, Brazil has transformed its health-care system in terms of both universalization and municipalization. Remarkably, this radical change was not characterized by disjointed shifts, "big bangs," or critical junctures. Instead, a series of gradual changes slowly refashioned health care even before the democratic transition (Falleti 2010; cf. Kaufman and Nelson 2004). The 1988 Constitution enshrined new health rights, but such advances accrued through quiet alterations by actors within the state that often occurred under the political radar (Falleti 2010). Thus, while reforms in health care in Brazil were more gradual than those in Argentina, they have been cumulatively transformative.

The greater success of slower reform owes to the absence of powering, which extended the time-horizon of change agents within the state. A group of health professionals faced problems that they addressed inch by inch within the existing policy process. They built consensus around transforming a system based on expensive, curative treatments into one based on preventative care. This process took time: It was marked by trial and error, plus it required learning from past mistakes. Yet these incremental improvements in the Brazilian health sector did not demand the same tremendously complex and comprehensive plans for reform as in Argentina and so were less likely to run up against cognitive constraints. When they did – when reform strategies or the changes themselves failed to produce expected outcomes – health officials were able to learn and adjust the reforms as well as the approach itself. Moreover, reformers in health tended to back away from revolutionary changes that would incite opposition and provoke the risk of reversal. The piecemeal approach had lower costs and better prospects for success.

The slow unfolding of change, which spanned some twenty-five years and spread through various levels of government, involved innumerable problem-solving reforms. Transparency in government contracting offers a telling case in point. The Ministry of Health has the largest budget of all Brazilian ministries and spends far more in terms of procurement than any other sector, even though much of the contracting for health occurs at the state and municipal levels.[1] In the past, the ministry has been particularly vulnerable to corruption and pharmaceutical cartels. An analysis of contracting demonstrates how gradual changes in one area of the federal administration can expand to others, then set in motion further changes that accumulate over time to enhance transparency and accountability. In addition, reform in health procurement illustrates two important advantages of the problem-solving approach: its ability to engender learning and to safeguard bureaucratic autonomy. The changes over the past few decades have been impressive and substantial, but the persistent challenges should not be understated. There is still much to be done to improve health and transparency in Brazil.

GRADUAL BUT POWERFUL TRANSFORMATION OF HEALTH CARE IN BRAZIL

The 1988 Constitution: One Step in a Long Reform Process

Prior to 1988, health care was centralized in the federal government, which contracted most services from the private sector. Coverage extended only to formal sector workers and tended to privilege curative treatment over preventative care, leaving much of the population without access to basic health services. Health indicators reflected the miserable conditions for those without care: In 1990, Brazil recorded the eighth-highest infant mortality rate among 105 developing countries, controlling for GDP per capita (McGuire 2010, 151). In this context, the 1988 Constitution would seem a watershed moment, a "big bang" for health in Brazil (Kaufman and Nelson 2004). The document, produced over

---

[1] Data from Siga Brasil and ComprasNet (2011).

some two years by a constituent assembly, enshrined the right to health care for all citizens, created provisions for decentralization, and formally established the Brazilian Unified Health System (*Sistema Único de Saúde,* SUS).

Yet the 1988 Constitution was far from a powering reform. As such scholars as Tulia Falleti (2010) have emphasized, the seemingly radical changes marked the culmination of a gradual reform process by actors who had "infiltrated" the state long before. Chief among them were the progressive health professionals of the Movimento Sanitário (public health movement), an activist group formed during the military dictatorship (1964–85). The movement criticized the care available to the rural and urban poor, insisted on health as a universal human right, and objected to the excessive reliance on curative as opposed to preventative medicine (Weyland 1995, 1702; Arretche 2005, 167). Beginning in the 1970s, many so-called *sanitaristas* became civil servants or filled appointed positions in the bureaucracy – first at the state and local levels and then in the federal government[2] (Escorel 1999, 183, 189; Falleti 2010). Using administrative rules and regulations, the *sanitaristas* helped extend legal entitlements and medical services to rural regions (Weyland 1995, 1703). These changes did not arouse significant opposition, because modifications and adjustments were gradual and consistent with a decades-long process of extension (Malloy 1979).

By the time the constituent assembly was convened, the *sanitaristas* had developed years of expertise through trial and error. They had built strong networks of support, so that even in a context of multiple veto players they were in a position to exercise strong influence. The codification and institutionalization of the practices they had perfected through the era of military rule were now politically feasible. Discussions about heath care within the constituent assembly debates were not without political conflicts, however, and opposition from those within the medical business resulted in the removal of provisions leading to the gradual statization of health care (Weyland 1996, 168).

Nevertheless, the 1988 Constitution was an achievement for the *sanitaristas* in enshrining sweeping principles like the universal right to health care and the decentralization as well as unification of the public health system. The changes in the Constitution regarding the health sector

---

[2] The Movimento Sanitário was not really an interest group: It never acquired a mass base and exercised its influence more like an issue network within the state than as a pressure group operating mainly in civil society (McGuire 2010, 177).

"brought to light change that had been percolating beneath the surface and been nurtured at the local level for more than a decade" (Falleti 2010, 58). Yet many of the general principles were left intentionally vague so as to avoid additional conflict (Weyland 1996, 169). Without enabling legislation and sustained, far-reaching institutional changes, the extension of health rights as an ideal would mean little in practice. The newly won rights had no teeth without operationalization, and there was every possibility that little would change.

From Failure to Progress: The Evolution of SUS (1990–2010)

Indeed, results were at first disappointing. Attempts to push through sweeping changes that would create a unified and decentralized health-care system were undermined by the diverse veto players, including not only the welter of political parties but also the private sector, institutions of horizontal accountability, states, municipalities, and all of the attendant bureaucracies. Some states had received federal transfers to assist them in assuming a greater role in the provision of health services, but such transfers were often used for other purposes. By the mid-1990s, actual change seemed negligible; scholars argued that "the movement achieved few improvements" (Weyland 1995, 1699; 1996), and Brazil was deemed a dilatory reformer by IFIs. Most countries, Argentina included, adopted neoliberal health reforms during this time, yet by strengthening the public system Brazil had moved in the opposite direction. A policy-based loan was secured from the IDB and the World Bank later in the 1990s, but in the end Brazil received a rare "unsatisfactory" rating for its performance (Weyland 2006, 152–4).

Since 1988, however, health care has made significant progress in realizing the initial objectives of the *sanitaristas*. Access is free, coverage universal, delivery decentralized, and services integrated. The private sector continues to exist as a complement to SUS, but the capacity of the public system has significantly expanded. The number of health-care facilities has grown from 22,000 to 75,000 in 2009 (Gragnolati, Lindelow, and Couttolenc 2013, 2; IBGE 2010). Much of the expansion reflects a new emphasis on primary care. The Family Health Strategy (*Estratégia de Saúde da Família*, ESF), developed from pilot programs in Ceará and other states during the 1980s, proved key to this expansion. Family health teams increased from 4,000 to more than 31,600 and are now present in over 90 percent of Brazil's 5,565 municipalities, providing coverage especially to families in the lowest-income quintiles (Macinko

2011; Ministry of Health DATASUS data). The gradual reallocation of resources to primary care and deployment of family health teams have reduced the hospital-centric nature of the system and increased preventative care. SUS has also reduced disparities across regions (Couttolenc 2011).

Such developments have yielded clear results. From 1960 to 1990, infant mortality decline was much slower than GDP per capita growth predicted, but this trend was reversed from 1990 to 2005. During that time, Brazil's infant mortality rate dropped very rapidly, despite slow economic growth. By 2005, infant mortality had fallen to the level predicted by Brazil's GDP per capita (McGuire 2010, 149). Recent World Bank reports confirm these findings. In terms of covering such health interventions as immunizations, antenatal care, and hospital deliveries, "Brazil is a stellar performer, with nearly universal coverage and limited geographic disparities" (Gragnolati, Lindelow, and Couttolenc 2013, 6).

Another approach to assessing the contribution of the health system is to evaluate trends in avoidable mortality (i.e., deaths that could have been avoided with timely and effective health care). Studies of avoidable (or amenable) mortality in Brazil suggest that SUS has played an important role in improving outcomes; mortality from avoidable causes declined significantly, while mortality from other causes remained stable (Abreu, Cesar, and Franca 2007, 2009; Malta et al. 2010; Gragnolati, Lindelow, and Couttolenc 2013, 8–9).[3]

Table 4 shows the change in health outcomes in Brazil and comparable countries. In Brazil, life expectancy has increased by 15.5 percent and infant mortality decreased by 71.3 percent. These advances far outpaced improvement in Latin America and other middle-income countries and are very close to levels in the best-performing countries. Thus, despite initial disappointments in advancing health reform, Brazil has transformed health care and posted impressive results in a number of areas.

Factors Contributing to Advances

Why were reforms successful? How did reformers achieve such complex transformations as universalization and decentralization given the vested

---

[3] In some cases mortality has increased. Socioeconomic changes in Brazil mean that first-world health problems, such as non-communicable diseases like heart disease and diabetes, are increasingly causes or contributors to mortality.

TABLE 4 *Change in Health Outcomes in Brazil and Comparable Countries by Percentage, 1985–2009*

Country or Group of Countries	Life Expectancy	Infant Mortality
Brazil	+15.5	−71.3
Latin America and the Caribbean	+7.1	−33.2
Middle-income countries	+6.1	−28.5
China and India	+11.1	−60.5
Best performers in group[a]	+16.5	−76.3

Source: Gragnolati, Lindelow, and Couttolenc 2013, 82, with data from IBGE 2004; Ministry of Health data (Ministry of Health, SVS 2011); World Bank 2011.
[a] Best performers are Peru in life expectancy and Turkey in infant mortality.

interests in the existing system? What sustained the reforms across decades? How did a unified system develop without focused political will? Two characteristics of the reform process were crucial: the scale and speed of reform, and the collective characteristics of the reformers.

Small-scale changes advanced over time, meaning there was no need to plan the whole reform at once. While many actors within the state were guided by goals like basic health care for all, they did not propose a specific model, nor they did attempt to make comprehensive changes all at once. Instead, their reform tactics were flexible, and they adapted their approaches along the way. This was not directionless incrementalism; rather, flexible modifications were guided by core principles. The ideal espoused by *sanitaristas* and collaborating groups was a shift in emphasis from curative to preventative health care. The means to this end evolved over time.

For instance, initially *sanitaristas* expected that municipalization – that is, bringing care closer to patients in municipalities – would result in greater levels of accountability and better care. Yet as reformers realized that the rent-seeking of local political leaders threatened quality care, and as more *sanitaristas* entered the federal government, they began to favor conditional funding at the municipal level. That is, as they observed the consequences of greater local autonomy, reform groups initially opposed to centralized rules began to support the Ministry of Health in influencing local policy (Barros 2001; Carvalho 2001). Similarly, as reformers discovered that smaller municipalities did not have the personnel or resources to effectively manage hospitals, they began to advocate a shift to greater regional coordination.[4] The inability of experts, including many of the well-educated *sanitaristas*, to foresee such problems in their initial reform objectives illustrates that even specialists can be cognitively constrained and struggle to anticipate the consequences of complex reforms. The learning that occurred as a result of sequencing adjustments proved crucial for the success of the reforms.

A more experimental approach then gave rise to one of Brazil's widely admired initiatives, the Family Health Program (*Programa Saúde da Família*, PSF). This program was designed to deliver basic health services to the poor in all parts of the country and served as a gateway for the health-care system. From 1994 on, the program expanded through a series of reforms that increased funding for basic preventative care (Weyland 2006, 175; Hunter and Borges Sugiyama 2009). Such reform successes often cascaded from one area of health policy to another.[5]

Additionally, the characteristics of reformers were crucial in shaping the success of Brazil's health reform. Broad expertise, accumulated experience, and diversity within organizational structures enhanced information processing. The *sanitarista* movement comprised academics along with others who were likewise well educated. Yet many relied most on their experience – their previous positions in local, state, and federal governments. Successes and failures over time proved crucial, not only for their contribution to the Constitution of 1988 but also for a wide variety of piecemeal changes.[6] The *sanitaristas* may have shared a few core principles, but they did not have a monolithic approach or a single set of objectives. Most wished to see a shift from curative to preventative care, but what that meant and what level of government should provide it varied dramatically.[7] Although the different objectives and experiences of reformers often slowed and complicated reform efforts, they also induced *sanitaristas* to explain and defend their proposals to those who disagreed. Divergence produced refinements.

---

[4] Author interview with Dr. Luciana Mendes (Health Coordinator, Institute of Applied Economic Research, 1983–present), January 26, 2012.

[5] Mendes, interview.

[6] Author interview with Dr. Jovita José Rosa (Diretora da Secretaria Executiva, Movimento de Combate a Corrupção Eleitoral, 2002–present; Auditor, Ministry of Health DENASUS, 1983–present; President, National Union of Health Auditors (UNASUS), 2003–8), January 16, 2012; author interview with *sanitarista* and high-level Ministry of Health official, December 5, 2011. Dr. Rosa also played a central role in negotiating the *ficha limpa* law.

[7] Author interview with *sanitarista* and high official in Rousseff's Ministry of Health, January 18, 2012.

And the diversity in the health sector seemed to grow over time. New groups developed; for example, the Primary Care Movement, a loose alliance made up of a large contingent of nurses, emerged in the early 1990s.[8] Over time the Movimento Sanitário itself began to further splinter and no longer held unified objectives (Arretche 2004, 185).[9] Such groups subjected their proposals to the scrutiny of an ever-more diverse set of actors, including experts outside of medicine. (The minister of health under Cardoso, José Serra, was an economist by training.) Reform proposals were crosschecked and vetted by a diverse group of individuals, so coalitions and their policies were less prone to "groupthink."

By including a wide array of approaches in the reform process, groups often made concessions to opponents, which had salutary effects on the reform process in the long run. Instead of foisting responsibility for health services onto local governments, the federal government provided municipalities with options assuming responsibility. By 2001, all Brazilian municipalities had qualified for the federal health-care decentralization program, while retaining the autonomy to reject the increased responsibility (Arretche 2004, 179). Along the way, numerous changes were made to ensure that reforms slid past points of resistance. Increases in the revenue that states, municipalities, and federal government are obliged to spend have been gradually phased in, for example (Piola and Biasoto 2001).

While such strategies often attenuated change, they ensured that reform was politically feasible in the moment and less subject to reversal later on. By seeking allies, developing networks, and building coalitions, reformers could make changes once resistance subsided. Longer time horizons meant that short-term failures generated learning and inspired future tactics. In summary, smaller-scale change sequenced over time allowed reformers to experiment, learn, adjust, and ultimately perfect reforms. Moreover, by advancing modifications incrementally and negotiating more substantial changes, reformers made improvements more sustainable.

---

[8] This group played an important role in persuading the Ministry of Health in 1991 to scale up to the national level the Health Agents Program in Ceará, which had been developed in 1987 (Tendler, 1997; Weyland 2006, 174–5, 207–9; McGuire 2010, 162). As a result, the national Community Health Agents Program (PACS) was created and later became a part of the Family Health Program (PSF).

[9] Author interview with Dr. Roberto Nogueira (Health Expert, IPEA), January 10, 2012; *sanitarista* and high-level Ministry of Health official, interview.

PROBLEM SOLVING: SLOW BUT SUSTAINED EXPANSION OF
TRANSPARENCY IN PROCUREMENT

Despite the incremental advance of health policy in the 1990s, powerful political and economic interests remained entrenched in the health sector, especially in public procurement. Spending on health services was slowly decentralized, but the Ministry of Health remained responsible for purchasing pharmaceuticals for SUS. As was the case in Argentina, many experts recognized pharmaceutical cartel behavior as the norm and knew that cartels were responsible for siphoning millions out of public health coffers.[10]

Strong civil service protections in Brazil do not extend to procurement officials. Their pay is low, and the work is undesirable (Motta 2010, 144–8). Those responsible for maintaining integrity in government contract bidding were often strategically positioned in the health-contracting unit to divert health resources.[11] Those who were selected based on merit often lacked training as well as the autonomy to hold contractors accountable.[12]

Such problems were only exacerbated by procurement Law 8666, passed in 1993.[13] Purchasing basic pharmaceutical products often took well over six months and could stretch on for years if the process ended up in court. Given the bottleneck in obtaining medications, surgical supplies, or hospital beds, for example, "emergency" procedures were used excessively. Instead of requiring competitive bids, emergency procedures allow government officials to buy from the supplier of their choosing with no limit on price. In true emergencies, this workaround is surely justified. Yet officials estimate, in some agencies, that emergency procedures were used for well over 70 percent of contracts in 1997,[14] opening the door to

---

[10] Rosa, interview.   [11] Rosa, interview.

[12] Author interview with Francisco Gaetani (Deputy Executive Secretary, Ministry of Planning, 2003–11), February 24, 2012. In contrast to the meritocratic recruitment and job security enjoyed by many Brazilian public employees, there are no careers or specific tenure protections for the approximately 20,000 procurement employees (Motta 2010). The situation is not much better at the policy-making level: Supervisory procurement positions in federal ministries are filled by the lowest-ranking non-clerical political appointees. And while supervisory appointees and the staff of the small contracting policy and technology department (DLSG) enjoy higher salaries, none of the positions are specifically reserved for civil servants (Motta 2010, 144–8).

[13] As Chapter 6 discussed, the rigid procurement rules tilted the legal framework in favor of construction companies that bid on public works contracts.

[14] Author interview with Marcos Ozorio de Almeida (Consultant, World Bank and SERPRO, 2007–14), August 7, 2009.

corruption and the privileging of cronies within the powerful pharmaceutical lobby. Recall that when President Cardoso and Minister of State Reform Bresser-Pereira attempted to push through comprehensive corrective legislation between 1995 and 1998, corrupt interests defended Law 8666.

A seemingly small change eventually led to the gradual introduction of a new system, *pregão*, which set in motion other changes that accumulated over time, enhancing transparency and accountability in government contracting generally and health in particular. *Pregão* is a simple online reverse auction: In a standard auction, the highest bidder wins, but in the "reverse" auction the lowest bidder wins the contract. This simple and initially limited strategy proved to have powerful and wide-ranging effects.

Problem Solving: *Pregão* Crafted under the Radar

In contrast to highly political attempts at change, problem-solving *pregão* reforms were developed by a small team of technical professionals in the little-known Department of Logistics and General Services (*Departamento de Logística e Serviços Gerais*, or DLSG) within the Ministry of Planning, Budget, and Management. In 1999, at the beginning of the second Cardoso administration, executives decided against the powering approach that had failed to reform procurement in the first administration; political appointees who supported comprehensive change then left the administration. Elisabeth Braga, a low-profile career civil servant from the Ministry of Finance, was appointed to lead the contracting policy and technology department; a few of the technical members from the prior team were appointed to join her in the DLSG (Fernandes 2010, 176). It was, according to these team members, precisely the absence of political interests in reforming procurement – along with the team's technical acumen – that allowed them to remain in positions related to procurement policy.[15] These professionals had learned from past reforms and their experience in other ministries that sweeping change was neither desirable nor feasible; most knew firsthand how the well-intentioned 1993 reform had only furthered corrupt practices. Seeking

---

[15] Author interview with Carlos Moreira (Director, DLSG, 2004–10), January 23, 2012. None of the positions in DLSG are specifically reserved for civil servants (Motta 2010, 144–8). Thus, the effective protections which guarantee meritocratic recruitment for much of the Brazilian federal administration do not extend to the *pregão* case.

simply to improve the existing situation, they did not have a clear reform program in mind but resolved to fix at least some of the issues created by Law 8666.

Procurement reform did not emerge from an extensive, systematic evaluation of all possible alternatives but from an existing alternative familiar to the team: the *pregão* contracting experiment within the newly created National Telecommunications Agency (*Agência Nacional de Telecomunicações*, Anatel), itself an example of a successful problem-solving reform (Monteiro 2005). In 1997, an exception to Law 8666 was created for Anatel that resulted in the use of the *pregão* online reverse auction, which increased efficiency and transparency in contracting while reducing costs. Braga's team began exploring possibilities for piloting *pregão* in other areas of the Brazilian federal administration, with the hope that such a change would provide a way around Law 8666.[16]

Key decision-makers intentionally employed a number of tactics to keep the *pregão* reform incremental while flying under the radar of political actors and construction companies.[17] Braga's team began drafting a *medida provisória* (provisional measure), an executive decree with legislative force that would extend the applicability of the Anatel law to other areas and agencies. The provision was strategically limited in three important ways. First, the change was not mandatory. *Pregão* would be one of many means that contracting officers could use to procure goods and services. Therefore, despite the adoption of *pregão*, opaque areas of the Brazilian federal administration could continue reaping ill-gotten gains from the use of emergency contracts and other loopholes. Second, public works were excluded from the measure. In Brazil, large *empreiteiras* (construction firms) that benefit from public works projects are known for their contributions to political campaigns through *caixa dois* (off-the-books accounts). According to Vera Monteiro, one of the drafters of the law, the exclusion of public works was crucial for the measure's survival against the powerful construction company representatives in the legislature who would halt any public-works related change to Law 8666.[18] Finally, while the provisional measure would initially have the force of law, it would later require the legislature's approval.[19] In these

---

[16] Author interview with Elisabeth Braga (Director, DLSG, 2000–4), May 18, 2012.
[17] Author interview with Vera Monteiro (Pregão Legal Consultant, Sundfeld Law Office), November 27, 2011.
[18] Monteiro, interview.
[19] For an explanation of provisional measures, see Pereira, Power, and Rennó (2008, 14).

ways, the team started small, hoping that, with time, perceptions regarding the reform would change in their favor.

Timing was also crucial. Braga and her team presented the *pregão* modification to Minister of Planning Martus Tavares, who in turn presented it to President Cardoso just as the high-profile Fiscal Responsibility Bill (*Lei de Responsabilidade Fiscal*, LRF) appeared on his desk.[20] Would-be opponents of *pregão* were focused on the LRF, the culmination of incremental changes aimed at stemming the financial drain caused by state governments' spending and at stabilizing the Brazilian economy (Schneider 2007). This important bill overshadowed the *pregão* proposal, which seemed but a harmless technical modification. Both the LRF and the provisional measure were passed on May 4, 2000 (Medida Provisória n. 2.026 of May 4, 2000). Could high-level decision-makers, such as the minister, really not have understood the important *pregão* change? Minister Tavares was familiar with the results of *pregão*, for example, but struggled to recall details of its approval; his efforts at the time were focused on the LRF.[21]

In sum, the *pregão* initiative was developed by technocrats in response to the day-to-day problems created by Law 8666. Learning from past failure was essential to their strategy, which at every turn was incremental so as to elude the attention of potential opponents. The new procedure proved both effective and enduring. Once begun, *pregão* was difficult to halt; with increased information, the new form of bidding then revealed the need for additional reforms.

An Incremental and Sustained Sequence of Reform

By 2002, when the provisional measure was brought before the legislature for approval as a permanent law (Monteiro 2010, 36–49), the advantages of *pregão* were undeniable. Numerous federal agencies had adopted the optional procedure in order to speed up the contracting process. Procurement processes for simple goods and services that had once dragged on for months could now be completed in fewer than fifteen working days (de Almeida 2006, 507). These agencies also demonstrated that *pregão* reduced costs considerably: The Inter-American Development Bank estimates a reduction of up to 24 percent in product acquisition costs

---

[20] Braga, interview.

[21] Author interview with Martus Tavares (Minister of Planning, 1999–2002), May 28, 2012.

(Pinto 2009, 20). Other benefits included increased transparency, a reduction in emergency contracts by approximately 20 percent (de Almeida 2006, 507–9), greater competition, and the elimination of intermediaries and geographic limitations on participation by making the process available nationwide via the web (Joia and Zamot 2002). Years earlier, any permanent change to Law 8666 would have seemed impossible; however, as the new method became entrenched, proven results made the reform so difficult to reverse that the reform process endured despite presidential turnover.

As the use of *pregão* spread during President Lula da Silva's first term, pressure increased to adopt the new approach, and public servants discovered additional areas that could benefit from such reforms. In 2004, the use of *pregão* resulted in the break-up of the "Vampire Mafia," a group of pharmaceutical companies, lobbyists, and Ministry of Health employees who had been manipulating bidding processes since the early 1990s. Auditing officials had long suspected a corruption ring in the Ministry of Health; after encountering irregularities in a bidding process for hemoderivatives – blood products (hence the "Vampire" Mafia) used to treat hemophilia, AIDS, and cancer – the external oversight agency (TCU) mandated a new, *pregão* bidding process.[22] The *pregão* system facilitated the entry of other bidders, pushed companies to compete, and reduced opportunities for public officials to rig the process. Prices dropped by 42 percent.[23] The Federal Police and the public prosecutors of the *Ministério Público* subsequently began an investigation that, in 2004, resulted in "Operation Vampire." Ultimately seventeen people were arrested, including government officials and high-ranking Ministry of Health employees. Officials estimated that the Vampire Mafia drained US$40 million from public coffers from 1997 to 2004.[24]

This episode had two important spillover effects. First, Brazilian states likewise affected by the Vampire Mafia began adopting *pregão* for hemoderivatives (and later for other goods and services). Although states and municipalities had access to federal online *pregão* systems as early as 2002, only after the shocking price reductions did they begin to use them.[25] Second, the adoption of *pregão* revealed the need for additional reforms. The Vampire episode uncovered a major loophole used to direct

---

[22] Author interview with senior TCU official, January 20, 2012; Rosa, interview.
[23] *Folha de São Paulo*, May 20, 2004.   [24] Ibid.
[25] Author interview with Adriana Pacheco Aurea (Consultant, Ministry of Health and Institution for Applied Economic Research), January 25, 2012.

contracts to cronies: Pharmaceutical products were often listed by brand names rather than generics (e.g., "Aspirin" instead of "acetylsalicylic acid"), which effectively reduced the number of potential suppliers and facilitated collusion among remaining bidders. Shortly after Operation Vampire, the Ministry of Planning discovered that this problem resulted from improper coding in the Catalog of Materials (*Catálogo de Materiais*, CATMAT). The group responsible for coding medications had no expertise in medical terminology; they did not know that they should code for "acetylsalicylic acid" when given a request for "Aspirin." In 2004, CATMAT coding of medical products was transferred to a team in the Ministry of Health (CGU 2005). Many experts claim that, in the end, this was one of the most important advancements in eradicating corruption.[26]

As the use of *pregão* increased, information regarding malfeasance and compliance emerged, revealing the need for the extension of *pregão* and triggering a cascade of reforms. If the powerful drug companies had been aware of *pregão* and its potential, perhaps they would have opposed the modification from the beginning. At the time of the initial reform, however, it was impossible to forecast the sequence of events that would result in Operation Vampire, demonstrating a key reason why *pregão* reform was successful: It caught potential opponents unaware.

Meanwhile, as the use of *pregão* in other ministries and agencies produced impressive results, public servants within the Ministry of Planning and the TCU watched for the right moment to make *pregão* mandatory.[27] Pressure to use the new method increased over time as contracting officials and middle-level managers realized *pregão* offered autonomy from outside influences by increasing transparency in the procurement process. Yet not all applied – or perhaps were allowed to apply – the new approach. Predictably, agencies with the highest levels of corruption were the last to adopt the method. Eventually, non-adopters appeared corrupt (see Hyde 2011). This was no surprise to the TCU, and it became clear that some areas of the government refused to use the new method precisely because *pregão* would clean up contracting offices rife with kickbacks, bribes, and campaign contributions. Thus, by the time another contracting scandal hit in 2005 in the Brazilian Post Office (the initial stages of the Mensalão Scandal, a corruption scandal that involved the highest levels of President Lula da Silva's administration), the Ministry

---

[26] Author interview with Mariana Ramos (Ministry of Health), March 23, 2012; Pacheco Aurea, interview.

[27] Senior TCU official, interview.

of Planning and the TCU had already drafted a law regulating *pregão*.[28] President Lula da Silva signed it, making *pregão* the preferred method of contracting not only for the federal government but also for states and municipalities using funds from voluntary federal transfers (Decree No. 5504 of August 5, 2005).

In 2011 a new law, the Differential Contracting Regime (*Regime Diferenciado de Contratações Públicas*, RDC), created the option to apply some of the concepts of *pregão* to public works projects related only to the World Cup and Olympics and only when "convenient" (Rosilho 2013). Yet RDC was soon extended to public works projects for health (SUS) and other areas. All of this would have been unthinkable in 2000, but the quiet, gradual changes spearheaded by civil servants slowly transformed the rigid procedures and eroded resistance to change.

Experiential Learning Results in New and Complex Reforms

As the *pregão* team learned from prior experiences what was feasible and how to sequence changes, their tactics became more sophisticated, and they took on new and more complex areas. One of the areas that reformers in both the Ministries of Planning and Health sought to conquer in their quest for transparency was federal transfers to states and municipalities.[29] A considerable sum of federal funds transferred through agreements to states and municipalities or to private, non-profit, non-governmental organizations never reached their intended recipient or purpose (TCU 2014). Such opaque transfers, often initiated via budget amendments linked to a specific congressperson (*emendas parlamentares*), were increasingly used as a loophole to divert funds when transparency increased at the federal level.[30]

In 2003, the same team that developed *pregão* and extended transparency to procurement in general, now under the leadership of one of its long-time members, Henrique Moreira, began a project that sought to bring federal transfers slowly under the same transparency regime. After discussions with the TCU, Moreira and his team began developing what came to be known as Sistema de Gestão de Convênios e Contratos de

---

[28] Ibid.

[29] Moreira, interview. In Portuguese, such transfers are known as *convênios e contratos de repasse*.

[30] Author interview with senior TCU, January 17, 2012. There are nearly 40,000 municipal partnerships. While the amount of money transferred is often small, the sheer quantity of transfers means that a significant amount of public funds is diverted.

Repasse (SICONV), a system that would track federal transfers from their originators in Congress to their final recipients. The development of the new system simply extended the model used for *pregão* into a new, and admittedly more complex, area.

The team had woven together a coalition of government officials who supported the effort and at first drew little attention. But as their work became more widely known, resistance emerged. According to Moreira, they maintained the support of a few key Ministry of Planning officials, but, because their reforms threatened the access of high-level political actors to important sources of funding, they sustained attacks from all sides – from deputies and senators, the Ministry of Planning, and the other ministries.[31]

The siege subsided, however, after a Federal Police investigation, code-named Operation Bloodsucker (or "leech," *sanguessuga*), uncovered the fraudulent purchase of ambulances using federal transfers. The investigation found that congressional aides had been bribed to write individual budget amendments financing the purchase of ambulances with Health Ministry funds; the bidding processes were rigged at the local level. A congressional inquiry committee (*Comissão Parlamentar de Inquérito*, CPI) recommended that seventy-two members of Congress be expelled (Praça 2011).

Thereafter, the TCU officials, who had been in touch with Moreira's team all along, issued a ruling mandating that the Ministry of Planning, within 180 days, present a technical study for the implementation of an information technology system that would allow online monitoring of all agreements and other legal instruments used to transfer federal funds to other organizations, federal agencies, and the private sector (Acórdão 2066/2006). Essentially, the TCU mandated that the Ministry of Planning develop the system that Moreira had told them three years earlier was necessary to track such expenditures.

Following the ruling, the reach of SICONV expanded (TC 012.075/2014–0), and it is now obligatory for most federal transfers.[32] Especially in the area of health, the system has increased the ability to track funds that flow from the federal governments to the states[33] and it has become a rich source of data for auditors, journalists, and citizens.[34]

---

[31] Moreira, interview.   [32] *O Globo*, November 12, 2011.

[33] Author interview with Orlando Neto (Consultor Geral, Consultoria de Orçamentos, 1996–present), May 9, 2012; Ramos, interview.

[34] Author interview with José Roberto de Toledo (Journalist, *Estado de São Paulo;* Founder, Associação Brasileira de Jornalismo Investigativo), July 30, 2009; author interview with

The Virtuous Circle of Problem Solving and Remaining Challenges

Advancing modest changes spearheaded by career administrators increases the success of institution building in a number of ways. Problem-solving reforms tend to deflect political struggles; in the case of *pregão*, for example, decision-makers intentionally avoided reforming public works contracts directly. Instead, they emphasized technical expertise. Furthermore, when the problem-solving process proves successful, the need for wholesale reform becomes less dire, reducing the impulse to start over from scratch. During the turnover between presidents Cardoso and Lula da Silva, there was no attempt at comprehensive procurement reform, because *pregão* reforms slowly improved the situation. This gradual process also had implications for personnel decisions. During the turnover, Alexandre Motta replaced Braga, but the rest of the skilled technical team remained in place at Motta's request.[35] The same situation applied when Henrique Moreira assumed the role. The Braga team's efforts were intentionally apolitical: They did not clearly serve one political side or another. And because they were effective, there was little incentive to attempt a completely new reform strategy or replace the team. The team was able then to learn from prior reforms what was feasible and how to sequence changes, transforming existing employees into reform experts. Experts became more sophisticated, eventually taking on new and complex areas such as federal transfers to states and municipalities. In this way, problem solving allowed bureaucratic autonomy and capacity to build over time.

By providing opportunities for learning over time, improvements in one area could reveal underlying problems in another (e.g., use of *pregão* revealed needed reforms in CATMAT). Brazil has strong civil service norms, yet improvements in the CATMAT coders' capacity happened only after *pregão* exposed the problem. And incremental problem-solving changes have, over the long run, enhanced the autonomy of the procurement staff and increased efforts to provide them with additional training. Motta long argued that *pregão* was not the solution to all procurement problems, and now as the director of the School of the Ministry of Finance, he spearheads training.[36]

Roberto Maltchik (Reporter, *O Globo*), October 10, 2011. Maltchik is the top reporter on corruption scandals for *O Globo*.

[35] Interview with Alexandre Motta (Director, DLSG, 2003–4), December 22, 2011.

[36] Motta, interview.

The problem-solving strategy has also contributed to preserving bureaucratic autonomy in a broader sense. Today, Brazil has strong civil service norms (Echebarría and Cortázar 2007). Twenty-five years ago, however, this was not necessarily true. Members of the elite team of governmental administrators, in the state since the return of democracy, credit the impressive level of meritocratic recruitment and adherence to civil service guarantees in Brazil to a long process of problem solving.[37] *Sanitaristas* have also worked to improve the quality of health professionals and reduce the staff working on short-term contracts.[38] Individuals throughout the public sector (some of whom call themselves the "Transparency Movement") have sought to improve competitive exams to select only the highest-quality candidates with a zeal for safeguarding state resources from corruption.[39] Argentina also developed an elite corps of civil servants[40] and guarantees of meritocratic recruitment.[41] Yet radical restructuring there halted many of these programs and disrupted the slow process of building up civil service norms and guarantees. Complete overhauls of programs tend to interrupt small but cumulatively substantial transformations.

Problem solving is not perfect, and certainly *pregão* is not a panacea for contracting corruption.[42] While there have been major advances in transparency, progress at the state and municipal levels has been uneven, especially in a country of continental size with high levels of inequality.[43] Much remains to be done to improve the Brazilian health

---

[37] Graef, interview; Santos, interview.   [38] Mendes, interview; Pacheco Aurea, interview.

[39] Author interview with Dr. Rommel Carvalho (Chief Data Scientist, CGU, 2005–17), April 19, 2012; author interview with André Luiz Furtado Pacheco (Auditor, Secretaria de Fiscalização de Tecnologia da Informação (Sefti), TCU, 1992–present), August 6, 2009; Gaetani, interview.

[40] Known as the *administradores gubernamentales* (governmental administrators). Author interview with Hugo Dalbosco (Administrador Gubernamental, Argentina, 2001–present), November 6, 2012.

[41] Author interviews with Guillermo Schweinheim (Director of Training and Development, Tribunal de Cuentas de la Nación, Argentina, 1984–92), August 22, 2012.

[42] Author interview with Dr. Florencia Ferrer (President, e-Stratégia Pública), November 20, 2011.

[43] Author interviews with Gil Castello Branco (Secretário-geral, Contas Abertas, 2005–present), October 28, 2011; Eduardo Cunha (no relation to the current president of the Chamber of Deputies of Brazil of the same name), senior executive and leader of Accenture's Global Service Strategy and Operations group in Latin America and formerly responsible for supply chain management in Brazil, July 18, 2009; Author interview with Roberta Clemente, Assessor Técnico. Assembleia Legislativa do Estado de Sao Paulo, September 24, 2011. A Brazilian NGO, Contas Abertas, conducted a comprehensive assessment of financial transparency at various levels of government. While the federal

system. Basic health care has improved, but a shortage of doctors remains a challenge for extending it to remote areas. Citizens have access to public hospitals, but the quality of care varies tremendously (e.g., many municipalities are too small to operate hospitals effectively and cannot provide funds to ensure quality care).[44] Brazil has successfully decentralized and brought care closer to citizens, but the coordination across autonomous levels of government has blurred defined roles and responsibilities. Civil servant protections are strong for many health workers, but state and local governments have increasingly augmented the health-care workforce with short-term contracted employees, producing problems with continuity and quality.[45] Finally, the strain on the health-care system due to the recession's depletion of public coffers cannot be overstated.

OPPORTUNITIES FOR CHANGE: INDIVIDUALLY SMALL CHANGES GAIN MOMENTUM TO TACKLE BIG PROBLEMS

Nevertheless, problem solving provides a way forward, as progress is made on seemingly intractable issues bit by bit. In many areas, the pressure of change has impelled the current cascade of revelations about corruption at the highest levels. The many efforts that have extended transparency illustrate how problem solving has contributed to tackling corruption and impunity at even the highest levels.

In a 2012 interview with lead Senate Budget Consultant Orlando Neto, the ambitions of the transparency movement developed since democratization were clear. Neto developed the web platform Siga Brasil, where users can access the full budget down to specific amendments and line items in addition to information on public revenues and expenditures shortly after execution (including *pregão* and federal transfer data) – another example of successful problem solving. Neto drew a detailed map of financial data in Brazil on a giant whiteboard to show exactly what his team members have gained access to and what they are still working to bring into their database. State enterprises (e.g., Petrobras) and BNDES, for instance, remained out of their control.[46] Access to federal transfers had expanded information on states and municipalities,

and many state governments ranked quite high, others ranked very poorly, providing only data at the most aggregate level.

[44] In states, such as Amazonas, interviewees suggest that pharmaceutical cartels still have a strong hold on the market for certain products. Ferrer, interview.

[45] Gaetani, interievw; Pacheco Aurea, interview.

[46] Given the recent corruption scandals around Petrobras, this is likely to change.

as had legislation that phased in requirements for municipalities of increasingly smaller sizes to make data accessible. Yet the team had gained access to most of the information over time by working with states, municipalities, and a vast network of individuals within the federal government who share the goal of expanding transparency. Such networks have been crucial to the quiet efforts of the elite team of budget consultants.[47]

Regarding health, experimentation continues, especially at the state and regional levels. To address the shortage of medical professionals, the government has piloted programs allowing foreign doctors to serve in remote areas.[48] Moreover, members from the National Health Council (*Conselho Nacional de Saúde*, CNS) have started to discuss developing small pilot programs to train physician assistants and nurse practitioners to extend services to these areas.[49] In recent years, the Ministry of Health has initiated a dialogue with the judiciary regarding the effects of their rulings on public policy, while also improving the systems and procedures for incorporating new technologies (Gragnolati, Lindelow, and Couttolenc 2013, 4).[50] Judicial decisions related to health care are also debated in Congress (Piola et al. 2009, 152–8). Furthermore, experiments with more effective and efficient ways to deliver health care have proliferated throughout the country.[51] In Bahia, for example, public–private partnerships have been used to develop and manage hospitals, and in São Paulo the state has turned to private non-profit management groups (i.e., Social Organizations in Health, OSS) to administer hospitals.[52] While it is too soon to assess such efforts, these experiments seem promising precisely because they engender a learning process.

Faced with persistent challenges, many auditors and health officials have developed innovative ways to reach outside their roles in the state

[47] They are among the highest-paid civil servants in the country. After each competitive exam to enter the civil service, the lead consultant – who wins the position through an election of the other consultants (Orlando Neto has been in this position for over fifteen years) – selects the candidates he would like on his team. Since it is one of the most coveted positions, the team usually gets who they would like, the pick of the litter.

[48] These are only for positions in which no Brazilian doctors have expressed interest.

[49] Rosa, interview.   [50] Ramo, interview.

[51] Brazil has also made significant strides in recent years in clarifying the roles and relationships across levels of government with ongoing efforts to modify the framework for contracting between federal government and health regions and institutional mechanisms for coordinating between municipalities, states, and federal government (Gragnolati, Lindelow, and Couttolenc 2013, 11).

[52] Mendes, interview.

and mobilize the public. For instance, auditors from a variety of different state entities have banded together to create NGOs that seek to engage citizens in combating corruption. One of the highest-profile results of their efforts was the passage of the *ficha limpa*, or "clean sheet" law (Law no. 135 of 2010), which was proposed by a popular initiative that garnered 1.3 million signatures in September 2009.[53] This law specified that candidates with "dirty" court records (i.e., convicted by a second-level court) would be ineligible to run for office. Other initiatives seek to educate citizens, especially in poor areas, about detecting, responding to, and reporting fraud. The Institute of Auditing and Monitoring (*Instituto de Fiscalização e Controle*), for instance, conducts "Caravans" that travel to poorer municipalities to educate citizens about corruption in health, facilitate meetings between citizens and mayors and health officials, conduct "civic audits," and develop municipal health councils.[54] Indeed, studies have shown that each additional year of health council experience reduces corruption incidence levels by 2.1 percent (Avelino, Barberia, and Biderman 2014, 694). In other cases auditors have moved into politics, running for office themselves.[55] Thus, in a variety of ways, individuals with expertise and experience have sought to make connections with citizens to increase their power, while loosening the cognitive constraints of those unfamiliar with the complex world of diversion of funds through health.

ANALYSIS OF COMPARATIVE CASES

Brazil has changed dramatically since the early 1990s, when its democratic institutions were labeled "feckless" (Mainwaring 1995). That change, however, has not hinged on any particular points. Instead,

---

[53] This effort was largely led by Articulação Brasileira Contra a Corrupção e a Impunidade (Abracci) (Rosa, interview). Only four laws have been passed in such a way in Brazil (*O Globo*, May 20, 2010).

[54] Author interviews with Henrique Ziller (Auditor Federal de Controle Externo, Tribunal de Contas da União, 2001–14); Founder and President, Instituto de Fiscalização e Controle, 2004–present), October 31, 2011; Rosa. Auditors have also sought to use their positions by serving as "guides" for citizens at participatory governing events. Through a process of dialogue, auditors explain the importance of advancing some measures over others to citizen delegates. Indeed, the proposed legislation from such participatory conferences looks strikingly similar to auditors' own proposals for reform. This author was an invited observer at the CONSOCIAL 2012, a national participatory conference. The legislation from the conference was to be sent on to Congress.

[55] Ziller, interview; Rosa, interview.

seemingly insignificant shifts, modifications, and adjustments have occurred over time, often nearly unnoticed, and led eventually to significant transformations. To observers at any single point in time, Brazil's policy process might have seemed relatively stable, even stagnant. Yet for those who visited Brazil in the 1990s, a trip to the country a decade or more later reveals real differences.

Consider the recent torrent of corruption scandals and the indictments of powerful political and economic actors. In the early 1990s such events would have been unthinkable. Over time, however, changes have accumulated. Reform movements have been built slowly but steadily, especially in the realms of transparency and accountability. Advances in agencies and ministries of the direct administration have then revealed new problems and additional areas of opacity (e.g., in the indirect administration, such as Petrobras and state-owned banks like BNDES). With such advances and revelations, reform coalitions have built momentum and organizational capacity over time for conquering new changes. The constant scandals, which have often been revealed by problem solvers, have increased public awareness of corruption and fueled popular outrage. NGOs and popular organizations that had been working to fight corruption, often in partnerships with civil servants and problem solvers within the government, are now well positioned to support corruption-fighting efforts. Indeed, the popular support for the Lava Jato proceedings may well have protected reformers from the interference of political actors. Such dramatic events focus the spotlight on corruption in Brazil, but they should not overshadow the many individual reform processes that pushed corruption to center stage.

An analysis of reforms in Brazil over twenty-five years reveals that gradual change has produced a remarkable transformation. Powering in transportation was followed by a long process of problem solving, which, while very slow, has made progress in rebuilding capabilities in this crucial sector for Brazil. In health, the absence of dramatic overhauls and the steady series of problem-solving changes have improved health indicators in many areas, such that Brazil is now held up as an example of successful basic health provision.

Both transportation and health have witnessed impressive advances in transparency and auditing. Whereas the constant powering in Argentina disrupted similar efforts, transparency and accountability have flourished in Brazil. Why? In Argentina the centralization of control in tight-knit reform teams facilitated powering, which disrupted efforts to increase transparency, monitoring, and oversight. By contrast, in Brazil, the president hands over many ministries and agencies to coalitional allies, and, as the recent corruption scandals have highlighted, such political actors often are much more concerned with rent seeking than advancing the executive's governance objectives. Presidents have incentives to keep rent seeking of coalitional allies in government agencies at bay (Bersch, Praça, and Taylor 2017b). At the same time, very often the executive's party is just as interested in rent seeking. As a result, presidents do not plunge headlong into transparency and audit reforms but often are pushed into them. There is a governance logic for enhancing the role of neutral technocrats who can advocate for greater transparency and install controls. In sum, the multiplicity of actors in the Brazilian policy process provides opportunities for civil servants and technocrats to advance their reform objectives.

What can be learned from the comparison between Brazilian reforms in health and transportation? First, even though political-organizational patterns make powering rare, an executive still retains agency. Political-organizational context does not preclude the rise of a president who would be willing and able to push through dramatic change. Collor pushed through powering measures. Thus, the Brazilian case study demonstrates the development of strong patterns of executive power sharing but does not guarantee their endurance.

Second, the comparison underscores the deleterious and enduring consequences of powering. Collor's destruction of transportation agencies left a lasting mark on Brazil. The years of neglect – the result of firing capable professionals in the transport sector (e.g., engineers, auditors, and accountants) – have been corrected very slowly. Rebuilding institutions and capacity takes time. Progress has been made, but Brazil has had to play catch-up in transportation investment and institution building as a result of large-scale blunders decades ago. By contrast, health was never subject to the same type of powering. Although advances have been uneven and have depended to a great degree on politics at other levels (parts of Brazil still have vestiges of authoritarian enclaves), the slow building of institutions over time has contributed to significant advances in health care for Brazilians.

CONCLUSION

This sea change in Brazil was not the result of a political leader rushing through the open door of crisis but rather the product of homegrown, novel, and indirect changes sequenced over time, often quietly and under the radar of political and social forces. Nor was the reorientation of health the product of a clear, comprehensive model; instead, many of the objectives arose from actors within the state addressing problems through existing policy approaches. Broad principles (such as an emphasis on preventative care) guided changes, but the specific means toward achieving broad objectives evolved. Experiential learning was crucial for the gains made in health. Efforts to resolve smaller problems drew on decision-makers' existing knowledge and experience, not abstract planning. And although proponents of reform may have wished for more extensive changes and a quicker process,[56] the multiplicity of actors involved often prompted health reformers to adjust their approach and consider a wider variety of alternatives. Reform coalitions were then crafted slowly along the way. As benefits became clear, coalitions grew strong enough to take on opposition that would have thwarted the entire effort if it had been presented up front, in total.

This chapter also highlighted an important factor underlying the analysis – the quality of the bureaucracy. It showed that not only were parts of the Ministry of Health dominated by clientelistic structures but also that the vast majority of contract officials in Brazil do not enjoy civil service protections and often have very low levels of bureaucratic autonomy and capacity. Nevertheless, civil service structure is subject to change. This chapter demonstrated how reform type significantly affects bureaucratic quality. As the previous chapters demonstrated, powering does not ameliorate but exacerbates governance maladies in the long term; worse, it may further weaken what civil service protections do exist. By contrast, problem solving has a salutary impact by building bureaucratic capacity over time. The existing structure of the civil service matters (Bersch, Praça, and Taylor 2017b), but improvements are possible in areas of weak civil service protection. One reform type – problem solving – has been shown to strengthen civil service norms.

---

[56] Mendes, interview; Nogueira, interview; Rosa, interview.

8

Theoretical Conclusions and Comparative Perspectives

This book advanced a theory of state building that explains why some reform strategies result in sustainable improvements and which political conditions encourage the adoption of successful strategies. The theory rests on evidence from nearly a quarter-century of reform in Latin America, ranging from micro-level details of changes to governmental contracting processes in health and transportation in Brazil and Argentina to cross-national trends of reform approaches.[1] Reform attempts in Brazil and Argentina demonstrate that incremental changes sequenced over time (targeted "problem-solving" reforms) are more effective in reducing corruption, increasing transparency, and enhancing accountability than swift, ambitious overhauls pushed through by political leaders ("powering" reforms).

Analyzing reform strategies and political contexts integrates bounded rationality micro-foundations with organizational macrofactors and to reveal the advantages of problem solving over powering. Existing explanations for successful reform tend to focus on aligning the interests of high-level political actors and building the political will for executing sweeping changes to reorder incentives. Undoubtedly, interests and incentives are important. Yet they alone cannot explain successful public sector reforms; capabilities are also crucial. Building roads and delivering health care are complex processes that require an understanding of congressional budgeting, financing, and procurement as well as issues that impede access. Continual adjustments and modifications engender an incremental learning process that allows reform tactics to evolve along the way. Such

---

[1] See Chapter 3 and the comparative extensions in this chapter.

change often brings results slowly and haltingly, but, over time, these changes often lead to impressive transformations.

Moreover, public sector reform is not a one-shot game. Capabilities change. Interests change. Choosing to pursue powering or problem solving influences the next iteration of changes and thus their durability. Ambitious transformations tend to breed resistance and backlash, but modifications sequenced over time make reform more sustainable and help preserve bureaucratic capacity and autonomy, especially in weak institutional environments. The type of change then not only affects a particular policy area but also shapes bureaucratic capacity for the next wave of reform.

The process-tracing analysis of reforms over time in Argentina and Brazil in the areas of health and transport reveals the failures of powering and the merits of problem solving. Instances of powering in some cases seemed successful in the short term but were plagued by performance problems, pushback, and credibility issues. As a result, powering reforms were subject to reversals in the long term. The deepest, most draconian overhauls of the state resulted in enduring problems. Such overhauls not only were problematic for one or two administrative terms but also in some cases sparked cycles of institutional deterioration, with one set of radical overhauls begetting another. In contrast, problem solving advanced in a frustratingly slow fashion, yet these cautious, gradual changes accumulated to become thorough transformations that tended to be more sustainable. Insiders played an important role in sustaining the reform process. Changes benefited from the scrutiny of a variety of diverse actors and experts within the state who possessed longer time horizons than did politicians and the political technocrats. Thus in both Brazil and Argentina, attempts to achieve short-term policy goals by rapidly revamping the state resulted in long-term problems, whereas problem solving advanced slowly but resulted in impressive transformations over time.

Reform choices are not made in a vacuum, of course, but are conditioned by political-organizational contexts. Exclusionary governing patterns, whereby executive power is concentrated in single-party cabinets, facilitate powering; the ability to appoint loyal experts to key positions in ministries and agencies means that unified reform teams can rapidly impose profound and sweeping changes. Argentine presidents have largely governed in an exclusionary fashion. In many cases, reform teams comprising like-minded loyalists and experts were tasked with designing complex transformations in uncertain conditions. To cope with uncertainty, ambiguity, overabundant information, and time pressure, policymakers – many of whom were newcomers to the federal administration – relied to a great extent on inferential shortcuts, often in the form of such ideological solutions as privatization or nationalization. To execute change before resistance mounted, reformers worked at a lightning pace. Ultimately the powering approach resulted in either poor performance or reversals once the will to sustain dramatic reforms dried up.

Inclusionary governing patterns frustrate big-bang change. Coalitional presidentialism in Brazil has limited the ability of presidents to implement sweeping public sector reforms. The absence of repeated overhauls, moreover, provided opportunities for technical experts within the government to make smaller changes that add up to larger reforms. Whereas policymakers in contexts of executive power sharing are still subject to cognitive limitations, their assumptions tend to be closer to the mark because the approach narrows the scope of changes and draws on the autonomy, experience, and expertise of bureaucratic technocrats. Additionally, the sequencing of reforms contributes to learning over time. In this context, experts can advance change without inciting opposition, so they remain in a position to defend and quietly extend their reforms. If the problem-solving process is successful then there is no need for wholesale overhauls. Paradoxically, however, successful reforms can actually make the situation appear worse in the short term because they expose just how bad corruption is.

The recent cascade of scandals in Brazil, stemming from the investigation into corruption schemes in the state-owned oil company's contracts, has revealed shocking and systematic corruption, implicating high-level political actors of all stripes. It is tempting to conclude that public sector reform in Brazil has largely failed to strengthen institutions and reduce corruption, yet passing judgment now would be premature. That corruption is being investigated and political actors from all parties prosecuted shows the strength of many institutions of accountability. In Brazil today, corruption has become quite sophisticated, especially at the federal level, involving Swiss bank accounts and artwork in exchange for contracts.

State building is a long process. In such countries as the United States and Sweden, making the transition from the spoils systems to a professionalized civil service took decades (Skowronek 1982; Grindle 2012; Teorell and Rothstein 2013). Brazil has taken important steps forward, but progress has been uneven. Different reform approaches applied within the same country or over time help explain the development of bureaucratic "islands of excellence" alongside incapable, and often corrupt, ministries and agencies (Bersch, Praça, and Taylor 2017b; see also Evans

1995, 257; Geddes 1994; Whitehead 2006, 96). Indeed, the coexistence of two different forces of change – high-level political elites and meritocratically recruited civil servants – results in a surprising situation wherein corruption proliferates at certain levels even while strident efforts to rein in corruption develop at others. The efforts of public-minded reformers to increase transparency and accountability have contributed to the unprecedented Lava Jato investigations and the political earthquake that shook Brazilian politics to its core.

At the same time, the implications of this current moment for the future of Brazil remain uncertain.[2] What is remarkable about earthquakes and other abrupt transitions is that they often generate unexpected results. Political crises that trigger sweeping change may reverse advances that have slowly accumulated over years or decades. Only time will tell whether unprecedented events in Brazil will contribute to entrenching or eradicating high-level political corruption.

My argument does not suggest that democracies ought to be left to technocrats. Problem solving does not take the place of politics; rather, problem solving is able to reach its fullest potential only when representative political institutions and civil society are involved. Prior studies of bureaucratic authoritarian regimes suggest that technocratic policymaking, which relies on depoliticizing the state, can empower elites at the expense of the majority (O'Donnell 1973; Garretón 1989). Many issues, such as labor or tax reform, cannot be resolved by problem solving alone (although applying principles of a problem-solving approach early on, before the problem becomes a crisis, may help). Lasting solutions require deeper political agreements. Although problem solving and public sector reform can lead to impressive changes, not all areas can or should be left to experts within the state. Moreover, high-level political actors and political technocrats are responsible for their decisions on political appointments and in such key areas as economic policy. The problem-solving approach cannot be blamed for presidents politicizing Petrobras, for example, nor can the experts in the economic ministries who tried to warn presidents about the consequences of their fiscal shenanigans be blamed for the economic crisis. Democratically elected leaders make crucial, high-level

---

[2] The same could be said of the current moment in Argentina. Although initial interviews suggest that President Mauricio Macri (2015–present) has taken a more gradual approach in many areas, it is still too early to assess the changes under the new administration. Author interviews with Dr. Carlos Javier Regazzoni, Director of PAMI (2015–present), June 28, 2016; interview with transportation official, 2016.

decisions in a number of policy areas, which can either foster or destroy opportunities for steady advances over time. In Latin America and beyond, the neglect of politics and deep political grievances may even set the stage for radical reforms. Indeed, across the developed and developing world, the swell of popular discontent with globalization and the failure of political leaders and the state to address its uneven effects seemed to have sparked a sea change in politics and set the stage for political outsiders to execute sweeping reforms – powering on a grand scale.

Thus, remaining responsive and at the same time providing space for problem solving is a delicate balance, one likely to take different forms depending on context. While the novel alliances between Brazilian bureaucratic actors and civil society highlighted in Chapter 7 are promising, this is clearly an area where more could be done. Nevertheless, as the example of Uruguay in the next section demonstrates, it is possible to marry politics and problem solving. Consensus-building around reforms in Uruguay has involved popular mobilization to a far greater degree than in such countries as Chile and Brazil (Pribble 2013, 40). This has clear implications for democracy. Whereas countries such as Chile and Brazil have low levels of satisfaction with democracy, Uruguay has maintained quite high levels of satisfaction with, and support for, democracy (Corporacion Latinobarometro 2016). Such examples, as well as the development of "civic audits," the *ficha limpa* law and publicly accessible budget data in Brazil suggest that problem solving can emphasize popular mobilization and political engagement. Problem solving and democratic accountability can go hand in hand.

REFORM APPROACHES IN LATIN AMERICA

While focus here falls on health and transportation infrastructure in Brazil and Argentina, my central argument travels well beyond these policy areas and cases. For a case to be consistent with my theory, problem solving would have to result in more effective and enduring change than powering, regardless of political-organizational context. Moreover, countries governed by coalitions or with long-established patterns of power sharing should pursue problem solving to a greater extent. To what extent do these conditions hold in Latin America? Consider five Latin American democracies: Chile, Uruguay, Venezuela, Colombia, and El Salvador.

The Chilean case closely conforms to expectations. Since democratization, Chile has been governed by two relatively stable, broad-based electoral coalitions, enhancing expectations that presidents will govern in an inclusionary manner (Boeninger 1997; Siavelis 2006). In this context, governmental officials should adopt problem solving as their dominant reform strategy, and, indeed, policy reform in Chile has been largely gradual – characterized by some scholars as technocratic (Boeninger 1997), by others as the result of seemingly quotidian processes (Barrientos 2000, 105–11).[3] This moderate approach has been applied in a variety of policy domains, including economic, health, transport infrastructure, contracting, and civil service reform. As expected, this approach has been largely successful in these particular policy areas.[4] Moreover, Chile is undoubtedly the region's leader in terms of establishing effective and enduring policies, outranking the rest of Latin America on a host of governance indicators.[5]

Chile's success is unsurprising, because the country has strong governmental institutions. Problem solving can strengthen institutions over time, but Chile already had a stronger state and a higher level of socio-economic development than its neighbors when it democratized in 1990. Thus ascertaining the cause of its success proves more difficult. The most useful tests in the Chilean context, then, are instances of powering. If powering is effective in states with higher capacity and economic development, then the central argument – that reform approach, independent of other factors, matters for successful change – does not hold.

When powering was applied in Chile, was it effective? The sweeping economic and pension changes during the Pinochet years occurred under an authoritarian, rather than a democratic, regime, so set those issues aside for the moment. But note that even the acclaimed reforms under Pinochet (transformative pension reform, for example, and the school voucher system) have run up against unanticipated problems, sparking public outrage and the largest protests since the return to democracy in 1990 (see Pribble 2017).

---

[3] Some explicitly argue that technocrats constitute a buffer zone between the president and the political parties, serving as mediators between contending social and political forces (Silva 2009, 222–3, 234).

[4] On health, see Barrientos (2000, 105–11); Pribble (2013); Ewig (2008); and Espinosa, Tokman, and Rodríguez (2005). On broader reforms, see Weyland, Madrid, and Hunter (2010). On transport infrastructure, see OECD (2017) and EIU (2014). On procurement, transparency, and models of service provision, see Garretón (2005) and Volosin (2010). On strengthening institutions and state modernization, see Echebarría and Cortázar (2007, 128–9); Armijo (2002); and Stein et al. (2006, 124).

[5] These include *The Economist*'s Infrascope Index, Heritage Foundation's Index of Economic Freedom, and the World Bank's Governance Indicators.

Other powering reforms in Chile have fallen short of expectations. For instance, Chile's Transantiago, a radical attempt to revamp the Santiago bus system, represented a significant instance of powering in country that has – as a democracy – tended to pursue problem solving. On paper, it seemed like a good idea to replace an informal system with one comprehensively planned to rely on large, modern buses so as to reduce noise, congestion, and exhaust fumes. Despite meticulous blueprints for the ambitious reform and extensive research on the informal bus system, however, the implementation of the new system created chaos, resulting in a nightmare for commuters.[6] As my theory predicts, the breadth and speed of the changes heighten the complexity of the feat, swamping cognitive abilities of even the most impressive planners. Despite subsequent problem-solving efforts and substantial increases in funding, ten years later *The Economist* titled its assessment of the ambitious scheme "Going Nowhere: The Capital's Public-transport System is Sputtering." A prominent think tank remarked that Transantiago was one of Chile's worst public-policy projects since the country's return to democracy. Notably this revamping of transportation was one of the few attempts at powering.[7] Thus, even in Chile, with its high levels of state capacity, when powering does occur it falls short of delivering the expected results.

Policymaking in Uruguay likewise relies on problem solving but for more complex reasons. Given Uruguay's formal institutional framework and its low rank on the index of coalitional necessity, Uruguayan presidents might be expected to employ an exclusionary approach, appointing single-party cabinets, and apply a powering approach more frequently than inclusionary countries like Chile. Yet because of the long-standing importance of factions in Uruguay, patterns of power sharing have developed, with presidents governing in an inclusionary fashion (Altman 2000; Magar and Moraes 2012). Thus policymaking in Uruguay proves the point that formal institutions contribute to, but do not determine, patterns of power sharing. Historical practices also matter.

The Uruguayan case also reveals that popular participation and problem solving can go hand in hand. Measures like the Constitution's Article 79, which allows a plebiscite to repeal legislation within one year of its passage (Panizza 2004, 10), have fostered a political climate of developing reform with broad popular support.[8] Thus, problem solving in Uruguay

---

[6] *The Economist*, February 7, 2008.   [7] *The Economist*, April 15, 2017.
[8] In other areas, such as civil service reform, change has been deliberately given a low profile (Panizza 2004).

seems to strike a balance between responding to popular opinion and limiting reform scope to advance change in a context of a plurality of political demands. Change becomes not only cognitively but also politically feasible.[9] Veto players can include their priorities in the debate and block policy choices, encouraging more inclusionary, consensual governing practices (Castiglioni 2000). The results of the problem-solving strategy have been remarkable in a range of policy areas.[10] Compared with its neighbors, Uruguay is cited as the least corrupt country and has made some of the greatest improvements in terms of strengthening institutions, all while maintaining high confidence in democracy.[11]

If the case of Uruguay illustrates the importance of historical patterns of power sharing, Venezuela demonstrates that these are not necessarily determinative. Venezuela could be expected to opt for a mixture of problem solving and powering, given that it lies between Argentina and Brazil on the index of coalitional necessity. Yet following the collapse of the country's party system in 1999 (Morgan 2011; Corrales and Penfold 2011; Hawkins 2010), Hugo Chávez relied on powering to a far greater extent than elsewhere in the region, extending the approach not only to state reforms but also to political institutions, which he reworked to his advantage.[12] It is beyond the scope of this book to explain popular support of Chávez, but the case of Venezuela suggests that determined reformers under certain circumstances can transform broader institu-

---

[9] Pribble notes in her analysis of health reform: "In Uruguay, the path toward health reform was characterized by a complicated process of political negotiation and coalition building, whereas in Chile the reform process was top-down and involved elite maneuvering but virtually no mobilization" (Pribble 2013, 40). Such accounts are typical of other policy areas as well.

[10] On health, see Pribble (2013); on broader reforms, see Weyland, Madrid, and Hunter (2010, 171). On public administration reform, see Echebarría and Cortázar (2007). On pensions, see Taylor (2008, 132–51) and Bergara et al. (2006). On transportation and neoliberal reforms, see Blake (1998) and Panizza (2004). On transparency and anti-corruption, see Martini (2016).

[11] For example, see Blake (1998) on specific reforms, Transparency International's Corruption Perceptions Index (2016), and the World Bank's Worldwide Governance Indicators (Kaufmann and Kraay 2016).

[12] For a summary of the dramatic changes and state intervention on constitutional changes, see Haggard and Kaufman (2008, 275–6). On changes to the public administration and mechanisms of accountability, see Corrales and Penfold (2011). On changes in "pockets of efficiency," see Monaldi et al. (2008, 410–11). On health and missions, see Hawkins, Rosas, and Johnson (2011); Hawkins (2010); Handlin (2012); Ortega and Rodríguez (2008, 7); D'Elia and Quiroz (2010, 8); and Pribble (2013, 158–68). For a summary of economic changes, see *The Economist* (February 14, 2015).

tional constraints.[13] Moreover, the results of Chávez's radical reforms conform to the expectation of my argument: Powering is less effective and enduring than problem solving. As I write, the situation in Venezuela could not be bleaker: Thousands of Venezuelans are fleeing starvation, a collapsed health system, hyperinflation, and political persecutions.

Given the crisis in Venezuela, it is easy to forget that, only a decade before, aspects of Chávez's sweeping powering approach seemed promising (Gibbs 2006; Weisbrot 2008; Ellner 2008).[14] Venezuela maintained some of the highest levels of growth in the region from 2003 to 2008 and achieved striking success in boosting popular well-being in the course of a few years (see Weyland, Madrid, and Hunter 2010, 142–3). Moreover, from 1996 to 2007, the percent of Latinobarometer survey respondents who were very or somewhat satisfied with democracy rose from 30 percent in 1996 to 59 percent in 2007 (Corporación Latinobarómetro 2007, 91).

The case of Venezuela, however, illustrates the paradox of powering on a grand scale. The first step of reform – attacking existing institutions – means that achievements are weakly institutionalized and short-lived. Sweeping changes such as the Misiones Bolivarianas, a series of social programs aimed at eliminating illiteracy, reducing poverty, and providing basic health-care services to low-income Venezuelans, seemed to achieve quick results in the short term (Hawkins, Rosas, and Johnson 2011). Nevertheless, the approach that made quick gains possible – concentration of power at the apex of the state, reliance on loyal reformers and outsiders to bypass opposition, use of off-budget oil revenues to circumvent legislative oversight, and creation of programs from scratch – weakened existing institutions. Mechanisms of horizontal accountability were gutted, polarization increased, and new institutions were so weak as to prove unsustainable. Any advances that might have occurred have largely been swept away in the devastating aftermath of dramatic powering reforms.

---

[13] While the power-sharing approach that preceded Chávez might suggest that Venezuela was characterized by inclusionary governing practices, the Puntofijo Pact ultimately resulted in the exclusionary dominance of the Democratic Action (*Acción Democrática*, AD) and Social Christian (*Partido Socialcristiano*, COPEI) parties, which may well have led to Venezuelan demand for a radical reformer.

[14] I do not include Chávez's successor, Nicolás Maduro, here because by the time he assumed power, democracy has been eroded to such an extent that Venezuela can no longer be classified as a democracy.

What would my theory predict in the cases of Colombia and El Salvador? Given their middle-range scores on the index of coalitional necessity, we would expect a mixture of reform approaches. The theory would also predict that policy areas where problem-solving reforms have been applied have seen more success than those where the powering approach was employed.

Colombia was governed for years by a pact determining that Liberals and Conservatives alternated in the presidency, with elected positions allocated in equal parts. Such power sharing has contributed to moderate policy change. The inclusionary approach continued under the new Constitution of 1991, which ended the pact but extended the powers of other political actors. Even under President Álvaro Uribe, who preferred a powering approach, political checks on exclusionary tendencies remained strong. In a wide variety of areas, Colombian technocrats have eschewed dramatic changes and applied a problem-solving approach. Neoliberal reforms that were implemented in the 1990s, for example, fell below the regional median in terms of their depth and level of change (Morley, Machado, and Pettinato 1999). The gradual, step-by-step approach has been credited for enhancing policy stability over the long run as well as for shielding the Colombian economy from sudden shocks (Botero 2005; Dargent 2015, 77).

As predicted, however, reforms that leaned toward powering led to unintended consequences, as in the case of Colombian health reform Law 100 (1993). Although the process included some elements of both powering and problem solving,[15] scholars have characterized the sweeping overhaul as one of the more – if not the most – comprehensive transformations of a national health system in the history of Latin America (Nelson 2004; Dargent 2011, 119). Its most ambitious aspect – the attempt to place all citizens into a single, two-tiered health-care system[16] – has produced the

---

[15] Some aspects of the process retained hallmarks of problem solving, such as the prominence of domestic expertise. Instead of relying on the pure Chilean blueprints, both pension and health reforms were modified considerably based on lessons learned from the limits of the private-sector approach and the Colombian context. The process of crafting changes was more consensual than pension reform in countries such as El Salvador (Mesa-Lago and Müller 2002) and afforded a larger role for domestic experts, who advocated for less radical reforms in order to sidestep anticipated resistance (Mesa-Lago, Córdova, and Lopéz 1994, 86–7; Weyland 2006, 105–7). Thus, the pension and health reforms in Colombia cannot be classified as a purely powering or problem-solving approach.

[16] The new health law technically placed all citizens into a single health-care system, but the regime had two tiers based on the ability to pay (Dargent 2011, 121), with the private

most disappointing outcomes. Years after implementation, the quality of care under the two systems varies dramatically,[17] owing in large part to models based on overly optimistic levels of growth and employment.[18] The expectation that two-thirds of the population would be covered by an expanded contributory scheme did not occur; as of 2015, over half belonged to the government-funded insurance, leading workers to remain in the informal economy.[19] Inaccurate models, combined with unpredictable rulings by the Constitutional Court mandating the same benefit plans and expensive pharmaceuticals for both systems, resulted in severe fiscal challenges.[20] At a mere 73.81 years, Colombia's life expectancy is one of the lowest in the region (World Bank 2013), and efforts to reduce avoidable mortality have stagnated (Yepes Luján 2010, 120–22). In these and many other ways, the sweeping overhaul to health care in Colombia has created unintended consequences and yielded disappointing outcomes.[21]

Yet instead of repealing Law 100 and attempting another overhaul to the health sector, Colombian policymakers have largely taken a problem-solving approach. To address problems created by the Court's rulings, for example, the health ministry has developed a body that makes decisions, on a case-by-case basis, about which drugs provide value for the money; the ministry has started to require payments from those who can afford prescriptions. The long follow-up to Law 100 has contributed to lower out-of-pocket costs, enhanced equity in rural–urban coverage, and improved targeting of subsidies for the poorest citizens (Yepes Luján 2010, 119–20). Thus, health reform in Colombia corroborates the argument that the challenges of crafting a sweeping reform result in unintended and enduring consequences. At the same time, this case also

---

scheme compensating the public system. The expectation was that the two programs would equalize by 2001. These expectations were not borne out.

[17] The Colombian ombudsman showed that between 2006 and 2008, 53 percent of the claims under the non-contributory system had been denied by insurance companies (Yepes Luján 2010, 119).

[18] Models expected the economy to grow by over 5 percent and unemployment be in the single digits (*The Economist*, February 4, 2010).

[19] *The Economist*, February 13, 2016. This was the argument of Health Minister Alejandro Gaviria.

[20] Moreover, the massive overhaul left countless grey zones, especially in terms of implementation. Health reform occurred together with decentralization and thus muddled clear lines of responsibility for instituting changes.

[21] Some scholars go as far as to argue that "the consequences of [Colombia's] ... model have been a consolidation of resources in the hands of the insurance companies, the widening of social inequalities, and the abandonment of public health" (Álvarez and Torres-Tovar 2010, 177).

suggests that following up powering with problem solving may gradually ameliorate some of the most problematic aspects of wholesale reforms.

The Colombian case reveals an additional important insight into the application of my theory in other contexts. Outsider technocrats in Colombia often emerge as the heroes of reform processes (see Dargent 2015). External to the state, technocrats are frequently non-bureaucratic actors hired to conduct reforms; often they adopt a problem-solving strategy.[22] This offers an important lesson for politicians in countries with weak states: Even outsider reformers can problem-solve. In many weak states throughout the developing world, no core of experts exists within the state, and politicians struggle to find internal experts. In such cases, outsiders can recognize their own limitations in understanding the bureaucratic context within which they work and can pursue a moderate approach to reform – phasing in reform steps and working with the existing bureaucratic framework to advance change.

Insights into powering and problem solving also help explain reform outcomes in El Salvador, long considered a paradox. After the return to democracy in El Salvador, presidents from the conservative Nationalist Republican Alliance (*Alianza Repúblicana Nacionalista*, ARENA) held power for twenty years (1989–2009). They employed a big-bang style of public policymaking, facilitated by their majority support in Congress. Under ARENA presidents, Salvadoran technocrats – supported by the expertise of economists and IFIs – implemented a coherent set of reforms that included trade liberalization, financial sector strengthening, privatization, and comprehensive tax reform (Lora 2007, 271; World Bank 2015, 2). Many economists and observers regarded El Salvador as a darling of reform, a textbook case for implementing reforms that increase growth (Spalding 2014, 45).[23] Yet according to my theory, these

---

[22] In a detailed study of the rise of economic technocrats in Colombia, Dargent (2011) demonstrates how technocrats – who were frequently outsiders, moving in and out of the state from positions in business, consulting, and academia – used their expertise to gain considerable autonomy from their political superiors over time. Taking a cautious and technical approach, and playing actors off one another, allowed them to safeguard their positions. Studies of Colombia by Dargent and the reflections of economic technocrats suggest that experts' deliberate but gradual changes shaped both policy and entrenched technical expertise and autonomy over time in a process that Botero, one of the first technocrats, calls "intelligent design" (Botero 2005; quoted in Dargent 2011, 77).

[23] Between 1990 and 1995, El Salvador's per capita GDP grew by almost 4 percent per year. In 1995, the World Bank's Country Economic Memorandum argued that "stabilization and adjustment measures implemented since 1989 and the return to peace have laid the foundations for sustained growth in El Salvador."

powering reforms should produce disappointing results, because the sheer complexity and uncertainty they entail push the cognitive abilities of designers and implementers past their limit. Moreover, we might expect that areas spared sweeping reforms experienced problem solving.

In fact, this is precisely what we see in El Salvador. Optimism about dramatic reforms gave way to disappointment as overhauls underperformed against expectations.[24] El Salvador was in many ways a "best-case" scenario for powering. The World Bank and other economists and experts agreed that the reforms were sound. The political party responsible for the reforms remained in power for twenty years, which precluded reform reversal. Nonetheless, the results proved disappointing. Thus, my theory sheds light on a compelling puzzle yet to be explained by economists.[25]

My argument can also help explain surprising advances in El Salvador. Areas such as health, where reform efforts appeared inadequate, have nevertheless gone on to make important advances. Health institutions were spared the dramatic changes that cut across so many other policy areas in El Salvador under ARENA. This problem-solving approach continued in 2009, when the opposition party FMLN assumed the presidency. Instead of upending social ministries and programs, the Funes and Sánchez Cerén administrations have steadily increased access to basic support by removing user fees for existing public institutions, an idea initiated by the previous administration (Perla and Cruz-Feliciano 2013, 89; Clark 2015, 103; PAHO 2014, 37).[26] Early indications suggest that the problem-solving approach to health has yielded impressive outcomes in improving care on a variety of indicators (see PAHO 2014). For

[24] Growth after 1996 slowed and, since 2000, fell well below the rates observed in lower-middle-income countries (World Bank 2015, 2). Out of seventy-two countries for which roughly comparable data on household income is available, only five had a lower growth of mean income than El Salvador since 2000 (World Bank 2015, 2). Despite the unbroken string of reforms led by ARENA governments until 2009, about 43 percent of the population remained in poverty throughout the 2000s, and El Salvador's rate of poverty reduction was well below its peers in Latin America and other lower-middle-income countries (World Bank 2015, ii). In the early 2000s, nearly half of the houses in the country were without water connections, and 1 million households – two-thirds of El Salvador's population – were without a sewerage connection (World Bank 2006, 4).

[25] The El Salvador paradox may have even contributed to some economists turning to a more incremental approach, by tackling "binding constraints" and an experimental approach (Rodrik 2010).

[26] Such efforts have been left to sector experts and have drawn on a nationwide poverty map, developed under previous administrations, which the Funes administration used to steer implementation toward the poorest municipalities first (Spalding 2014, 219).

example, while infant mortality rates remain relatively high for the region, the Salvadoran health sector has seen striking improvements over time, with rates falling from 45.9 deaths per 1,000 live births in 1990 to 15.4 in 2013 (World Bank 2013). Thus, even in a context where sweeping reforms were the norm and political polarization was high, problem solving and gradual institution building are possible.

Despite the failures of the powering approach in El Salvador and promises of problem solving, a recent World Bank publication calls for doubling down on the powering strategy, arguing that to break vicious circles, a "big push" is needed (World Bank 2015, 7). Other recent reports on social infrastructure have argued for the "implementation of an integrated legal, regulatory, institutional and financial strategy" (World Bank 2006, 1). The argument advanced in this book suggests that this strategy is wrongheaded and likely to create more problems than it solves. Designing changes that are both cognitively and politically feasible is essential for policy reform and the success of state building over the long haul.

What do we learn from these additional cases? Problem-solving reforms are: (a) more common in countries with coalitional governments and countries with long-established power-sharing approaches; and (b) more likely to succeed. Coalitions and inclusionary governing patterns in Chile, Uruguay, and Brazil have contributed to policy stability and a problem-solving approach. In these cases, authority to craft details has often been relegated to experts within the state in order to advance changes in the midst of complex negotiations between political parties and factions. We would not expect Uruguay to undertake problem solving, based on the index of coalitional necessity, yet entrenched patterns of factional power sharing have contributed to an inclusionary approach. This case, then, strengthens the argument and underscores the importance of established political arrangements. As expected, Colombia and El Salvador have largely taken mixed approaches, with policy changes in Colombia falling closer to the problem-solving side of the reform spectrum and those in El Salvador falling closer to the powering side. Finally, exclusionary governing styles in Venezuela and Argentina have contributed to powering. The extreme nature of powering in Venezuela underscores that political-organizational patterns can change and illustrates that determined reformers in some cases can transform broader institutional constraints. Thus, while contextual factors are important for influencing change, examining reform choices remains essential for understanding successful state building and institutional change.

The additional cases provide further evidence of the second claim: Problem solving is more effective and enduring than powering. In the long run, countries that have pursued problem solving as the predominant reform strategy have outperformed those that employed a powering approach. Undoubtedly, this brief assessment of reforms cannot account for all of the factors that shape reform outcomes. Nonetheless, the cases that provide the clearest illustration of the argument are those where reforms have diverged from the dominant reform approach, revealing that reform choices matter regardless of a priori levels of state capacity and political-organizational context. Powering reforms tend to produce failed results, even in countries such as Chile and Colombia with higher state capacity. Conversely, problem-solving reforms have resulted in more effective and enduring changes, even in countries such as El Salvador where, despite relatively lower levels of state capacity ex ante, health reform has gone on to produce notable achievements.

Comparative Extensions

To what extent can these considerations be applied to other contexts? What about notable big-bang reforms in other countries: Thatcherism in Britain, Chile under Pinochet, Hong Kong's rapid reduction of corruption, police reform in the Republic of Georgia, or the development of Indonesia's Anti-Corruption Commission? While the argument that crafting comprehensive transformations requires tremendous computational capacity and imposing radical changes breeds resistance (as well as backlash) should apply broadly, it plays out in slightly different ways that highlight the importance of a priori levels of state capacity, time horizons of reformers, and levels of democratic accountability.

Developed democracies, which tend have higher levels of state capacity and political autonomy than developing countries, initially seem less susceptible to the perils of powering. Problems are less likely to lead to crises when institutions are strong in the first place, weakening the allure of the powering approach. When dramatic overhauls are instituted, they are more likely to be implemented by professional civil services and other actors with longer time horizons that follow up the changes with problem solving so as to mitigate long-term damage. For instance, compared to most cases in the developing world, the civil service that implemented Thatcherism in Britain was quite capable. Moreover, strong institutions mean that powering is more likely followed up with the types of second-order changes that render grand reform plans viable.

Although such developed-world mechanisms may attenuate resistance and backlash to such changes, they do not eliminate the possibility of reversals. Recent US health reform, known as Obamacare, though far from a pure powering reform[27] was closer to powering than many policy changes in the country and shows that the threat of backlash and reversal is ever-present, even in developed countries. A strong state can buffer the effect of powering, but the dangers of the approach should not be dismissed in the developed world.

Institution building is a long process. Institutional destruction, however, is rapid, and the polarization it can cause is enduring. Argentina's initial success in state building and subsequent reversal of fortune offers a clear example of this. The lesson for the developed world, then, is the same: Powering can eviscerate the state and leave the political landscape so polarized that frequent, radical change becomes the norm rather than the exception.

What, then, can be said of powering in non-democracies? After all, Pinochet pursued comprehensive transformations and employed a powering approach in Chile, which emerged from this period with a stable economy and some of the most effective institutions in the region. Other countries such as Singapore and Hong Kong have also made great strides in reducing corruption and improving service delivery. In authoritarian regimes, the nature of time horizons and veto players is fundamentally distinct; government officials do not have the same type of preoccupations about the next election and often are able to crush resistance. Accordingly, a cautious and careful approach to policy change in such a context may proceed more quickly than in democracies. Yet even in Chile, Pinochet's application of powering was not free from the reform strategy's characteristic flaws. His dramatic overhaul resulted in economic collapse in 1982, and only after a long problem-solving process did the situation improve. Thus, regardless of context, consistent effort over an extended period of time proves more effective. China's steady transformation seems to have relied on strategies akin to problem solving, which Chinese revolutionary Deng Xiaoping described as *mozhe shitou guo he*, or "crossing the river by feeling for stones" (qtd. in Cook 2016, 229). Admittedly, evaluating reform in non-democratic settings sets aside issues of accountability, which changes the parameters within which reformers

---

[27] Obamacare built on successful experiments and was in some respects piecemeal. The transition to a single-payer system would have pulled the change closer to the powering side of the reform spectrum.

work, but nonetheless these other case studies resonate with elements of the core argument.

What of other powering exemplars, such as police reform in Georgia, the development of the Corruption Eradication Commission (*Komisi Pemberantasan Korupsi*, KPK) in Indonesia, and the Independent Commission Against Corruption (ICAC) in Hong Kong? Changes to increase the meritocracy, capacity, and autonomy of the public sector often do not require the same type of comprehensive, coherent planning as single-shot attempts to transform the health sector. Because such reforms tend to be less complex than overhauls of nationwide systems such as health care or transportation, cognitive constraints do not come into play in the same way as for other types of reforms. In democracies and non-democracies alike, perhaps the most successful powering efforts transform the characteristics of those in the government through impartial recruitment of the best and brightest.

Nonetheless, other risks of the powering approach remain, and charging boldly ahead may endanger the whole reform enterprise. Even when recruitment is meritocratic and politically impartial, if it is carried out swiftly it will very often trigger resistance and become associated with the instigator of reforms, tainting the perception of impartiality. Thus, the paradox of powering comes into play: After the instigator leaves, the successor may consider even an impartial police force to be loyal to the politician who led the changes. The same concentrated power used to transform the force may again be used to dismantle the reforms. It is too early to draw conclusions, but this seems to be the case of police reform in Georgia. What was initially considered a success story now seems like a presidential overreach by Mikheil Saakashvili (Kupatadze 2016). As a result, the staying power of even this exemplar is questionable. The same dynamics may eventually play out for the KPK in Indonesia as well. Nonetheless, thanks to its incremental approach, which allowed popular support to build slowly over time, the KPK seems to hold a degree of protection from changes in political forces (Bolongaita 2010).

The conclusion that can be drawn from such notable cases is that the powering approach, even if it brings short-term benefits in certain circumstances, entails tremendous risks in terms of sustainability. For powering efforts to succeed in creating or replacing agencies or police forces, the cautious application of power over longer time horizons is required. It is not surprising, therefore, that in Hong Kong, under the stable rule of a British-appointed governor, efforts were more successful in building state capacity over time (Klitgaard 1988). The rarity of such stability suggests that powering is a very risky strategy in most cases.

There is, of course, an alternative option, which provides some of the advantages of boldly reforming the public sector without the high risks: namely, implementing meritocratic recruitment more gradually. In Brazil, for instance, instead of firing public sector workers, reformers enhanced meritocratic recruitment as holdovers from prior years slowly retired. There is no one surefire strategy for such step-by-step improvements, but in a variety of cases a competent civil service has emerged from small efforts that accumulate over time (Grindle 2012).

Finally, while the lessons from this analysis of public sector reform in Latin America ought to apply to other developing democracies, they do not necessarily hold true for countries in the midst of violent conflict or those emerging from authoritarian regimes. In such situations, the very process of establishing democratic institutions could be considered a sweeping reform. Yet even in those contexts, preserving whatever ability the state has to carry out essential functions has proven an important element in transitions. In Iraq, for example, the dismantling of existing institutions and process of de-Baathification has left the state unable to provide many basic goods and services, potentially jeopardizing democratizing efforts. Thus a certain type of problem solving may be advisable even in dire situations.

Broader Theoretical Implications

It has been well established that political rationality is distinctly bounded (Simon 1990; Baumgartner, Jones, and Wilkerson 2011). The cognitive constraints on policymakers mean that, instead of proactively seeking out alternatives, calculating advantages and disadvantages, and using balanced logical calculations to select a solution, they regularly deviate from such rational standards, often by seeking a satisfactory rather than an optimal solution (Simon 1956; Bendor 2003). It has also been well established that the extent to which cognitive constraints bind depends on the computational capabilities of the actor (Simon and Simon 1962). Grandmasters in chess outperform duffers, just as a well-trained engineer will be more successful than a construction worker at designing a bridge. The bounds of rationality are not uniform.

What has often been overlooked, however, is a second vital factor important for shaping the bounds of rationality: namely, the complexity of the task at hand (Simon 1990, 7; Bendor 2003, 435; 2010, 3).

Policymaking tasks in the twenty-first century vary tremendously, from minor adjustments (e.g., increasing public health insurance recipients) to radical overhauls that aim to get to the root of numerous problems simultaneously. Therefore, cognitive constraints are determined not only by computational capabilities but also by the correspondence between ability and the complexity of the problem. Simon explains that "the structure of task environments and the computation capabilities of the actor" have joint effects and are like "scissors [with] two blades" (Simon 1990, 7; Bendor 2003, 435). It is, then, the relationship between a decision-maker's mental abilities and the information-processing demands of the problem at hand that determines whether cognitive constraints will "show through" (Simon 1996).

This point is often missed by social scientists (Bendor 2010, 3). Yet theories of bounded rationality, as Bendor highlights, have cutting power – especially relative to rational choice – only when the two blades operate (Bendor 2003, 435). And both do operate in my framework: Problem solving leads to both (1) more experienced and competent decision-makers and (2) more manageable tasks by dividing complex reforms into pieces. By contrast, powering results in (1) less experienced decision-makers and (2) terrifically complex task environments. Accordingly, we might expect cognitive limitations to always bind in the case of powering, whereas bounds of rationality loosen when experienced decision-makers modify an existing policy or experiment with a new approach.

Moreover, problem solving results in an additional advantage: learning over time. In the sequential process of solving smaller problems, reformers acquire a repertoire of pragmatic moves and their results, increasing their ability to recognize solutions to a given problem (Simon 1990, 1996). This engenders a learning process whereby policymakers enhance their cognitive resources via experiential learning. By contrast, powering requires getting reforms right in one shot. As President Collor of Brazil once famously said, "I have only one bullet to kill the tiger of inflation." Powering requires an optimal solution, whereas problem solving works even with decision-makers who seek not the best option but an acceptable option. They can then learn and correct later (Simon 1956).

The cognitive resources of decision-makers are often conceptualized in terms of expertise; i.e., the education and sophistication of actors. As regards Latin American policymaking, foreign-educated technocrats might come to mind. Certainly education-derived knowledge is important, but often such high-profile experts have been brought in to implement grand, one-size-fits-all solutions, only to leave office with the political leader who appointed them. My theory and empirical cases emphasize a different component of expertise: experience, which allows capabilities to build over time.

Bureaucrats have often been given a bad name: They drag their feet, resist change, and would prefer to go home early. This is fair in some cases, but often is not. In countless hours spent interviewing civil servants in Brazil and Argentina, I heard story after story about their efforts to resist political leaders' sweeping overhauls of the public sector because the changes either did not address the problems at hand or would not be sustainable. Deep contextual understanding is especially crucial for designing administrative reform. This knowledge develops over time, with experience. Furthermore, longer time horizons free such technocrats and civil servants from the need to advance their preferred changes all at once. Thus, my application of bounded rationality to reform decision-making highlights not only the importance of considering the complexity of the problem at hand but also the importance of expertise developed by experiential learning over time.

By applying these insights to my analysis of state reform and integrating them with macrofactors, this study also contributes to the literature on historical institutionalism. The classical version of historical institutionalism is well suited to explain continuity but not change. According to this paradigm, critical junctures – rare moments of uncertainty when the rules of the game are in flux – are followed by long stretches of continuity.

This historical institutional model does not, however, characterize the empirical reality of the reforms in this study. Instead of a big bang followed by continuity, radical change in Argentina has been recurring. Over the course of the twentieth century, the country's trains have been nationalized, then privatized, then nationalized, and on it goes. The same has been true in a number of different areas, with some agencies experiencing complete overhauls during each executive term. Scholars like Steven Levitsky and Victoria Murillo (2014), focusing on such overarching institutional changes as constitutional replacement, argue that radical and recurring change, or serial replacement, is quite common in Latin America. The change pendulum swings back and forth, but more quickly than most models of change would suggest, as if the clock of change sped up. But where are the long stretches of continuity? Such patterns of frequent and radical change do not follow the patterns postulated by historical institutionalists or by punctuated equilibrium theorists (Jones and Baumgartner 2005; Mahoney and Thelen 2010; cf. Levitsky and Murillo 2014).

Changes in Brazil likewise fail to conform to the historical institutionalist models. Incremental changes in Brazil were seldom triggered by a critical juncture yet often went on to be transformative and lasting. At the same time, policymaking cannot be accurately characterized as stable and unchanging. Brazil has changed substantially since the early 1990s (cf. Mainwaring 1995). Nevertheless, that change is hard to pin to particular events. Even the unprecedented corruption investigations, while perhaps seeming like a turning point, represent the accumulation and culmination of changes over time.

Neither radical and recurrent nor incrementally transformative change is explained by existing paradigms. My theory addresses this lacuna and contributes to efforts at theory construction within historical institutionalism by drawing on the work of scholars who focus on micro-foundations of change (e.g., Simon 1990; Baumgartner, Jones, and Wilkerson 2011) while embedding such insights in organizational context (Weyland 2014). Why do we see patterns of radical recurring change in some countries and incremental transformations in others? Under what conditions might we expect more proportionate changes? What explains variation in collective information processing?

This study has demonstrated how established governing patterns mediate the bounds of rationality and help explain patterns of policy change. Patterns of executive power sharing and expectations regarding coalitional formation – concepts of classical historical institutionalism – play a crucial role in this theory because they shape who is involved in the reform process and the type of reform that will likely be selected.

The importance of history in the study of politics has long been underscored by scholars of historical institutionalism. This study integrates this approach with bounded rationality and provides micro-foundations that explain why history is so important. Overhauling institutions and dismissing large swaths of the public sector have long-lasting effects because they shape collective cognitive capabilities. Cognitive capabilities are built over time and enhanced by experience and memory; when they are lost, no amount of political will can recreate them quickly. Nearly twenty-five years after powering reforms in Brazil wiped out almost all the engineers, accountants, and auditors in the transport sector, the country is still struggling to rebuild capacity in those areas. By developing this line of reasoning, my study draws theoretical connections between historical institutionalism and bounded rationality, in addition to explaining new types of institutional change.

Additionally, the findings of this book have important implications for the study of state reform. Policy studies often focus on specific episodes, such as the passage, implementation, or initial effects of an important policy. Problem solving in any of these isolated instances appears quite unimpressive: a small adjustment here, a modification there. This research, however, shows that we only understand the impact of reform type fully if we look at a whole sequence of modifications. An observer of only the first stretch of the race between the tortoise and the hare would declare the hare the champion. Likewise, victory should not be declared before reforms have withstood three or more administrative cycles. A significant time frame is also important for evaluating problem solving because it allows researchers to demonstrate continuity and to see how small improvements accumulate into more impressive transformations. In sum, employing longer time horizons, as this and other studies demonstrate (Patashnik 2008; Jacobs 2011), reveals previously obscured factors crucial for understanding successful governance reforms.

Finally, this study has important implications for policymakers and practitioners. My argument suggests that established governing patterns limit the option to power or problem solve in a given country. When a choice exists between relying on political leaders to support institutional overhauls or working within the bureaucracy to sequence modest changes over time, decision-makers would be wise to opt for the latter and work with the institutions they inherit. The current cascade of corruption scandals in Brazil, and the resulting protests that erupted in 2013 over corruption and poor quality of services, might seem an opportunity to press for grand, sweeping change. The findings of this study, however, suggest that this would be a mistake. Progress in institution building in Brazil has occurred gradually and haltingly, but its advancements have been significant. Public interest in corruption and the quality of service delivery indeed play an essential role in continuing such advancements; however, the lessons of this study suggest that the most ambitious reforms aimed at increasing transparency and enhancing accountability, paradoxically, can weaken institutions over time.

Abbreviations

Chapter 3

FREPASO: Front for a Country in Solidarity (*Frente por un País Solidario*)

PFL: Liberal Front Party (*Partido da Frente Liberal*)

PMDB: Brazilian Democratic Movement Party (*Partido do Movimento Democrático Brasileiro*)

PRN: National Reconstruction Party (*Partido da Reconstrução Nacional*)

PSDB: Brazilian Social Democracy Party (*Partido da Social Democracia Brasileira*)

PT: Workers' Party (*Partido dos Trabalhadores*)

UCR: Radical Civic Union (*Unión Cívica Radical*)

Chapter 4

ADIF: Administración de Infraestructura Ferroviarias S.E.

AGP: General Port Administration (*Administración General de Puertos*)

AGN: National Audit Body (*Auditoría General de la Nación*)

ALL: América Latina Logística

CNRT: National Transportation Regulatory Commission (*Comisión Nacional de Regulación del Transporte*)

DNU: Decreto de Necesidad y Urgencia

DNV: National Highway Agency

OCCOVI: Agency of Road Concessions

SOFSE: Sociedad Operadora Ferroviaria Sociedad del Estado, or Trenes Argentinos

UGOFE: Unidad de Gestión Operativa Ferroviaria de Emergencia

Chapter 5
BNDES: Development Bank
DNIT: National Department of Transport Infrastructure (*Departamento Nacional de Infraestrutura de Transportes*)
DNER: National Department of Roads and Highways (*Departamento Nacional de Estradas de Rodagem*)
FRN: National Road Fund (*Fundo Rodoviário Nacional*)
GEIPOT: Transport Planning Agency (*Grupo Executivo de Integração da Política de Transporte*)
PAC: Growth Acceleration Program (*Programa de Aceleração do Crescimento*)
PNLT: National Logistics and Transport Plan (*Plano Nacional de Logística de Transportes*)
PPI: Pilot Project for Investment (*Projecto Piloto de Investimento*)
RDC: Differential Contracting Regime (*Regime Diferenciado de Contratações Públicas*)
TCU: Federal Court of Accounts (*Tribunal de Contas de União*)

Chapter 6
AGN: National Audit Body (*Auditoría General de la Nación*)
APE: Administration of Special Programs (*Administración de Programas Especiales*)
INAP: National Office of Employment (*Instituto Nacional de la Administración Pública*)
PAMI: Program of Integrated Medical Assistance (*Programa de Atención Médica Integral*)
SSS: Superintendency of Health Services (*Superintendencia de Servicios de Salud*)

Chapter 7
Anatel: National Telecommunications Agency (*Agência Nacional de Telecomunicações*)
CATMAT: Catalog of Materials (*Catálogo de Materiais*)
CNS: National Health Council (*Conselho Nacional de Saúde*)
CPI: congressional inquiry committee (*Comissão Parlamentar de Inquérito*)
DLSG: Department of Logistics and General Services (*Departamento de Logística e Serviços Gerais*)
ESF: Family Health Strategy (*Estratégia de Saúde da Família*)
LRF: Fiscal Responsibility Bill (*Lei de Responsabilidade Fiscal*)
OSS: Social Organizations in Health

PSF: Family Health Program (*Programa Saúde da Família*)

RDC: Differential Contracting Regime (*Regime Diferenciado de Contratações Públicas*)

SICONV: *Sistema de Gestão de Convênios e Contratos de Repasse*

SUS: Unified Health System (*Sistema Único de Saúde*)

TCU: Federal Court of Accounts (*Tribunal de Contas de União*)

Chapter 8

ARENA: Nationalist Republican Alliance (*Alianza Repúblicana Nacionalista*)

ICAC: Independent Commission Against Corruption

KPK: Corruption Eradication Commission (*Komisi Pemberantasan Korupsi*)

Bibliography

Abers, Rebecca, and Margaret E. Keck. 2013. *Practical Authority: Agency and Institutional Change in Brazilian Water Politics.* New York: Oxford University Press.

Abranches, Sérgio. 1988. "Presidencialismo de Coalizão: O Dilema Institucional Brasileiro." *Dados* 31 (1): 5–34.

Abreu, D., C. Cesar, and E. Franca. 2007. "The Relationship between Deaths That Are Avoidable with Adequate Health Care and the Implementation of the Unified Health System in Brazil." *Revista Panamericana de Salud Pública* 21 (5): 282–91.

———. 2009. "Gender Differences in Avoidable Mortality in Brazil (1983–2005)." *Cad. Saúde Pública* 25 (12).

Acemoglu, Daron, Simon Johnson, and James A. Robinson. 2001. "The Colonial Origins of Comparative Development: An Empirical Investigation." *The American Economic Review* 91 (5): 1369–1401.

Acemoglu, Daron, and James Robinson. 2012. *Why Nations Fail: The Origins of Power, Prosperity, and Poverty.* New York: Crown Publishers.

ACIJ (Asociación Civil por la Igualdad y la Justicia). 2007. "Transporte sin Control, Usuarios Indefensos: Informe sobre la Comisión Nacional de Regulación del Transporte."

———. 2008. "La Situación Institucional Actual en los Entes de Control de Servicios Públicos."

Acuña, Carlos H., and Mariana Chudnovsky. 2002. "El Sistema de Salud en Argentina." Buenos Aires.

Acuña, Carlos H., and M. F. Tuozzo. 2000. "Civil Society Participation in World Bank and Inter-American Development Bank Programs: The Case of Argentina." *Global Governance* 6 (4): 433–56.

AGN (Auditoría General de la Nación). 1999. "Apoyo a la Reconversión del Instituto Nacional de Servicios Sociales para Jubilados y Pensionados (INSSJP)." Resolusion Number: 146–02.

———. 2004. "Informe de Auditoria 39."

———. 2006. "Informe de Auditoria 82: Informe Especial."

de Almeida, Marcos Ozorio. 2006. "The Role of ICT in Diminishing Collusion in Procurement." In *International Public Procurement Conference Proceedings*, 477–516. Rome.

Altman, David. 2000. "The Politics of Coalition Formation and Survival in Multiparty Presidential Democracies: The Case of Uruguay, 1989–1999." *Party Politics* 6 (3): 259–83.

Álvarez, Mario Hernández, and Mauricio Torres-Tovar. 2010. "Colombia's New Health Reform: Keeping the Financial Sector Healthy." *Social Medicine* 5 (4): 177–81.

Amann, Edmund, Werner Baer, Thomas Trebat, and Juan M. Villa. 2014. *IRIBA Working Paper 10: Infrastructure and Its Role in Brazil's Development Process.*

Ames, Barry. 2001. *The Deadlock of Democracy in Brazil.* Ann Arbor, MI: University of Michigan Press.

Ames, Barry, Miguel Carreras, and Cassilde Schwartz. 2012. "What's Next? Reflections on the Future of Latin American Political Science." In *Routledge Handbook of Latin American Politics*, edited by Peter Kingstone and Deborah J. Yashar, 485–511. New York and London: Routledge.

Amorim Neto, Octavio. 1998. "Of Presidents, Parties, and Ministers: Cabinet Formation and Legislative Decision-Making under Separation of Powers." University of California at San Diego.

2002. "Presidential Cabinets, Electoral Cycles, and Coalition Discipline in Brazil." In *In Legislative Politics in Latin America*, edited by Scott Morgenstern and Benito Nacef, 48–78. Cambridge, UK: Cambridge University Press.

2006. "The Presidential Calculus: Executive Policy Making and Cabinet Formation in the Americas." *Comparative Political Studies* 39 (4): 415–40.

Andrews, Matt. 2013. *The Limits of Institutional Reform in Development.* Cambridge, UK: Cambridge University Press.

Andrews, Matt, Lant Pritchett, and Michael Woolcock. 2013. "Escaping Capability Traps Through Problem Driven Iterative Adaptation (PDIA)." *World Development* 51: 234–44.

2017. *Building State Capability: Evidence, Analysis, Action.* New York: Oxford University Press.

Ang, Yuen Yuen. 2017. "Do Weberian Bureaucracies Lead to Markets or Vice Versa? A Coevolutionary Approach to Development." In *States in the Developing World*, edited by Deborah J. Yashar, Miguel A. Centeno, Azul Kohli, 280–308. New York: Cambridge University Press.

Armijo, Leslie Elliott. 2002. *Debating the Global Financial Architecture.* Albany: State University of New York Press.

Armijo, Leslie Elliott, and Sybil D. Rhodes. 2017. "Explaining Infrastructure Underperformance in Brazil: Cash, Political Institutions, Corruption, and Policy Gestalts." *Policy Studies* 38 (3): 231–47.

Arretche, Marta. 2004. "Federalismo e Políticas Sociais No Brasil." *São Paulo Em Perspectiva* 18 (2): 17–26.

2005. "Perspectivas de Uma Agenda Para a Política Social Brasileira." *Teoria & Sociedade (UFMG).* Belo Horiz: 44–55.

Åslund, Anders. 1994. "The Case for Radical Reform." *Journal of Democracy* 5 (4): 63–74.

Avelino, G., L. G. Barberia, and C. Biderman. 2014. "Governance in Managing Public Health Resources in Brazilian Municipalities." *Health Policy and Planning* 29 (6): 694–702.

Axelrod, Robert M. 1970. *Conflict of Interest: A Theory of Divergent Goals with Applications to Politics*. Chicago: Markham Pub. Co.

Azzoni, Carlos, Joaquim Guilhoto, Eduardo Haddad, Geoffrey Hewings, Marco Laes, and Guilherme Moreira. 2009. "Social Policies, Personal and Regional Income Inequality in Brazil." In *Brazil under Lula: Economy, Politics, and Society under the Worker-President*, edited by Joseph Love and Werner Baer, 243–62. New York: Palgrave Macmillan.

Baer, Werner, and Gabriel Montes-Rojas. 2008. "From Privatization to Re-Nationalization: What Went Wrong with Privatizations in Argentina?" *Oxford Development Studies* 36 (3): 323–37.

Bambaci, Juliana, Pablo T. Spiller, and Mariano Tommasi. 2007. "The Bureaucracy." In *The Institutional Foundations of Public Policy: A Transactions Theory and an Application to Argentina*, edited by Pablo Spiller and Mariano Tommasi. Cambridge, UK: Cambridge University Press.

Barat, Josef. 2007. *Logística, Transporte e Desenvolvimento Econômico*. São Paulo: Editora CLA.

Barrientos, Armando. 2000. "Getting Better after Neoliberalism: Shifts and Challenges of Health Policy in Chile." In *Healthcare Reform and Poverty in Latin America*, edited by Peter Lloyd-Sherlock, 94–111. London: Institute of Latin American Studies.

Barros, Maria Elizabeth. 2001. "Implementação do SUS: Recentralizar Será o Caminho?" *Ciência e Saúde Coletiva* 6 (2): 307–10.

Baumgartner, Frank R., Bryan D. Jones, and John Wilkerson. 2011. "Comparative Studies of Policy Dynamics." *Comparative Political Studies* 44 (8): 947–72.

Behn, R. D. 1988. "Management by Groping Along." *Journal of Policy Analysis and Management* 7 (4): 643–63.

Belmartino, Susana. 2005. *La Atención Médica Argentina en el Siglo XX: Instituciones y Procesos*. Buenos Aires: Siglo XXI Editores.

Bendor, Jonathan. 2003. "Herbert A. Simon: Political Scientist." *Annual Review of Political Science* 6 (1): 433–71.

    2010. *Bounded Rationality and Politics*. Berkeley and Los Angeles, CA: University of California Press.

    2015. "Incrementalism: Dead yet Flourishing." *Public Administration Review* 75 (2): 194–205.

Bennett, Andrew. 2008. "Process Tracing: A Bayesian Perspective." In *Oxford Handbook of Political Methodology*, edited by Janet Box-Steffensmeier, Henry Brady, and David Collier, 702–21. Oxford: Oxford University Press.

Bergara, Mario, Andrés Pereyra, Ruben Tansini, Adolfo Garcé, Daniel Chasquetti, Daniel Buquet, and Juan Andrés Moraes. 2006.

"Political Institutions, Policymaking Processes, and Policy Outcomes: The Case of Uruguay." R-510. Inter-American Development Bank.

Berliner, Daniel, and Aaron Erlich. 2013. "Competing for Transparency: Political Competition and Administrative Reform in Mexican States." In *American Political Science Association Annual Meeting*, 1–25.

Bersch, Katherine. 2016. "The Merits of Problem-Solving over Powering: Governance Reform in Brazil and Argentina," *Comparative Politics* 48 (2): 205–25.

Bersch, Katherine, and Sandra Botero. 2014. "Measuring Governance: Implications of Conceptual Choices." *European Journal of Development Research* 26 (1): 124–41.

Bersch, Katherine, Sérgio Praça, and Matthew M. Taylor. 2017a. "Bureaucratic Capacity and Political Autonomy Within National States: Mapping the Archipelago of Excellence in Brazil." In *States in the Developing World*, edited by Miguel Angel Centeno, Atul Kohli, and Deborah Yashar, 157–83. Cambridge, UK: Cambridge University Press.

2017b. "State Capacity, Bureaucratic Politicization, and Corruption in the Brazilian State." *Governance* 30 (1): 105–24.

Biedermann, Carlos, and Hazem Galal. 2013. "*Crunch Time for Brazilian Infrastructure.*" PwC: Gridlines Spring.

Blake, Charles H. 1998. "Economic Reform and Democratization in Argentina and Uruguay: The Tortoise and the Hare Revisited?" *Journal of Interamerican Studies and World Affairs* 40 (3): 1–26.

Blustein, P. 2005. *And the Money Kept on Rolling In (and Out): Wall Street, the IMF and the Bankrupting of Argentina.* New York: Public Affairs.

Boeninger, Edgardo. 1997. *Democracia en Chile: Lecciones para la Gobernabilidad.* Sanitago, Chile: Editorial Universidad Andrés Bello.

Bolongaita, Emil. 2010. *An Exception to the Rule? Why Indonesia's Anti-Corruption Commission Succeeds Where Others Don't.* Bergen: Chr. Michelsen Institute.

Botero, Rodrigo. 2005. "Una Nota sobre la Tecnocracia Colombiana." *Coyuntura Económica* 2: 17–24.

Brinks, Daniel, and Abby Blass. 2015. "Inclusion-Exclusion: Constitutional Governance and the Politics of Judicial Design." In *2015 International Congress of the Latin American Studies Association.* San Juan, Puerto Rico.

Buchanan, Paul G. 1985. "State Corporatism in Argentina: Labor Administration under Peron and Ongania." *Latin American Research Review* 20 (1): 61–95.

Bunse, Simone, and Verena Fritz. 2012. "Making Public Sector Reforms Work: Political and Economic Contexts, Incentives, and Strategies." 6174. World Bank Policy Research Working Paper.

Cabot, Diego, and Francisco Olivera. 2008. *Hablen con Julio: Julio de Vido y las Historias Ocultas del Poder Kirchnerista.* Buenos Aires: Sudamericana.

Camp, Roderic A. 1985. "The Political Technocrat in Mexico and the Survival of the Political System." *Latin American Research Review* 20 (1): 97–118.

Campos-Méndez, Javier, Antonio Estache, and Lourdes Trujillo. 2001. "Processes, Information, and Accounting Gaps in the Regulation of

Argentina's Private Railways." 2636. World Bank Policy Research Working Paper.

Carbajo, José C., and Antonio Estache. 1996. "Railway Concessions: Heading Down the Right Track in Argentina." *Viewpoint: Public Policy for the Private Sector*, no. 88. Washington, DC.

Cardoso, Fernando Henrique. 1994. *Mãos à Obra, Brasil: Proposta de Governo*. Brasília: Fernando Henrique Cardoso.

Carvalho, Gilson. 2001. "A Inconstitucional Administração Pós-Constitucional do SUS Através de Normas Operacionais." *Ciência & Saúde Coletiva* 6 (2): 435–44.

Castiglioni, Rossana. 2000. "Welfare State Reform in Chile and Uruguay: Cross-Class Coalitions, Elite Ideology, and Veto Players." In Meeting of the Latin American Studies Association, *Mar 16–18, 2000*. Miami, FL.

De Castro, Newton. 1999. "Privatization of the Transportation Sector in Brazil." In *Privatization in Brazil: The Case of Public Utilities*, edited by Armando C. Pinheiro and Kiichiro Fukasaku, 177–218. Rio de Janeiro: Brazilian Development Bank (BNDES).

Cavalcanti, Celso de Oliveira Bello. 1995. "Impactos Da Reforma Administrativa Do Governo Collor Na Modelagem Organizacional Do DNER." Fundação Getúlio Vargas.

Centeno, Miguel Angel. 1994. *Democracy Within Reason: Technocratic Revolution in Mexico*. 2nd ed. University Park, PA: Penn State University Press.

———. 2002. *Blood and Debt: War and the Nation-State in Latin America*. University Park, PA: Penn State University Press.

Centeno, Miguel A., and Patricio Silva, eds. 1998. *The Politics of Expertise in Latin America*. Latin American Studies Series. London: Palgrave Macmillan.

Centro de Estudios Económicos de la Regulación (CEER). 2001. *Las Empresas Privadas de Servicios Publicos en la Argentina. Un Analisis de Su Contribucionala Competitividad del Pais*. Buenos Aires: Universidad Argentina de la Empresa.

Cerra, Valerie, Alfredo Cuevas, Carlos Goes, and Izabela Karpowicz. 2016. "Highways to Heaven: Infrastructure Determinants and Trends in Latin America and the Caribbean." *IMF Working Papers*.

CGU (Controladoria-Geral da União) - Secretaria Federal de Controle Interno. 2005. *Tomada de Contas Anual Agregada*. Report No. 175662, Brasília, 223.

Chaisty, Paul, Nic Cheeseman, and Timothy J. Power. 2014. "Rethinking the 'Presidentialism Debate': Conceptualizing Coalitional Politics in Cross-Regional Perspective." *Democratization* 21 (1): 72–94.

Charosky, Hernán. 2009. "¿Obstáculos o Herramientas? Los Usos de las Investigaciones de Casos sobre Corrupción en las Políticas Públicas." In *La Revisión Judicial de Políticas Sociales*, edited by Víctor Abramovich and Laura Pautassi, 329–56. Buenos Aires: Editores del Puerto.

Chavez, Rebecca Bill. 2004. *The Rule of Law in Nascent Democracies: Judicial Politics in Argentina*. Stanford, CA: Stanford University Press.

Cheibub, José Antonio, Adam Przeworski, and Sebastian M. Saiegh. 2004. "Government Coalitions and Legislative Success Under Presidentialism and Parliamentarism." *British Journal of Political Science* 34 (4): 565–87.

Cipoletta Tomassian, Georgina, and Ricardo J Sánchez. 2009. *Análisis del Régimen de Concesiones Viales en Argentina 1990–2008. Serie Recursos Naturales e Infraestructura.* CEPAL.

Clark, Mary A. 2015. "The New Left and Health Care Reform in El Salvador." *Latin American Politics and Society* 57 (4): 97–118.

CNI (Confederação Nacional da Indústria). 2005. *Agenda Mínima para a Infraestrutura.* Brasília.

CNT (Confederação Nacional Do Transporte). 2014. *Pesquisa Rodoviária 2014.* Brasília: CNT.

Collier, Ruth, and David Collier. 1991. *Critical Junctures and Historical Legacies.* Princeton, NJ: Princeton University Press.

Cook, Alexander. 2016. *The Cultural Revolution on Trial Mao and the Gang of Four.* Cambridge, UK: Cambridge University Press.

Corporacion Latinobarómetro. 2016. "Informe 2016." Buenos Aires.

Corrales, Javier, and Michael Penfold. 2011. *Dragon in the Tropics.* Washington, DC: Brookings Institution.

Correa, Paulo, Carlos Pereira, Bernardo Mueller, and Marcos Melo. 2006. *Regulatory Governance in Infrastructure Industries: Assessment and Measurement of Brazilian Regulators.* Washington, DC: World Bank.

Correia, Marcelo Bruto da Costa. 2011. "Por Que as Reformas Permanecem? A Trajetória Gradualista de Mudanças No Setor de Infraestrutura Rodoviária No Brasil Entre 1985–2010." Fundação Getúlio Vargas.

Coutinho, Maria Eugenia. 2007. "Un Análisis Institucional de la Organización de la Presidencia en la Argentina." *Colección.*

Couttolenc, Bernard. 2011. "Taking Stock of Performance Reforms at the Sub-National Level in Brazil: Recent Performance Gains Achieved in the Health Sector, Hypotheses on Possible Drivers of Good and Bad Performance." Washington, DC: World Bank.

D'Elia, Yolanda, and Cristyn Quiroz. 2010. "Las Misiones Sociales: ¿Una Alternativa Para Superar la Pobreza?" Caracas: Instituto Latinoamericano de Investigaciones Sociales (ILDIS).

Dargent, Eduardo. 2011. "Agents or Actors?: Assessing the Autonomy of Economic Technocrats in Colombia and Peru." *Comparative Politics,* 43 (3): 313–32.

——— 2015. *Technocracy and Democracy in Latin America: The Experts Running Government.* Cambridge, UK: Cambridge University Press.

Davis, Kevin E. 2010. "Does the Globalization of Anti-Corruption Law Help Developing Countries?" In *International Law, Economic Globalization and Development,* edited by Julio Faundez and Celine Tan. Cheltenham, UK: Edward Elgar.

Deheza, Grace Ivana. 1997. "Gobiernos de Coalicion en el Sistema Presidencial: America del Sur." Florence: European University Institute.

Demsetz, Harold. 1967. "Toward a Theory of Property Rights." *The American Economic Review* 57 (2): 347–59.

Diamond, Jared. 1997. *Guns, Germs and Steel*. New York: W. W. Norton and Co.

Dirección Nacional de Vialidad (DNV). 2007. "Informe: Evolución de la Dotación de Personal - Planta Permanente." Buenos Aires.

Dollar, David, and Aart Kraay. 2003. "Institutions, Trade, and Growth." *Journal of Monetary Economics* 50 (1): 133–62.

Domínguez, Jorge I. 1997. *Technopols: Freeing Politics and Markets in Latin America in the 1990s*. University Park, PA: Penn State University Press.

Doner, Richard F., Bryan K. Ritchie, and Dan Slater. 2005. "Systemic Vulnerability and the Origins of Developmental States: Northeast and Southeast Asia in Comparative Perspective." *International Organization* 59 (02): 327–61.

Dunning, Thad. 2012. *Natural Experiments in the Social Sciences: A Design-Based Approach*. New York: Cambridge University Press.

Durand, Francisco, and Rosemary Thorp. 1998. "Reforming the State: A Study of the Peruvian Tax Reform." *Oxford Development Studies* 26 (2): 133–51.

Echebarría, Koldo, and Juan Carlos Cortázar. 2007. "Public Administration and Public Employment Reform in Latin America." In *The State of State Reform in Latin America*, edited by Eduardo Lora. Palo Alto, CA: Stanford University Press.

Edital Esaf. 2012. "Concurso Público para Provimento de Cargos Do Quadro de Pessoal Efetivo do Departamento Nacional de Infraestrutura de Transportes – DNIT." 66.

EIU (Economist Intelligence Unit). 2014. "Evaluating the Environment for Public-Private Partnerships in Latin America and the Caribbean: The 2014 Infrascope." New York.

Ellner, Steve. 2008. *Rethinking Venezuelan Politics: Class, Conflict, and the Chávez Phenomenon*. Boulder, CO: Lynne Rienner.

Escorel, Sarah. 1999. *Reviravolta Na Saúde*. Rio de Janiero: Editora Fiocruz.

Espinosa, Consuelo, Marcelo Tokman, and Jorge Rodríguez Cabello. 2005. "Finanzas Públicas de La Reforma." In *Reforma de la Salud en Chile: Desafíos de la Implementación*. Santiago, Chile: Universidad de Andrés Bello.

Estache, Antonio, and José C. Carbajo. 1996. *Designing Toll Road Concessions: Lessons from Argentina*. Washington, DC: World Bank.

Estache, Antonio, José C. Carbajo, and Gines de Rus. 1999. "Argentina's Transport Privatization and Re-Regulation." 2249. Policy Research. Washington, DC: World Bank.

Estache, Antonio, Andrea Goldstein, and Russell Pittman. 2001. "Privatization and Regulatory Reform in Brazil: The Case of Freight Railways." *Journal of Industry, Competition and Trade* 1 (2): 203–35.

Evans, Peter. 1995. *Embedded Autonomy: States and Industrial Transformation*. Princeton, NJ: Princeton University Press.

Evans, Peter, Evelyne Huber, John D. Stephens. 2017. "The Political Foundations of State Effectiveness." In *States in the Developing World*, edited by Miguel

A. Centeno, Atul Kohli, and Deborah J. Yashar, 380–408. Cambridge: Cambridge University Press.

Evans, Peter, and James E. Rauch. 1999. "Bureaucracy and Growth: A Cross-National Analysis of the Effects of 'Weberian' State Structures on Economic Growth." *American Sociological Review* 64 (5): 748–65.

Ewig, Christina, and Stephen J. Kay. 2008. "New Political Legacies and the Politics of Health and Pension Re-Reforms in Chile." In *Public and Private Social Policy*, 249–68. London: Palgrave Macmillan.

Falleti, Tulia G. 2010. "Infiltrating the State: The Evolution of Health Care Reforms in Brazil, 1964–1988." In *Explaining Institutional Change: Ambiguity, Agency, and Power*, edited by James Mahoney and Kathleen Thelen, 38–62. New York: Cambridge University Press.

Fernandes, Ciro Campos Christo. 2010. "Política de Compras e Contratações." Fundaçao Getulio Vargas.

Ferraro, A. 2006. "Una Idea Muy Precaria: El Nuevo Servicio Civil y los Viejos Designados Políticos en Argentina." *Latin American Research Review* 41 (2).

Figueiredo, Argelina Cheibub, and Fernando Limongi. 1999. *Executivo e Legislativo Na Nova Ordem Constitucional*. São Paulo: Editora Fundação Getúlio Vargas.

2000. "Presidential Power, Legislative Organization, and Party Behavior in Brazil." *Comparative Politics* 32 (2): 151.

Forester, John. 1984. "Bounded Rationality and the Politics of Muddling Through." *Public Administration Review* 44 (1): 23–31.

Fukuyama, Francis. 2014. *Political Order and Political Decay: From the Industrial Revolution to the Globalization of Democracy*. London: Profile Books.

Fundación de Investigaciones Económics Latinoamericanas (FIEL). 1999. "La Regulación de la Competencia y de los Servicios Públicos: Teoría y Experiencia Argentina Reciente." Buenos Aires.

Gaetani, Francisco. 2003. "Public Management Policy Change in Brazil: 1995–1998." *International Public Management Journal* 6 (3): 327–41.

Gallamore, R. E. 1999. "Regulation and Innovation: Lessons from the American Railroad Industry." In *Essays in Transportation Economics and Policy: A Handbook in Honor of John R. Meyer*, edited by José A. Gómez-Ibáñez, William B. Tye, and Clifford Winston, 493–529. Washington, DC: Brookings Institution Press.

Garretón, Manuel Antonio. 1989. *The Chilean Political Process*. Boston, MA: Allen & Unwin, Inc.

2005. "Social Sciences and Society in Chile: Institutionalization, Breakdown and Rebirth." *Social Science Information* 44 (2–3): 359–409.

Geddes, Barbara. 1994. *Politician's Dilemma: Building State Capacity in Latin America*. Berkeley, CA: University of California Press.

George, Alexander. 1979. "Case Studies and Theory Development: The Method of Structured, Focused Comparison." In *Diplomacy: New Approaches in History, Theory, and Policy*, edited by P. G. Lauren, 43–68. New York: The Free Press.

Gerchunoff, Pablo, and German Coloma. 1993. "Privatization in Argentina." In *Privatization in Latin America*, edited by Manuel Sanchez and Rossana Corona, 251–300. Baltimore, MD: The Johns Hopkins University Press.

Gertler, P. J., Pi Giovagnoli, and Sebastián Martínez. 2014. "Rewarding Provider Performance to Enable a Healthy Start to Life: Evidence from Argentina's Plan Nacer." *World Bank Policy Research Working Paper* 6884 (May).

Gibbs, Terry. 2006. "Business as Unusual: What the Chávez Era Tells Us about Democracy under Globalisation." *Third World Quarterly* 27 (2): 265–79.

Gingerich, Daniel W. 2012. "Governance Indicators and the Level of Analysis Problem: Empirical Findings from South America." *British Journal of Political Science* 43 (3): 505–40.

2013. *Political Institutions and Party-Directed Corruption in South America: Stealing for the Team*. New York: Cambridge University Press.

Ginsburg, Tom. 2003. *Judicial Review in New Democracies: Constitutional Courts in Asian Cases*. Cambridge, UK: Cambridge University Press.

Goldsmith, Arthur A. 2007. "Is Governance Reform a Catalyst for Development?" *Governance* 20 (2): 165–86.

Gómez-Ibáñez, José A. 2003. *Regulating Infrastructure: Monopoly, Contracts, and Discretion*. Cambridge, MA: Harvard University Press.

Gomide, Alexandre de Ávila. 2011. "A Política Das Reformas Institucionais No Brasil." Fundação Getulio Vargas.

González, Lucas I. 2010. "Primus Contra Pares: Presidents, Governors, and the Struggles over the Distribution of Power in Federal Democracies." University of Notre Dame.

Gragnolati, Michele, Magnus Lindelow, and Bernard Couttolenc. 2013. *Twenty Years of Health System Reform in Brazil*. Washington, DC: World Bank.

Graham, Carol, and Moisés Naím. 1998. "The Political Economy of Institutional Reform in Latin America." In *Beyond Tradeoffs: Market Reforms and Equitable Growth in Latin America*, edited by Nancy Birdsall, Carol Graham, and Richard A. Sabot, 321–61. Washington, DC: Inter-American Development Bank.

Grindle, Merilee S. 1977. "Power, Expertise and the 'Tecnico': Suggestions from a Mexican Case Study." *The Journal of Politics* 39 (2): 399–426.

2004. *Despite the Odds: The Contentious Politics of Education Reform*. Princeton, NJ: Princeton University Press.

2010. "Good Governance: The Inflation of an Idea." 10–023. HKS Faculty Research Working Paper Series.

2012. *Jobs for the Boys: Patronage and the State in Comparative Perspective*. Cambridge, MA: Harvard University Press.

Grzymala-Busse, Anna. 2007. *Rebuilding Leviathan: Party Competition and State Exploitation in Post-Communist Democracies*. Cambridge, UK: Cambridge University Press.

Guasch, J. Luis. 2004. *Granting and Renegotiating Infrastructure Concessions*. World Bank.

Guillan Montero, A. 2011. *As If: The Fiction of Executive Accountability and the Persistence of Corruption Networks in Weakly Institutionalized Presidential Systems. Argentina (1989–2007)*. Washington, DC: Georgetown University.

Haggard, Stephan, and Robert R. Kaufman. 2008. *Development, Democracy and Welfare States*. Princeton, NJ: Princeton University Press.

Hall, Peter A. 1993. "Policy Paradigms, Social Learning, and the State: The Case of Economic Policymaking in Britain." *Comparative Politics* 25 (3): 275–96.

Handlin, S. 2012. "Social Protection and the Politicization of Class Cleavages During Latin America's Left Turn." *Comparative Political Studies* 46 (12): 1582–609.

Hausmann, Ricardo, Dani Rodrik, and Andres Velasco. 2005. "Growth Diagnostics." In *The Washington Consensus Reconsidered: Towards a New Global Governance*, edited by Narcís Serra and Joseph E. Stiglitz, 324–55. New York: Oxford University Press.

Hawkins, Kirk A. 2010. *Venezuela's Chavismo and Populism in Comparative Perspective*. New York: Cambridge University Press.

Hawkins, Kirk, Guillermo Rosas, and Michael Johnson. 2011. "The Misiones of the Chávez Government." In *Venezuela's Bolivarian Democracy*, edited by David Smilde and Daniel Hellinger. Durham and London: Duke University Press.

Heclo, Hugh. 1974. *Modern Social Politics in Britain and Sweden: From Relief to Income Maintenance*. New Haven, CT: Yale University Press.

Hirschman, Albert. 1967. *Development Projects Observed*. Washington, DC: Brookings Institution.

Hirschman, Albert O. 1971. *A Bias for Hope: Essays on Development and Latin America*. New Haven, CT: Yale University Press.

1973. *Journeys Toward Progress: Studies of Economic Policy-Making in Latin America*. New York: Norton.

Holt, Jordan, and Nick Manning. 2014. "Fukuyama Is Right about Measuring State Quality: Now What?" *Governance* 27 (4): 717–28.

Huber, Evelyne, and John D. Stephens. 2000. "Partisan Governance, Women's Employment, and the Social Democratic Service State." *American Sociological Review* 65 (3): 323–42.

Huber, Evelyne, and John D. Stephens. 2012. *Democracy and the Left: Social Policy and Inequality in Latin America*. Chicago: University of Chicago Press.

Huber, John D. 1998. "How Does Cabinet Instability Affect Political Performance? Credible Commitment, Information, and Health Care Cost Containment in Parliamentary Politics." *American Political Science Review* 92 (3): 577–92.

Hunter, Wendy. 2007. "The Normalization of an Anomaly: The Workers' Party in Brazil." *World Politics* 59 (3): 440–75.

2010. *The Transformation of the Workers' Party in Brazil, 1989–2009*. Cambridge, UK: Cambridge University Press.

Hunter, Wendy, and Natasha Borges Sugiyama. 2009. "Democracy and Social Policy in Brazil: Advandng Basic Needs, Preserving Privileged Interests." *Latin American Politics and Society* 51 (2): 29–58.

Hyde, Susan D. 2011. "Catch Us If You Can: Election Monitoring and International Norm Diffusion." *American Journal of Political Science* 55 (2): 356–69.

IBGE (Instituto Brasileiro de Geografia e Estatística). 2004. "Projeção Da População Do Brasil Por Sexo e Idade Para o Período 1980–2050." Rio de Janeiro.

   2010. "Estatísticas Da Saúde: Assistência Médico-Sanitária (AMS) 2009." Rio de Janeiro.

IDB (Inter-American Development Bank). 1998. *Argentina: Programa de Modernización y Reforma Del Sector Salud.* Washington, DC: IDB.

Instituto para el Desarrollo Social Argentino (IDESA). 2012. "En 6 Años Se Triplicaron Los Subsidios a Los Trenes." 430.

Jacobs, Alan M. 2011. *Governing for the Long Term: Democracy and the Politics of Investment.* Cambridge, UK: Cambridge University Press.

Janis, Irving. 1982. *Groupthink: Psychological Studies of Policy Decisions and Fiascoes.* New York: Houghton Mifflin.

Johnston, Michael. 2014. *Corruption, Contention, and Reform.* New York: Cambridge University Press.

Joia, Luiz Antonio, and Fuad Zamot. 2002. "Internet-Based Reverse Auctions by the Brazilian Government." *Information Systems* 9 (6): 1–12.

Jones, Bryan D. 1999. "Bounded Rationality." *Annual Review of Political Science* 2 (1): 297–321.

Jones, Bryan D., and Frank R. Baumgartner. 2005. *The Politics of Attention. How Government Prioritizes.* Chicago, IL: University of Chicago Press.

   2012. "From There to Here: Punctuated Equilibrium to the General Punctuation Thesis to a Theory of Government." *Policy Studies Journal* 40 (1): 1–19.

Jones, Mark P., Sebastian Saiegh, Pablo T. Spiller, and Mariano Tommasi. 2002. "Amateur Legislators – Professional Politicians: The Consequences of Party-Centered Electoral Rules in a Federal System." *American Journal of Political Science* 46 (3): 656–69.

Kahneman, Daniel. 2011. *Thinking, Fast and Slow.* New York: Farrar, Straus and Giroux.

Katz, Ricardo Santiago. 2006. *Historia de las Elecciones Presidenciales Argentinas.* la Plata: R. S. Katz.

Kaufman, Robert R., and Joan M. Nelson. 2004. *Crucial Needs, Weak Incentives: Social Sector Reform, Democratization, and Globalization in Latin America.* Washington, DC: Woodrow Wilson Center Press.

Kaufmann, Daniel, and Aart Kraay. 2002. "Growth without Governance." World Bank Policy Research Working Paper.

Kaufmann, Daniel, and Aart Kraay. 2016. "Worldwide Governance Indicators." Washington, DC: World Bank.

Kaufmann, Daniel, Aart Kraay, and Massimo Mastruzzi. 2010. "The Worldwide Governance Indicators: Methodology and Analytical Issues." 5430. World Bank Policy Research Working Paper Series.

Klitgaard. 1988. *Controlling Corruption.* Berkeley and Los Angeles, CA: University of California Press.

Klitgaard, Robert. 2011. *Review: The Quality of Government: Corruption, Social Trust, and Inequality in International Perspective. Perspectives on Politics.* Vol. 10. Chicago, IL: University of Chicago Press.

Knack, Stephen, and Philip Keefer. 1995. "Institutions and Economic Performance: Cross-Country Tests Using Alternative Institutional Measures." *Economics & Politics* 7 (3): 207–27.

Kogan, Jorge H. 1999. "Experiencias Ferroviarias: Una Revisión Del Caso de Buenos Aires." In *Presentation Made to the World Bank Seminar on Transport Regulation.* Las Palmas, Spain.

Kupatadze, Alexander. 2016. "The Quest for Good Governance: Georgia's Break with the Past." *Journal of Democracy* 27 (1): 110–23.

Kurtz, Marcus. 2013. *Latin American State Building in Comparative Perspective.* New York: Cambridge University Press.

Lameirão, Camila. 2011. "A Casa Civil Como Instituição Do Executivo Federal." *Desigualdade & Diversidade Dossiê Especial,* no. 2: 143–84.

Leff, Nathaniel H. 1964. "Economic Development Through Bureaucratic Corruption." *American Behavioral Scientist* 8 (3): 8–14.

Levitsky, Steven, and María Victoria Murillo. 2012. "Institutional Change and State Capacity in Weak Institutional Environments: Reflections on the Latin American Experience." *Princeton State Building Workshop.*

2013. "Building Institutions on Weak Foundations." *Journal of Democracy* 24 (2): 93–107.

2014. "Building Institutions on Weak Foundations: Lessons from Latin America." In *Understanding Imperfect Democracies: The Legacy of Guillermo O'Donnell for the Study of Democracy,* edited by Daniel Brinks, Scott Mainwaring, and Marcelo Leiras. Baltimore, MD: Johns Hopkins University Press.

Levy, Brian. 2014. *Working with the Grain: Integrating Governance and Growth in Development.* New York: Oxford University Press.

Leys, Colin. 1965. "What Is the Problem about Corruption?" *The Journal of Modern African Studies* 3 (2): 215.

Lijphart, Arend. 1971. "Comparative Politics and the Comparative Method." *The American Political Science Review* 65 (3): 682–93.

2012. *Patterns of Democracy.* New Haven, CT: Yale University Press.

Lindblom, Charles E. 1959. "The Science of 'Muddling Through.'" *Public Administration Review* 19 (2): 79–88.

1968. *The Policy-Making Process.* Englewood Cliffs, NJ: Prentice-Hall.

Linz, Juan. 1994. "Presidential or Parliamentary Democracy: Does It Make a Difference?" In *The Failure of Presidential Democracy: Comparative Perspectives,* edited by Juan Linz and Arturo Valenzuela, 3–87. Baltimore, MD: Johns Hopkins University Press.

Lipset, Seymour Martin. 1960. *Political Man: The Social Bases of Politics.* New York: Doubleday.

Llanos, Mariana, and Ana Margheritis. 2006. "Why Do Presidents Fail? Political Leadership and the Argentine Crisis (1999–2001)." *Studies in Comparative International Development* 40 (4): 77–103.

Lloyd-Sherlock, Peter. 2005. "Health Sector Reform in Argentina: A Cautionary Tale." *Social Science & Medicine* 60 (8): 1893–1903.

2006. "When Social Health Insurance Goes Wrong: Lessons from Argentina and Mexico." *Social Policy and Administration* 40 (4): 353–68.

Lora, Eduardo. 2007. *The State of State Reform in Latin America*. Washington, DC: Inter-American Development Bank.

Loureiro, Maria Rita, and Fernando Abrúcio. 1999. "Política e Burocracia no presidencialismo brasileiro: o papel do ministério da fazenda no primeiro governo Fernando Henrique Cardoso." *Revista Brasileira de Ciências Sociais* 14 (41): 69–89.

Maceira, Daniel. 2009. "Inequidad en El Acceso a la Salud en la Argentina." *Cuadernos del CLAEH* 33 (99): 7–17.

Macinko, James. 2011. "*A Preliminary Assessment of the Family Health Strategy (FHS) in Brazil.*" Washington, DC: World Bank.

Madrid, Raul. 2002. "The Politics and Economics of Pension Privatization in Latin America." *Latin American Research Review* 37 (2): 159–82.

Magar, E., and J. A. Moraes. 2012. "Factions with Clout: Presidential Cabinet Coalition and Policy in the Uruguayan Parliament." *Party Politics* 18 (3): 427–51.

Mahoney, James. 2001. *The Legacies of Liberalism: Path Dependence and Political Regimes in Central America*. Baltimore, MD: Johns Hopkins University Press.

Mahoney, James, and K. Thelen. 2010. *Explaining Institutional Change: Ambiguity, Agency, and Power*. Cambridge, UK: Cambridge University Press.

Mainwaring, Scott. 1993. "Presidentialism, Multipartism, and Democracy: The Difficult Combination." *Comparative Political Studies* 26 (2):198–228.

1995. "Brazil: Weak Parties, Feckless Democracy." In *Building Democratic Institutions: Party Systems in Latin America*, edited by Scott Mainwaring and Timothy Scully. Stanford, CA: Stanford University Press.

1999. *Rethinking Party Systems in the Third Wave of Democratisation: The Case of Brazil*. Stanford, CA: Stanford University Press.

Malloy, James. 1979. *The Politics of Social Security in Brazil*. Pittsburgh, PA: University of Pittsburgh Press.

Malta, D., E. Duarte, J. Escalante, M. Almeida, L. Sardinha, and E. Macario. 2010. "Avoidable Causes of Infant Mortality in Brazil, 1997–2006: Contributions to Performance Evaluation of the Unified National Health System." *Cadernos de Saúde Pública* 26 (3): 481–91.

Manzetti, Luigi. 1999. *Privatization South American Style*. Oxford: Oxford University Press.

2003. "Political Manipulations and Market Reforms Failures." *World Politics* 55 (3): 315–60.

2009. "Public Opinion Backlashes and the Risk of Re-Nationalization in Latin America." *Law and Business Review of the Americas* 15 (63): 63–80.

2014. "Accountability and Corruption in Argentina During the Kirchners' Era." *Latin American Research Review* 49 (2): 173–95.

March, James, and Herbert Simon. 1993. *Organizations*. 2nd ed. Cambridge, MA: Blackwell.

Martin, Helen, Sophie Sirtaine, and Cecilia Briceno-Garmendia. 2014. *Caribbean Infrastructure PPP Roadmap*. Washington, DC: World Bank Group.

Martínez-Gallardo, Cecilia. 2010. "*Designing Cabinets: Presidential Politics and Cabinet Instability in Latin America.*" Working Paper# 375. Kellogg Institute, Notre Dame, IN.

2011. "Out of the Cabinet: What Drives Defections From the Government in Presidential Systems?" *Comparative Political Studies* 45 (1): 62–90.

Martínez Nogueira, Roberto. 2002. "Las Administraciones Públicas Paralelas y la Construcción de Capacidades Institucionales." *Reforma y Democracia*, no. 24: 1–24.

Martini, Maíra. 2016. "Uruguay: Overview of Corruption and Anti-Corruption." Transparency International.

Martins, Luciano. 1985. *Estado Capitalista e Burocracia No Brasil Pós-64*. Rio de Janeiro: Paz e Terra.

McDermott, Rose. 2004. *Political Psychology in International Relations*. Ann Arbor: University of Michigan Press.

McGuire, James W. 2010. *Wealth, Health, and Democracy in East Asia and Latin America*. New York: Cambridge University Press.

Meireles, Fernando. 2016. "Oversized Government Coalitions in Latin America." *Brazilian Political Science Review*. 10 (3): 1–31.

Mejía Acosta, Andrés. 2009. *Informal Coalitions and Policymaking in Latin America: Ecuador in Comparative Perspective*. New York: Routledge.

Mejía Acosta, Andrés, and John Polga-Hecimovich. 2011. "Coalition Erosion and Presidential Instability in Ecuador." *Latin American Politics and Society* 53 (2): 87–111.

Melo, Marcus André, and Carlos Pereira. 2013. *Making Brazil Work: Checking the President in a Multiparty System*. New York: Palgrave Macmillan.

Melo, Marcus André, Carlos Pereira, and Carlos Mauricio Figueiredo. 2009. "Political and Institutional Checks on Corruption: Explaining the Performance of Brazilian Audit Institutions." *Comparative Political Studies* 42 (9): 1217–244.

Meneguello, Rachel. 1998. *Partidos e Governos No Brasil Contemporaneo (1985–1997)*. São Paulo: Paz e Terra.

Mesa-Lago, Carmelo, Ricardo Córdova Macías, and Carlos Mauricio López Grande. 1994. *El Salvador: Diagnóstico y Propuesta de Reforma de la Seguridad Social*. San Salvador: Centro Internacional para el Desarrollo Económico.

Mesa-Lago, Carmelo, and Katharina Müller. 2002. "The Politics of Pension Reform in Latin America." *Journal of Latin American Studies* 34 (3): 687–715.

Ministry of Health, SVS (Secretariat of Health Surveillance). 2011. "Sistema de informações sobre mortalidade." Brasília: Ministério da Saúde.

Mistree, Dinsha. 2015. "Review Article Party-Directed Corruption in the Developing World." *Comparative Politics* 47 (3): 354–74.

Moe, Terry. 1990. "The Politics of Structural Choice: Towards a Theory of Public Bureaucracy." In *Organization Theory from Chester Barnard to the Present and Beyond*, edited by Oliver E. Williamson. New York: Oxford University Press.

Monaldi, Rancisco, Rosa Amelia González, Richard Obuchi, and Michael Penfold. 2008. "Political Institutions and Policymaking in Venezuela: The Rise and Collapse of Political Cooperation." In *Policymaking in Latin America: How Politics Shapes Policies*, edited by Pablo T. Spiller, Ernesto Stein, Mariano Tommasi, and Carlos G. Scartascini. Cambridge, MA: Harvard University, David Rockefeller Center for Latin American Studies.

Monteiro, Vera. 2005. "Pregão." In *Seminario Nacional de Direito Administrativo*, 517–29. Coordenação Técnica.

2010. *Licitação Na Modalidade de Pregão*. 2nd ed. São Paulo: Malheiros.

Montoya, S, and J. Colina. 1998. "Reforma de Obras Sociales en Argentina: Avances y Desafíos Pendientes." IDB.

Morgan, Jana. 2011. *Bankrupt Representation and Party System Collapse*. University Park, PA: Pennsylvania State University Press.

Morley, Samuel, Roberto Machado, and Stefano Pettinato. 1999. *Indexes of Structural Reform in Latin America*. Santiago, Chile: United Nations Economic Commission for Latin America and the Caribbean.

Motta, Alexandre. 2010. "O Combate Ao Desperdício No Gasto Público." Universidade Estadual de Campinas.

MT (Ministério dos Transportes). 1994. *GT – DNER – Versão Preliminar*. Brasília: MT.

2007. *Plano Nacional de Logística de Transportes*. Brasília: MT.

2011. *Política de Recursos Humanos Para o DNIT Período 2012–2014*. Brasília: MT.

Mungiu-Pippidi, Alina. 2015. *The Quest for Good Governance: How Societies Develop Control for Corruption*. Cambridge, UK: Cambridge University Press.

Murillo, Maria Victoria. 2001. *Labor Unions, Partisan Coalitions and Market Reforms in Latin America*. New York: Cambridge University Press.

2009. *Political Competition, Partisanship, and Policy Making in Latin American Public Utilities*. 1st ed. New York: Cambridge University Press.

N'haux, Enrique. 1993. *Menem-Cavallo: El Poder Mediterráneo*. Buenos Aires: Ediciones Corregidor.

Naím, Moisés. 1994. "Latin America: The Second Stage of Reform." *Journal of Democracy* 5 (4): 32–48.

Natale, Alberto A. 1993. *Privatizaciones en Privado*. Buenos Aires: Planeta.

Nelson, Joan. 2004. "The Politics of Health Sector Reforms: Cross-National Comparisons." In *Crucial Needs, Weak Incentives*, edited by Robert Kaufman and Joan Nelson. Washington, DC: Woodrow Wilson Center Press.

Newell, Allen, and Herbert Simon. 1972. *Human Problem Solving*. Englewood Cliffs, NJ: Prentice-Hall.

Niedzwiecki, Sara. 2014. "The Effect of Unions and Organized Civil Society on Social Policy: Pension and Health Reforms in Argentina and Brazil, 1988–2008." *Latin American Politics and Society* 56 (4): 22–48.

Nóbrega, Mailson da. 2005. *O Futuro Chegou: Instituições e Desenvolvimento No Brasil*. São Paulo: Editora Globo.

Nóbrega, Mailson da, and Gustavo Loyola. 2006. "The Long and Simultaneous Construction of Fiscal and Monetary Institution." In *Statecrafting Monetary Authority: Democracy and Financial Order in Brazil*, edited by Lourdes Sola and Laurence Whitehead, 57–84. Oxford: Oxford University Centre for Brazilian Studies.

North, Douglass. 1990. *Institutions, Institutional Change and Economic Performance*. Cambridge, UK: Cambridge University Press.

Nunes, R. M. 2010. "Politics Without Insurance: Democratic Competition and Judicial Reform in Brazil." *Comparative Politics* 42 (3): 313–31.

O'Donnell, Guillermo. 1973. *Modernization and Bureaucratic-Authoritarianism: Studies in South American Politics*. Berkeley: Institute of International Studies.

OECD (Organization for Economic Growth and Development). March 2017. *Gaps and Governance Standards of Public Infrastructure in Chile*.

——— 2008. *OECD Reviews of Regulatory Reform: Brazil. Strengthening Governance for Growth*.

Ortega, Daniel, and Francisco Rodríguez. 2008. "Freed from Illiteracy? A Closer Look at Venezuela's Misión Robinson Literacy Campaign." *Economic Development and Cultural Change* 51 (1): 1–30.

Oscar, Rinaldi, and Damián Staffa. 2006. *Control de la Ejecución de Los Fondos Fiduciarios Estatales: Debilidades en la Presentación de Informes Del Poder Ejecutivo y Su Tratamiento Por El Congreso*. CIPPEC & CEP.

PAC (Programa de Aceleração do Crescimento). 2009. *10° Balanço*. Brasília: Brazilian Federal Government.

Page, Scott. 2008. *The Difference: How the Power of Diversity Creates Better Groups, Firms, Schools, and Societies*. Princeton, NJ: Princeton University Press.

PAHO (Pan American Health Organization). 2014. "*El Salvador en el Camino Hacia la Cobertura Universal de Salud: Logros y Desafíos*." San Salvador: PAHO.

Panizza, Francisco. 2004. "A Reform Without Losers: The Symbolic Economy of Civil Service Reform in Uruguay, 1995–96." *Latin American Politics and Society* 46 (3): 1–28.

Patashnik, Eric M. 2008. *Reforms at Risk: What Happens After Major Policy Changes Are Enacted. Princeton Studies in American Politics*. Princeton, NJ: Princeton University Press.

Pereira, Anthony W. 2016. "Is the Brazilian State 'Patrimonial'?" *Latin American Perspectives* 43 (2): 135–152.

Pereira, Carlos, Timothy J. Power, and Lucio R. Rennó. 2008. "Agenda Power, Executive Decree Authority, and the Mixed Results of Reform in the Brazilian Congress." *Legislative Studies Quarterly* 33 (1): 5–33.

Pérez, Verónica. 2014. "Cambios y Continuidades en la Organización Social de los Servicios de Trenes del Área Metropolitana de Buenos." *Revista Transporte y Territorio* 11: 114–34.

Perla, H., and H. Cruz-Feliciano. 2013. "The Twenty-First-Century Left in El Salvador and Nicaragua: Understanding Apparent Contradictions and Criticisms." *Latin American Perspectives* 40 (3): 83–106.

Pierson, P. 2000. "Increasing Returns, Path Dependence, and the Study of Politics." *American Political Science Review* 94 (2): 251–67.

Pinheiro, Armando Manuel da Rocha Castelar. 2011. "Two Decades of Privatization in Brazil." In *The Economies of Argentina and Brazil: A Comparative Perspective*, edited by Werner Baer and David V. Fleischer, 252–78. Rio de Janeiro: Edward Elgar.

Pinto, Solon Lemos. 2009. "Subastas Inversas Electrónicas y Su Aplicación en las Compras Gubernamentales: La Experiencia de Latinoamérica."

Piola, Sergio, Elisabeth Diniz Barros, Roberto Passos Nogueira, Luciana Mendes Servo, Edvaldo Batista de Sá, and Andrea Barreto Paiva. 2009. "Vinte Anos Da Constituição de 1988: O Que Significaram Para a Saúde Da População Brasileira?" In *Políticas Sociais: Acompanhamento e Análise*, edited by IPEA, 97–174.

Piola, Sérgio Francisco, and Geraldo Biasoto Júnior. 2001. "Financiamento Do SUS Nos Anos 90." In *Radiografia Da Saúde*, edited by B. Negri and G. Giovanni, 219–32. Campinas: Instituto de Economia.

Porta, Rafael La, Florencio Lopez-de-Silanes, Andrei Shleifer, and Robert Vishny. 1999. "The Quality of Government." *Journal of Law, Economics, & Organization* 15 (1): 222–79.

Portugal, Maurício, and Lucas Navarro Prado. 2007. *Comentários à Lei de PPP: Parceria Público-Privada: Fundamentos Econômico-Jurídicos*. São Paulo: Malheiros.

Power, Timothy J. 1998. "Brazilian Politicians and Neoliberalism: Mapping Support for the Cardoso Reforms, 1995–1997." *Journal of Interamerican Studies and World Affairs* 40 (4): 51–72.

2010a. "Brazilian Democracy as a Late Bloomer: Reevaluating the Regime in the Cardoso-Lula Era." *Latin American Research Review* 45: 218–47.

2010b. "Optimism, Pessimism, and Coalitional Presidentialism: Debating the Institutional Design of Brazilian Democracy." *Bulletin of Latin American Research* 29 (1): 18–33.

Power, Timothy J., and Matthew M. Taylor. 2011. *Corruption and Democracy in Brazil*. Notre Dame, IN: University of Notre Dame Press.

PR (Presidência de República). 1990. "Programa de Reconstrução Nacional." Brasília.

Praça, Sérgio. 2011. "Corrupção e Reforma Institucional No Brasil, 1988–2008." *Revista Opinião Pública* 17 (1): 137–62.

Praça, Sergio, Andréa Freitas, and Bruno Hoepers. 2011. "Political Appointments and Coalition Management in Brazil, 2007–2010." *Journal of Politics in Latin America* 3 (2): 141–72.

Praça, Sérgio, and Matthew M. Taylor. 2014. "Inching Toward Accountability: The Evolution of Brazil's Anticorruption Institutions, 1985–2010." *Latin American Politics and Society* 56 (2): 27–48.

Pribble, Jennifer. 2013. *Welfare and Party Politics in Latin America*. New York: Cambridge University Press.

———. 2017. "Chile's Elites Face Demands for Reform." *Current History* 116 (787): 49–54.

Przeworski, Adam, and Henry Teune. 1970. *The Logic of Comparative Social Inquiry*. New York: Wiley-Interscience, John Wiley & Sons.

Raigorodsky, Nicolás. 2007. *El Estado de Las Contrataciones: Mapa de Condiciones de Transparencia y Accesibilidad En Las Adquisiciones Públicas*. Buenos Aires: Ministerio de Justicia, Seguridad y Derechos Humanos, Oficina Anticorrupción; Embajada Británica y UNDP.

Raile, Eric. D., Carlos Pereira, and Timothy J. Power. 2010. "The Executive Toolbox: Building Legislative Support in a Multiparty Presidential Regime." *Political Research Quarterly* 64 (2): 323–34.

Rezende, Flávio da Cunha. 2008. "The Implementation Problem of New Public Management Reforms: The Dilemma of Control and the Theory of Sequential Failure." *International Public Management Review* 9 (2): 40–65.

de Rezende, Renato Monteiro. 2011. "O Regime Diferenciado de Contratações Públicas: Comentários à Lei N° 12.462, de 2011." Brasília: Núcleo de Estudos e Pesquisas do Senado.

Ribeiro, Marcelo. 1990. *Atuação Do Ministério Da Infra-Estrutura – Setor de Transportes. Pronunciamento Do Secretário Nacional de Transportes Na Escola de Guerra Naval*. Brasília: MINFRA.

Rinaldi, Oscar, Carlos Salazar, and Damián Staffa. 2005. *Fondos Fiduciarios Estatales: Dinero Público con Escaso Control*. Buenos Aires: CIPPEC y CEPP.

Rodrik, Dani. 2010. "Diagnostics before Prescription." *Journal of Economic Perspectives* 24 (3): 33–44.

Rodrik, Dani, Arvind Subramanian, and Francesco Trebbi. 2004. "Institutions Rule: The Primacy of Institutions Over Geography and Integration in Economic Development." *Journal of Economic Growth* 9 (2): 131–65.

Romero, Luis Alberto, and James P. Brennan. 2013. *A History of Argentina in the Twentieth Century*. University Park, PA: Penn State University Press.

Rose-Ackerman, Susan. 2017. "What Does 'Governance' Mean?" *Governance* 30 (1): 23–27.

Rosilho, André. 2013. "Regime Diferenciado de Contractações e Seu Controle." In *Contratações Públicas e Seu Controle*, edited by Carlos Ari Sundfeld, 1–29. São Paulo: Malheiros.

Ross, Michael L. 2001. "Does Oil Hinder Democracy?" *World Politics* 53 (3): 325–61.

Rothstein, Bo. 2011a. "Anti-Corruption: The Indirect 'Big Bang' Approach." *Review of International Political Economy* 18 (2): 228–50.

———. 2011b. *The Quality of Government: Corruption, Social Trust, and Inequality in International Perspective*. Chicago: University of Chicago Press.

Sachs, Jeffery. 2006. *The End of Poverty: Economic Possibilities for Our Time.* New York: Penguin.

Saiegh, Sebastian. 2010. "Active Players or Rubber-Stamps? An Evaluation of the Policy-Making Role of Latin American Legislatures." In *How Democracy Works: Political Institutions, Actors, and Arenas in Latin American Policymaking*, edited by Carlos Scartascini, Ernesto Stein, and Mariano Tommasi, 47–75. Cambridge, MA: Harvard University Press.

Schafer, Mark, and Scott Crichlow. 2010. *Groupthink versus High-Quality Decision Making in International Relations.* New York: Columbia University Press.

Scherlis, Gerardo. 2010. "Patronage and Party Organization in Argentina: The Emergence of the Patronage-Based Network Party." Faculty of Social and Behavioral Sciences, Leiden University.

2013. "The Contours of Party Patronage in Argentina." *Latin American Research Review* 48 (3): 63–84.

Schneider, Aaron. 2007. "Governance Reform and Institutional Change in Brazil: Federalism and Tax." *Commonwealth & Comparative Politics* 45 (4): 475–98.

Schneider, Ben Ross. 1987. "*Politics within the State: Elite Bureaucrats and Industrial Policy in Authoritarian Brazil.*" University of California, Berkeley.

Scott, James C. 1998. *Seeing Like a State: How Certain Schemes to Improve the Human Condition Have Failed.* New Haven, CT: Yale University Press.

Sharp, Richard. 2005. "Results of Railway Privatization in Latin America." TP-6. Transport Papers. Washington, DC: World Bank.

Shepsle, Kenneth A. 1989. "Studying Institutions: Some Lessons from the Rational Choice Approach." *Journal of Theoretical Politics* 1 (2): 131–47.

Siavelis, Peter. 2006. "Accommodating Informal Institutions and Chilean Democracy." In *Informal Institutions and Democracy: Lessons from Latin America*, 33–55. Baltimore, MD: Johns Hopkins University Press.

Simon, Herbert. 1955. "A Behavioral Model of Rational Choice." *The Quarterly Journal of Economics* 69 (1): 99–118.

1956. "Rational Choice and the Structure of the Environment." *Psychological Review* 63 (2): 129–38.

1976. *Administrative Behavior.* 3rd ed. New York: Free Press.

1990. "Invariants of Human Behavior." *Annual Review of Psychology* 41: 1–19.

1996. *The Sciences of the Artificial.* Cambridge, MA: MIT Press.

Simon, Herbert, and Peter Simon. 1962. "Trial and Error Search in Solving Difficult Problems." *Systems Research and Behavioral Science* 7 (4): 425–29.

Skowronek, Stephen. 1982. *Building a New American State.* Cambridge, MA: Cambridge University Press.

Soifer, Hillel. 2015. *State Building in Latin America.* New York: Cambridge University Press.

Spalding, Rose J. 2014. *Contesting Trade in Central America: Market Reform and Resistance.* Austin, TX: University of Texas Press.

Spiller, Pablo T., and Mariano Tommasi. 2007. *The Institutional Foundations of Public Policy in Argentina: A Transactions Cost Approach*. Cambridge, UK: Cambridge University Press.

Stein, Ernesto, Mariano Tommasi, Koldo Echebarria, Eduardo Lora, and Mark Payne. 2006. *"The Politics of Policies: Economic and Social Progress in Latin America."* Washington, DC: Harvard University Press.

Stepan, Alfred, and Cindy Skach. 1993. "Constitutional Frameworks and Democratic Consolidation: Parliamentarianism versus Presidentialism." *World Politics* 46 (1): 1–22.

Streeck, Wolfgang, and Kathleen Thelen. 2005. "Introduction: Institutional Change in Advanced Political Economies." In *Beyond Continuity: Institutional Change in Advanced Political Economies*, edited by Wolfgang Streeck and Kathleen Thelen. Oxford: Oxford University Press.

Summerhill, William. 1998. "Market Intervention in a Backward Economy: Railway Subsidy in Brazil, 1854–1913." *The Economic History Review* 51 (3): 542–68.

Sundfeld, Carlos Ari. 2007. *Parcerias Público-Privadas*. São Paulo: Malheiros.

Swann, Abram de. 1973. *Coalition Theory and Government Formations*. Amsterdam: Elsevier Ltd.

Taylor, Matthew M. 2008. *Judging Policy: Courts and Policy Reform in Democratic Brazil*. Stanford, CA: Stanford University Press.

2009. "Institutional Development Through Policy-Making: A Case Study of the Brazilian Central Bank." *World Politics* 61 (1): 28–57.

TCU (Tribunal de Contas da União). 2005. "Fiscobras: Fiscalização de obras públicas pelo TCU." Brasília.

2014. "Auditoria No Sistema de Gestão de Convênios e Contratos de Repasse (SICONV) Do Governo Federal." Brasília.

Teichman, Judith A. 1997. "Mexico and Argentina: Economic Reform and Technocratic Decision Making." *Studies in Comparative International Development* 32 (1): 31–55.

2004. "The World Bank and Policy Reform in Mexico and Argentina." *Latin American Politics & Society* 46 (1): 39–74.

Tendler, Judith. 1997. *Good Government in the Tropics*. Johns Hopkins Studies in Development. Baltimore, MD: Johns Hopkins University Press.

Teorell, Jan, and Bo Rothstein. 2013. "Getting to Sweden: Malfeasance and Bureaucratic Reform, 1720–1850." *APSA 2013 Annual Meeting Paper*, 1–34.

Tetlock, Philip. 2005. *Expert Political Judgment: How Good Is It? How Can We Know?* Princeton, NJ: Princeton University Press.

Tilly, Charles. 1990. *Coercion, Capital and European States*. Cambridge, MA: Wiley-Blackwell.

Tobar, Frederico. 2004. *Políticas para Promoción del Acceso a Medicamentos: El Caso del Programa Remediar de Argentina*. Washington, DC: IDB.

Torres, Rubén. 2004. *Mitos y Realidades de las Obras Sociales en la Argentina*. Buenos Aires: iSalud.

Transparency International. 2016. "Corruption Perceptions Index." Berlin: Transparency International.

Trotta, Nicolás Alfredo. 2008. "Sistema Electrónico de Compras y Contrataciones Públicas: La Experiencia del SECOP, Buenos Aires, Argentina, 4–7 Nov. 2008." In *XIII Congreso Internacional del CLAD Sobre la Reforma del Estado y de la Administración Pública*. Buenos Aires, Argentina.

Tsebelis, George. 1995. "Decision Making in Political Systems: Veto Players in Presidentialism, Parliamentarism, Multicameralism and Multipartyism." *British Journal of Political Science* 25 (3): 289–325.

Uña, Gerardo. 2007. "Fondos Fiduciarios En la Argentina: Los 'Todo Terreno' de la Política Económica." Buenos Aires.

Verbitsky, Horacio. 1993. *Hacer la Corte: La Construcción de un Poder Absoluto sin Justicia ni Control*. Buenos Aires: Planeta.

Volosin, Natalia. 2010. "*Promoviendo Compras Publicas Electronicas para el Desarrollo.*" Buenos Aires: Poder Ciudadano.

Vuolo, Rubén Lo, and Fernando Seppi. 2006. *Los Fondos Fiduciarios en la Argentina: La Privatización de los Recursos Públicos*. Buenos Aires: CIEPP.

Weisbrot, Mark. 2008. "*An Empty Research Agenda: The Creation of Myths About Contemporary Venezuela.*" Washington, DC: Center for Economic and Policy Research.

Weiss, Andrew, and Edward Woodhouse. 1992. "Reframing Incrementalism: A Constructive Response to the Critics." *Policy Sciences* 25 (3): 255–73.

Weyland, Kurt. 1995. "Social Movements and the State: The Politics of Health Reform in Brazil." *World Development* 23 (10): 1699–1712.

    1996. *Democracy without Equity: Failures of Reform in Brazil*. Pittsburgh, PA: University of Pittsburgh Press.

    1997. "The Brazilian State in the New Democracy." *Journal of Interamerican Studies and World Affairs* 39 (4): 63–94.

    1998. "The Politics of Corruption in Latin America." *Journal of Democracy* 9 (2): 108–121. Johns Hopkins University Press.

    2006. *Bounded Rationality and Policy Diffusion: Social Sector Reform in Latin America*. Princeton: Princeton University Press.

    2008. "Toward a New Theory of Institutional Change." *World Politics* 60 (2): 281–314.

    2014. *Making Waves: Democratic Contention in Europe and Latin America since the Revolutions of 1848*. New York: Cambridge University Press.

Weyland, Kurt, Raúl L. Madrid, and Wendy Hunter. 2010. *Leftist Governments in Latin America: Successes and Shortcomings*. New York: Cambridge University Press.

Whitehead, Laurence. 2006. *Latin America: A New Interpretation*. New York: Palgrave Macmillan.

Wildavsky, Aaron. 1964. *The Politics of the Budgetary Process*. Boston, MA: Little, Brown.

Willis, Eliza J. 1986. "The State as Banker: The Expansion of the Public Sector in Brazil." University of Texas at Austin.

Willis, Eliza J. 1995. "Explaining Bureaucratic Independence in Brazil: The Experience of the National Economic Development Bank." *Journal of Latin American Studies* 27 (3): 625–61.

Winston, Clifford. 2005. "The Success of the Staggers Rail Act of 1980." AEI-Brookings Joint Center for Regulatory Studies.

World Bank. 1993. *Road Maintenance and Rehabilitation Sector Project.* Washington, DC: World Bank.

1996a. *Argentina Country Assistance Review.* Washington, DC: World Bank.

1996b. *Federal Railways Restructuring and Privatization Project.* Washington, DC: World Bank.

1996c. *Health Insurance Reforms Argentina Report No. P-6851-AR.* Washington, DC: World Bank.

1999. *Implementation Completion Report: Argentina Health Insurance Reform Project.* Washington, DC: World Bank.

2002. *The World Bank Health Insurance Technical Assistance Project.* Washington, DC: World Bank.

2003. *Federal Railways Restructuring and Privatization Project.* Washington, DC: World Bank.

2006. *El Salvador: Recent Economic Developments in Infrastructure – Strategy Report (REDI-SR).* Washington, DC: World Bank.

2011. *World Development Indicators.* Washington, DC: World Bank.

2013. *Implementation Completion and Results Report: Road Transport Project.* Washington, DC: World Bank.

2014. *2014 Global PPI Update.* Washington, DC: World Bank.

2015. *El Salvador Building on Strengths for a New Generation: Systematic Country Diagnostic.* Washington, DC: World Bank.

Yepes Luján, Francisco José. 2010. "Luces y Sombras de la Reforma de la Salud en Colombia." *Revista Gerencia y Políticas de Salud* 9 (18): 118–23.

Zuvanic, Laura, and Mercedes Iacoviello. 2010. "The Weakest Link: The Bureaucracy and Civil Service Systems in Latin America." In *How Democracy Works: Political Institutions, Actors and Arenas in Latin American Policymaking*, edited by Carlos Scartascini, Ernesto Stein, and Mariano Tommasi. Inter-American Development Bank, David Rockefeller Center for Latin American Studies.

Index